The Ways of Friendship

The Ways of Friendship

Anthropological Perspectives

Edited by
Amit Desai and Evan Killick

Berghahn Books
NEW YORK • OXFORD

First published in 2010 by
Berghahn Books
www.berghahnbooks.com

First paperback edition published in 2013

Library of Congress Cataloging-in-Publication Data
The ways of friendship : anthropological perspectives / edited by Amit
Desai and Evan Killick.
    p. cm.
Includes bibliographical references and index.
ISBN 978-1-84545-731-0 (hardback : alk. paper) 1. Friendship.
2. Humanism. I. Desai, Amit. II. Killick, Evan.
GN486.3.W39 2010
144--dc22

                                            2010018548

British Library Cataloguing in Publication Data
A catalogue record for this book is available
from the British Library

Printed in the United States on acid-free paper.

ISBN 978-0-85745-792-9 (paperback)
ISBN 978-0-85745-825-4 (retail ebook)

Contents

Acknowledgements

All the papers in this collection (except one) were originally presented at a workshop entitled 'The Anthropology of Friendship', held at the London School of Economics in June 2006. We are grateful to the LSE Department of Anthropology for their support and encouragement.

Chris Fuller, Eric Hirsch, Deborah James, Peter Loizos, Caroline Osella and Charles Stafford kindly agreed to be our workshop discussants and we thank them for their astute comments. We also thank Atreyee Sen and David Pratten for their valuable contributions to the workshop. Simon Coleman's opening and closing remarks at the workshop helped us immensely in framing this collection and we thank him for the unwavering enthusiasm and support he has given the project from conception to conclusion. Finally, we thank those who contributed papers to the workshop and to this volume for providing such stimulating material with which to discuss the anthropology of friendship.

We wrote the Introduction and edited the volume while we both held Economic and Social Research Council postdoctoral fellowships (Killick – PTA-026-27-1354; Desai – PTA-026-27-1681); we gratefully acknowledge the ESRC's support.

Amit Desai and Evan Killick
April 2009

Introduction

Valuing Friendship

EVAN KILLICK AND AMIT DESAI

The study of friendship is haunted by the problem of definition. 'Who (or what) are friends?' is a common refrain in much of the sociological and anthropological discussion of the subject. This problem has led naturally to attempts to stabilize the category, and has resulted in typologies enumerating different kinds of friendship, organized by privileging some criteria over others (for example Paine 1969: 518; Adams and Allan 1998: 9–10). Is friendship a relationship characterized by autonomy, sentiment, individualism, lack of ritual and lack of instrumentality? Or are these requirements peculiarly Western expressions of friendship imposed on other places and times? A clear picture seldom emerges from such discussions and even less a consensus to use them as a basis for future work. In response to this academic reality this collection uses only the broadest of criteria for considering a relationship as one of friendship, that it is not primarily thought of as being one of kinship, in whatever manner the latter might be locally understood. This position means that we include relationships that might be considered as kinship and emphasize that relationships of friendship do not necessarily map neatly on to local conceptions of kin and non-kin.

Rather than dissect the category of friendship itself, we aim to study the spaces, histories and ideologies that allow and shape its constitution as a particular type of relationship (in the context of other types of relationships) in different places around the world. As such, the chapters in this volume show the analytical benefit of opening up the definition of friendship. For us friendship is interesting precisely because it evades definition: the way in which friendship acts to express fixity and fluidity in diverse social worlds is exciting and problematic for the people that practice friendship, and for the social scientists that study it.

In focusing on friendship's contrast to kinship our aim is not to show that friendship and kinship are mutually exclusive; indeed several of the chapters in this collection demonstrate the close interweaving, and at times inseparability, of the two concepts. Rather, this approach emphasizes what we feel is usually the most important aspect of friendship to its practitioners, that it is a relationship that stands in contrast to other ways of relating. Furthermore, while recent developments in anthropological thought suggest that we dispense with a narrow definition of kinship (i.e. one that is based on biology) and expand it by using concepts such as 'relatedness' (Carsten 2000, 2004) that can also encompass friendship relations, we contend that such an approach is not a sufficiently powerful analytical category to explain how friendship is constituted in the way that it is in different places. As we will discuss in more detail below, it is imperative to retain the analytical distinction between friendship and kinship since it is this aspect that appears to be of crucial importance in giving friendship its moral force in so many societies around the world.

One view has been to link a perceived rise in the contemporary importance of friendship, particularly in Western societies, to economic transformations associated with the rise and spread of capitalism since the eighteenth century. In this view a more collective past has given way to a more individualized present in which kinship is reduced to the nuclear family and ties of friendship have increased in importance (Adams and Allan 1998: 9–10; Oliker 1998; Giddens 1992, 1999). Such conclusions have been questioned from a variety of positions, not least by work that has shown the importance of friendship in European societies prior to the industrial revolution (Hanawalt 1986: 267; see also Brain 1977; Bell and Coleman 1999; Spencer and Pahl 2006). While economic change may affect the way in which different relationships are constituted – as attested to by Rodgers, Obeid and Santos in this volume – the idea of a clear progression from an emphasis on kinship to one on friendship is clearly simplifying a complex reality. Rather, alternative ways of structuring relations emerge in relation to ideologies of kinship and personhood. Indeed, if there is something that all the contributors to this volume demonstrate it is that friendship is not confined to European and North American societies, it is not a new phenomenon, and it cannot be associated with the so-called onset of modernity.

The argument for a link between friendship and modernity is implicitly linked to the idea that the notion of the person as individual was, as Mauss put it, 'formulated only for us, among us' (1985 [1938]: 22; see also Paine 1969; Allan 1996; and Course in this volume). In some societies people are understood to be constituted through social relations, such that no pre-existent, individual self can be said to exist and persons themselves are partible (e.g. Strathern 1988). As Spencer and Pahl note, if this is the case then 'consequently, there is, as it were, no internal source for the creation of personal, spontaneous affection that is characteristic of some forms of Western friendship' (2006: 40). Some of the chapters in this collection appear to contest this position and question the notion of Western individualism. For example, as Course notes among the Mapuche in Chile, relations with friends appear to constitute an indigenous realization and demonstration of the autonomous volition that they believe lies at the heart of the person. In the case of the Mapuche, persons can be said to create themselves through a constant process of engaging with others. Evans, in her work on southeast London, also problematizes the stereotype of the Western person as an individual. Drawing on a phenomenological preoccupation with inter-subjectivity, she reveals the inescapable sociality at the heart of what it is to be a child.[1] She suggests that:

> Rather than thinking about human relations in terms of a dichotomy between those societies characterized by situated persons engaged in personalized relations of exchange and those typified by autonomous individuals participating in the impersonalized relations of the market (Carrier 1999), we might more usefully think of a continuum of situated-ness... Along this continuum it becomes clear that, due to particular historical circumstances, some people have more choice than others, both within any one society and when comparing one society with another, about whom they are able to bring themselves into being in relation to. (Evans this volume)

Finally, the study of the ideologies and practices associated with friendship relations cross-culturally brings up a whole raft of issues, from the place of sentiment and construction of the person, to the importance of equality between participants through the relative significance of debt in maintaining or negating relationships. Here the diversity of local approaches to friendship becomes clear. While Desai shows that in rural India love and affection are taken to be the cornerstone of ritual friendship, Killick argues that in Peruvian Amazonia it is precisely the delayed, reciprocal exchange of objects that lies at the heart of friendship relationships. Similarly, Evans attests to the constant negotiation that occurs in friendship relations among boys in London while Obeid shows how fixed and inescapable relationships of friendship can become in a Lebanese village. Such examples emphasize the value of bringing together examples from a broad range of different places. This applies to the conduct of ethnographic research too, since fieldwork is often carried out through the idiom of friendship between the ethnographer and 'informants'. Thus, friendship is not only a valid subject of anthropological inquiry but also an important part of the process of ethnographic knowledge production itself.[2]

Friendship and Kinship

Even though it appears as a central feature of many people's lives around the world, friendship has received little intensive consideration. While political and economic relationships or those based on kinship have been studied in great detail, those of friendship are often implicitly seen as less important. In part, the relative lack of scholarly investigation of the ideas and practices of friendship can be linked, particularly in anthropological studies, to a continuing emphasis on the importance of kinship. This preoccupation was due in part to what was seen as the important organizing role of kinship in stateless societies. It can also be connected to the discipline's early attempts to 'establish ethnology as a science as exact as physics or chemistry' (Bouquet 1993: 114) and to researchers who saw in the apparent laws and structures of kinship the potential for a methodology more akin to that of the natural sciences (see Holy 1996: 144–55). Even with the advent of the new kinship studies brought on by Schneider's critique of traditional anthropological approaches to the subject (1980 [1968], 1984) and developed by scholars such as Strathern (1981, 1992a, 1992b, 1992c), Weston (1997 [1991]) and Carsten (1997, 2000, 2004), this focus has, in important respects, been retained.

Within anthropology the general approach has been to analyse relations of friendship in terms of kinship. According to this view such relationships are 'pseudo-' or 'fictive' kinship modelled on the ideas and structures of kinship within a given society.[3] More recently, Viveiros de Castro has suggested that relations of 'formal or ceremonial friendship' should be considered in many indigenous Amazonian societies as 'para-kinship' relationships, because of their use of the 'conceptual and practical symbols of affinity' (1995: 14).[4] Such a view has had two consequences. The first is that kinship connections between two people tend to be emphasized at the expense of other aspects of their relationships. As Paine has written: 'For example, where we observe behaviour in the field between persons who are known to us to be cousins, we are very likely to analyse this behaviour in our writings as 'cousin behaviour'; but it may be no such thing; rather it may be behaviour between friends' (Paine 1969: 505). The second outcome of this view has been that anthropologists have tended to subsume their discussion of friendship within the study of kinship. This trend has continued even with the movement away from structuralist understandings of kinship relations.

Ever since Schneider's (1984) blistering exposition of the biological assumptions inherent in much anthropological scholarship on kinship, the process by which the latter is socially created has been emphasized. One corollary of this view has been to move beyond ideas of kinship based on reproduction and genealogical connection and instead to use more general concepts such as 'relatedness' (Carsten 2000, 2004). The discussion of 'cultures of relatedness', while usefully opening up the categories by which human beings regard themselves as connected to one another, a project under which this volume falls, also carries a danger of masking the boundaries that people might themselves posit in the articulation of those relationships. In this case, by subsuming friendship under a general category of relatedness, we miss what friendship does differently to kinship for the people who practice it, and the different ways in which the two general forms of relationship might be constituted in a particular society (see also Santos, this volume).

Little space is given to the discussion of friends and friendship in any of the chapters of *Cultures of Relatedness*; where it is mentioned, it is regarded as relatedness. This is most clear in Stafford's contribution. Having noted that the cycle of *laiwang* in China 'centres mostly on relationships between friends, neighbours, and acquaintances' (Stafford 2000: 38), he writes that 'the point is that the cycle of *laiwang*... is a crucial element in the building up of relatedness between those who are *not* related (or not closely related) by kinship' (Stafford 2000: 47). Stafford argues that this shows that 'in China, as elsewhere, people *make* kinship' and stresses 'the social malleability of such connections' (Stafford 2000: 52). His aim is to show how Chinese forms of relatedness are a continuum stretching from the formality of patrilines to the informality of secret friendships. However, our contention is that in taking this position there is a danger that indigenous distinctions between such social institutions become invisible.

In contrast to Stafford's chapter stands Alan Smart's (1999) contribution to Bell and Coleman's volume on friendship. In this chapter he argues, following Yang (1994), that *guanxi,* which Stafford noted is usually linked in scholarly analysis to the cycle of *laiwang* (2000: 44), is both associated and contrasted with friendship: 'friendship is simultaneously a base on which *guanxi* ties can be built, and a cultural resource for criticism of (certain kinds of) *guanxi* practice' (Smart 1999: 129). Hence, if all of these forms of relating are merged under one term then the distinctions between them, and the use of those distinctions by their participants, are liable to be masked. Santos (this volume) makes a similar point for Chinese society, and thus emphasizes the usefulness of retaining separations between different types of relationship.

In addition to 'relatedness', other encompassing concepts for all forms of intimate relations have been put forward. Pitt-Rivers (1973) proposed using the concept of 'amiable relations' while Brain even suggested using the term friendship itself in this manner. For Brain, friendship referred to feelings of 'amicability' or 'love', and he argued that '

> There would even be a case for maintaining that all kin relations within our kinship group are based on friendship and personal choice. One chooses this or that uncle, this or that cousin, even this or that brother and sister to be friendly with' (Brain 1977: 16).

Such instances highlight one of the main problems with the use of such general or encompassing terms, which is, as Holy notes, that they '[do] not specify what precisely "relatedness" is meant to involve, how it is to be defined and how it should be distinguished from any other kind of social relationship' (Holy 1996: 168). Carsten has responded to Holy's criticism by arguing that the real value of the concept of 'relatedness' is that it allows anthropologists to make comparisons between very different ways of conceptualizing relations 'without relying on an arbitrary distinction between biology and culture, and without presupposing what constitutes kinship' (2000: 5). Thus, Carsten notes that '

> Rather than beginning with a domain of kinship already marked out, the authors in this volume describe relatedness in terms of indigenous statements and practices – some of which may seem to fall quite outside what anthropologists have conventionally understood as kinship' (Carsten 2000: 3).

While we embrace this expansiveness, we believe, as shown in the discussion of the Chinese example above, that such an approach can mask indigenous distinctions in their relationships by replacing talk of kinship with yet another all-encompassing, if more fluid, analytical category. Nuanced understandings of the place and forms of friendship may be unexpected casualties of this approach. Our position is thus to follow Carsten's advice about not beginning with social categories and domains already marked out but rather allowing for broad and multiple definitions of what counts as friendship. The authors in this volume all take the statements and actions of the people under study as their departure point for analysis. This means that we consider the very real differences (as well as similarities) in the types of relations with others that people talk about and use.

There are clearly some societies in which ties centring on ideas of kinship do take precedence over any other relations. Campbell (1964), in his work among Saraktsani pastoralists in the Greek mountains, shows how the overarching claims of kinship and affinity can reduce any other forms of relations, particularly those with outsiders, to little more than economic transactions (cf. Loizos and Papataxiarchis 1991: 20). Papataxiarchis makes a similar argument for married women on the Greek island of Lesbos: 'Friends are conceived as of "the (same) house"… and assist each other in tasks that otherwise are assigned to female relatives. Friendship among women, then, is a substitute for kinship, it is expressed in the terms of domestic kinship, it is susceptible to the fluctuations of domestic life, and it usually fades in time' (Papataxiarchis 1991: 157).

Yet, the view of women contrasts with those of men in the same society. Papataxiarchis argues that men in the uxorilocal village of Mouria find the burdens of affinal kinship oppressive and thus seek out unrelated men from the locale with whom to form close friendships, 'friends of the heart' (Loizos and Papataxiarchis 1991: 21). For such men this leads to the two realms, of kinship and friendship, being 'kept strictly apart' (Papataxiarchis 1991: 160–1).

In this volume, both Rodgers and Obeid write about societies (Southern Mozambican villages and Lebanese pastoral centres respectively) which similarly place a greater moral emphasis on kinship relations. They argue that these relationship types should not be considered as mutually exclusive. Rodgers suggests that 'Good friendship and good kinship existed in a kind of dialectical arrangement. In some instances, kinship even appeared to me to be invented or exaggerated in the course of enthusiastic efforts to establish or develop friendships.' Similarly, Obeid argues that friendship, even though considered a separate type of relationship constituting an autonomous realm, 'is part of an all encompassing ideology of sociality at the heart of which lies kinship'. Both friendship and kinship have value for the people of this Lebanese village, but they are in no way commensurable: it is largely kinship that furnishes the concepts that constitute the ideology of friendship. Such examples emphasize the complex processes of identification and separation of kinship and friendship concepts in the practice of everyday life.

In contrast to societies in which ideologies of kinship dominate social relations, stand those where friendship is a central idiom. In his study of Telefolmin society in the Western Highlands of New Guinea, Craig notes that an emphasis on their kinship structures would obscure the central essence of Telefolmin social organization – individuality:

Despite the feeling of group pride, there is little practical reinforcement of group unity… Moreover, as personal obligations are not defined in terms of common group membership or formal kinship, a man cannot rely on others just because they are fellow villagers or are particular kin of his. Rather, it is the number and quality of his personal friendships that count. That is, the Telefolmin do not think in terms of kin and non-kin, but in terms of friends (i.e. kin with whom there is a long history of close association) and strangers (who may be known kin). (Craig 1969: 177)

In this volume Killick similarly stresses the importance that Ashéninka people in Peruvian Amazonia place on independence and their similar reasons for preferring relationships of friendship to those of kinship.

Again this apparently fixed separation is complicated by the evident blurring of distinctions between kinship and friendship. In her work with gays and lesbians in San Francisco, Weston reports the varying attitudes of gay people in considering friends as family. On the one hand she notes that 'gay (or chosen) families', encompassing as they do lovers, co-parents, adopted children, children from previous heterosexual relationships, and offspring conceived through alternative insemination, appear to dispute the old saying that 'You can pick your friends, but you can't pick your relatives' (Weston 1997: 2–3). On the other, however, she quotes individuals such as Lourdes Alcantara:

I know a lot of lesbians think that you choose your own family. I don't think so. Because, as a Latin woman, the bonds that I got with my family are irreplaceable. They can't be replaced. They cannot. So my family is my family, my friends are my friends. My friends can be *more important* than my family, but that doesn't mean they are my family... 'Cause no matter what, they are just friends – they don't have your blood. (Weston 1997:36)

This example emphasizes that no relationship is ever either one thing or another. Indeed, it is this very fluidity that makes friendship such an important form of sociality.

Sentiment and the Person

We have suggested above that the task of defining friendship, either by attempting to uncover its 'essence' or by proposing typologies, is likely to frustrate as much as it illuminates. Yet there is a fundamental question, which is one of definition, that requires some discussion: is the concept of friendship so dependent on particular, culturally specific concepts of the person that to assume that it exists everywhere is wrong?

At the heart of this discussion is sentiment. Most scholars suggest that without sentiment, one cannot talk about friendship. In some societies, friendship appears to its practitioners as being constituted by nothing else. Looking at Greece, Papataxiarchis writes that 'in friendship the feeling *is* the relationship' (1991: 178). Taking a somewhat broader view, Brain asserts that 'no culture fails to emphasise the essential loyalty and love between friends… Affection and loyalty are implicit in all friendships and in all societies' (1977: 18). In this view, just as sentiment (or the appearance of it) makes the relationship possible, so the lack of it (or more precisely, the *mutual* lack of it) will eventually cause its demise (Pitt-Rivers 1973: 97).

By way of contrast, Carrier (1999) offers a critical perspective on the whole issue of sentiment and friendship. Agreeing that unconstrained sentiment lies at the basis of friendship, he argues that this very fact prevents it from being a human universal. For the idea of friendship and the unconstrained sentiment it involves presupposes a very particular concept of the person, one that is capable of such sentiment. As he writes, 'without people who can be friends … we cannot speak of friendship' (1999: 21). This concept of the person as an individual, or autonomous, self has, according to this view, a specifically European and North American genealogy. In the West, as a result of profound changes which have separated the spheres of economy and society, the self has come to be identified as being prior to social relations, and thus the sentiment that makes friendship possible is seen as emanating from within the person. As such it is beyond the messiness of social or economic interest and is thus able to offer unconditional affection. Drawing in part on Strathern's *The Gender of the Gift*, Carrier contrasts this situation with that of Melanesia where there is no stable category of the self. In Melanesia, social relations actually constitute personhood and there is no irreducible or inviolate core of the individual. Of course sentiment exists, but it cannot be of the unconstrained internal type that characterizes friendship; affection is not regarded by Melanesians as *enabling* relations between people, but rather *results from* the kinds of relations one engages in. Sentiment that is embedded in this way cannot, by definition, be unfettered and free. Melanesians, in Carrier's analysis, are people that cannot be friends.

These are valuable insights and the link between constructions and histories of the person and ideas of friendship is important and needs further study. But in highlighting two ideal types (the West and Melanesia),[5] Carrier neglects to pursue the exciting possibilities that his analysis suggests. For us, his conclusions raise a number of issues. Firstly, just as the West and Melanesia have developed particular notions of the self due to different histories of social transformation, we must be able to envisage multiple configurations and possibilities of the relationship between history, personhood, sentiment and friendship. We cannot claim that just because the West has a particular history of the development of the individual with a corresponding construction of unconstrained sentiment, others cannot have similar notions of an autonomous self (with or without the same articulation of sentiment) having had very different histories. After all, a pre-Christian and pre-industrial Aristotle asserts that friendship is only really possible between people who see themselves in each other (Sherman 1993: 98).[6] Such a claim requires that there is something essential and innate about persons and therefore that there is a fairly stable concept of the person. What we would suggest is that while social relations such as friendship may be culturally specific, the presence of a particular set of formations in one society does not preclude a similar set of formations in a very different society. As Course shows in this volume, the Mapuche of Chile have a concept of the autonomous individual self, together with the capacity to make friends. Indeed, for the Mapuche this capacity is a necessary element of personhood. But unlike the Western 'person who can be a friend' that Carrier describes, unconstrained sentiment is not at the heart of the Mapuche's articulation of this crucial relationship. Friendship in this case is about something else, and is doing something else; but it nevertheless involves an idea of the individual. This particular articulation is not derived from 'the West' as a result of colonialism, but is, as Course makes clear, an indigenous category intrinsic to a peculiarly Mapuche ontology of the person.

A further issue raised by Carrier's discussion is his proposition that the development of the ideology of friendship in the West is essentially a reflection of an elite male social position. Others have made similar arguments. Allan laments the fact that many sociologists have understood friendship in fairly limited terms: they have seen it as being primarily about sentiment, which, in their view, can have little or no social consequence (1989: 2). As such, friendship for them has been regarded as fairly unimportant and idiosyncratic. Allan suggests that researchers ought to examine what kinds of power relations are masked by the ideology of autonomy and personal freedom in the making of friends. Carrier takes up the challenge and puts a theory of power at the heart of his argument about the cultural uniqueness of friendship for the West.

An understanding of power is essential as Carrier shows; so, however, are processes of negotiation and creativity whereby dominant models of personhood are contested or sidestepped by alternative configurations of friendship and sentiment. Caste in India, for example, has long been seen as a major constituent of personhood. But it cannot be the all of personhood. The way in which friendship is articulated and experienced serves in many cases to provide an alternative basis for thinking about personhood distinct from caste (see Osella and Osella 1998). This raises a possibility that Carrier seems to ignore in his contrasting and exclusive vision of the West and Melanesia: that there may be multiple ideas of personhood in any given society, which are held and acted through by the same persons in different contexts. The chapters by Desai and Froerer in this volume demonstrate how contradictory models of personhood (and thus of the relations between persons) do exist alongside one another: ones in which caste is clearly important, and others (in friendship relations particularly) where it is less so. In contrast to studies of Indian society, which have emphasized the importance of caste and kinship in the making of personhood, Froerer demonstrates how proximity and locality are important sources of personhood too: to a great extent it is where you live, even within a small village, that determines your friendships which may cut across caste and kinship lines. Similarly Desai shows how the articulation of sentiment provides an alternative basis for thinking about relations between people, away from the undoubtedly important ones of caste and kinship. He also demonstrates how unconstrained sentiment – seen to constitute the basis of ritual friendship in central India – does not have to be located in any one person but can provide the rationale for such relationships over several generations.

Sentiment may have a role to play in various constructions of friendship and personhood, both in the West and elsewhere. We recognize, however, that friendship need not be understood as involving sentiment as a primary constituent. This is particularly clear in Killick's discussion of inter-ethnic relations in Peruvian Amazonia. He shows how relationships that are couched in local idioms of friendship are not built around sentiment. Rather the primary characteristic of such relationships is that they stand outside of kinship and thus carry different types of expectation, drawing people together even as a degree of separation is maintained. While sentiment may be present in such relationships, it is not their foundation. Such a view emphasizes the instrumental and structural basis of such relationships: the reciprocal exchange of desired objects enables and constitutes both persons and friends.

At another level, the capacity to make friends seems to be one way in which to achieve full and perfected personhood, and thus enjoy a successful social career. The chapters by Course and Evans in particular demonstrate this aspect of friendship. For example, Evans argues that it is through their friendships that Bermondsey boys come to understand what kind of social person they are becoming. Friendship is thus revealed to be as much about potentiality as it is about being, as oriented to the future as it is to the past. The reverse side of this is the consequences of the failure to conduct friendships, and thus the failure of the social quest for 'true' personhood. This is an aspect that none of the papers in our collection address explicitly though it is undoubtedly important.

Returning then to the question of definition, our understanding of friendship differs considerably from Carrier's. For us the key feature is not unconstrained sentiment emanating from an autonomous self, simply because, as discussed above, this construction, while inspiring, is problematic given the ethnographic record and entails glossing over meaningful local categories. It is clear that societies with varied constructions of personhood find a place for relationships that might be considered friendship. Hence our belief that the latter category is best left as open as possible. This very elasticity, however, raises problems of its own, which we will consider towards the end of this Introduction.

Equality and Debt

Following Leach (1968: 57), Paine notes that, in contrast to many social relationships which involve 'opposed pairs' (e.g. father-son, employer-employee, husband-wife) friendship is based on 'persons paired in the *same* role' (Paine 1969: 507; cf. Rezende 1999). Allan makes a similar point in suggesting that 'friendship is a bond in which issues of hierarchy and authority have no bearing' (Allan 1989: 20, see also Froerer in this volume). This often seems to be the most important reason why friendship is put in opposition to kinship, which is so often associated with hierarchical distinctions based on age or status as an affine or consanguine. In many of the chapters in this volume the importance of equality for friendship is clear. Evans suggests that friendship among boys in Bermondsey is founded on relations of 'competitive equality' with groups of boys vying to be equally good at particular activities. Similarly, among the Mapuche studied by Course, he notes that their term for friends and trading partners, *trafkin* or *trauki*, carries an idea of equality such that it is often used to replace other terms that are perceived as alluding to an unequal relationship. As one man explained to Course: 'I call my son-in-law *trauki* so as not to offend him as we are friends.' Furthermore, Desai reports that those who dislike ritual friendship in rural India do so because it operates outside the bounds of caste and untouchability, while Froerer shows how everyday friendship cuts across a variety of local social distinctions. Similarly, Killick argues that the Ashéninka's aversion to kinship can be linked to their emphasis on egalitarianism. Not only do Ashéninka individuals want to be able to maintain their autonomy from their kin but they also do not want any individual to have power over them.

Yet, even this apparent universal characteristic of friendship is questioned by the Amazonian case where Killick argues that those *mestizos* (people of mixed heritage) who enter into relationships with Ashéninka retain certain ideas of a hierarchical separation from their indigenous friends. Their use of the ideology of *compadrazgo* (ritual co-parenthood) retains hierarchical differences between the 'spiritual' godparent and the 'natural' parent (see Gudeman 1972, 1975). However,

Killick argues that such relationships are better understood in terms of friendship, rather than kinship, because they are used by *mestizos* precisely in order to avoid the use of idioms of kinship. Such an example may appear to push at the limit of what might be counted as friendship but it also serves to underline how even participants in the same relationship can have a diversity of views as to its implications and importance.

This Amazonian example also shows the role that gifts, reciprocity and debt can play in the instigation of relationships. In the West, where the egalitarian nature of friendship is stressed, friends are generally thought not to be indebted to each other. Moreover, they should be completely generous with each other. Silver suggests that 'Friendship is diminished in moral quality if friends consciously monitor the balance of exchange between them, for this implies that the utilities friends offer each other constitute their relationship, rather than being valued as expressions of personal commitment' (Silver 1990: 1477). This view can be linked to a generally negative Western view of debt. Deborah Durham argues that Mauss's view of the gift 'supports and repeats the tenets of a Western liberal individualism, acknowledging (or assuming) the equal agency of individual actors prior to social' (1995: 115).[7] She goes on to write that:

> The consequence of this classical Maussian approach to gifts, then, is to emphasize the agency of the giver, and the power of the gift. It is the giver who seems to have ultimate control over the transaction: his demand for a return overwhelms the ability of the recipient to determine a response. This deprivation of independence for the recipient, and the material debt engendered in receipt, may produce a hierarchical relationship between the two parties: the recipient, chained to the giver by the gift, is thereby subordinated to the giver, who attains a superior status. (Durham 1995: 115)

In contrast she argues that the exchange of gifts, while making a connection between people or, in her ethnography of people in Botswana, emphasizing their individual agency, does not necessarily carry an idea of inequality. Similarly the indigenous people in Killick's Amazonian example seem to want to base their relationships precisely on the delayed exchange of goods that binds individuals in long-term relationships. Here the emphasis on giving is precisely predicated on an egalitarian ideal that both men are equally able both to accept and to repay the objects and, further, that neither can force the other as to how and when to make repayments. Rodgers also describes how objects link people across the 'hard' border between Mozambique and South Africa and notes how those linked through debt 'could reasonably encapsulate the respective acts of lending and borrowing as both reflective and constitutive of a friendship'.

This emphasis on debt and the role of objects in linking people together connects to a wider argument about the non-instrumental character of 'true' friendship. This common, lay view of friendship in Western societies has led writers such as Allan to suggest that while many friendships do involve instrumental assistance, they 'must not be defined in these terms' (Allan 1989: 19–20). The development of this ideology is linked to the rise of the market economy, which is predicated on people making calculated and instrumental decisions and thus emphasizes a separate 'social sphere' in which sentiment and free gifts are all important (Parry 1986; Carrier 1999). In the same manner in which we have questioned sentiment as a *sine qua non* of friendship relationships, so too the ethnographic examples in this volume attest to the diversity of views on the issue of giving and receiving.

Rodgers shows how important friendship relations can be in facilitating migration across the Mozambique-South African border and explicitly notes how, in contrast to Aristotelian ideals, friendships often incorporated expectations of social and material obligation and 'seemed to include the overtly self-serving elements of utility, pleasure and companionship'. Obeid also shows the material benefits of herders' wives making friendships in the desolate Lebanese highlands. Less explicitly, Evans shows how friendships offer protection and power to the boys of Tenter Ground School. Desai, by way of contrast, argues that for ritual friends in India, 'what is emphasised is not what ritual friends should and could do for one another, but simply that they have love (*prem*) for one another.' Even where the ideology of friendship emphasizes the non-instrumental basis of the relationship, the material benefits of such relationships are often clear. Desai gives the example of the itinerant bullock seller for whom 'having a ritual friend in Markakasa means that on a cold winter's night he is fed and housed during his stay'. Finally, Killick's work seems to suggest that the most important characteristic of Ashéninka-*mestizo* relations in Peruvian Amazonia is the access to goods for the Ashéninka and access to labour for *mestizos* that they provide. By including such purely formal and pragmatic relationships within our volume, we may be pushing our definition of friendship to its limit, and straying too far into areas of social life where others would simply see an economic, patron-client relationship. But this follows our central argument that it is useful to make such connections, particularly in cases where people are using the concept of friendship to consider, and control, these relationships.

The Fluidity of Friendship

We have considered some of the obstacles that seemed to lie in the way of useful cross-cultural comparisons of friendship, from the 'relatedness' debates of kinship theory to the yoking of a culturally-specific concept of the individual to the capacity to make friends. Perhaps one of the greatest constraints on studying friendship has been the fear of imposing a 'Western' conception of friendship on other places and people. We have argued that one way to avoid this is by opening up the definition of friendship as widely as possible to include a variety of relationships – patron-client, childhood friends, ritual friends – in order to draw out the social importance of these types of relationships and the things that they offer. This is the principal achievement of the chapters in this collection.

A problem with this approach, however, (and one which it shares with the concept of 'relatedness'), is that in setting the criteria so wide, we may be obscuring important local distinctions between relationships we class as 'friendship'. Thus, in Bermondsey, a person's relationship with a schoolmate may be markedly different from someone with whom they work, and thus may involve very different notions of friendship (if indeed that is the correct concept in either case). We suggest that it is up to individual studies to highlight these nuances, and thus complicate the notion of friendship further, by paying attention to social context and the interplay of relations. In his preface to Bell and Coleman's edited volume *The Anthropology of Friendship*, Firth notes that, 'The concept of friendship can vary greatly in intensity, from simple well-wishers to familiar, close, dear, intimate, bosom, boon-companion friend, each with its own subtle quality' (Firth 1999: xiv). We endorse this view, and are most interested in how these different formulations relate one to another and to concepts of kinship and constructions of personhood. Santos' observation that in contemporary rural South China, 'the fact that friendship is less formally valued and visible than other forms of sociality (e.g. agnatic kinship) does not mean that it is less *important* to people or less *ubiquitous* in society', is instructive for any attempt at an anthropology of friendship.

Putting the study of friendship at the centre of any anthropological analysis can be extraordinarily fruitful. It enables us to determine how this key social relationship is articulated with ideas of being related, and ideas of being a person. The diversity shown by the eight studies included in this volume attest to the myriad ways in which relations of friendship come into being, are conducted, and are valued in different cultures and societies.

Notes

1. This work on child friendships is a potentially fruitful source of new research in this area where it might be shown, for example, that kinds of sociality that pertain in childhood become impossible among adults.
2. While this issue is touched on in a number of the chapters, most clearly in those by Rodgers and Evans, we have decided not to make it a central concern of this volume, choosing instead to focus on local usages and conceptions of friendship in which anthropologists naturally become engaged.
3. See also Pitt-Rivers' critique of this position (1973).
4. Viveiros de Castro's argument that friends are best understood in terms of affinity can be questioned on a number of levels. First, as Santos-Granero notes in Amazonia:

   > If formalized intertribal friendships are indeed an actualization of potential affinity, one would expect either that they are phrased exclusively in the language of affinity, or that they, at least, lead to some kind of symbolic affinal exchange. Instead, what we observe is that these relationships are equated to affinal or consanguineal relationships interchangeably, and that they seldom culminate in symbolic exchanges. (Santos-Granero 2007:14)

   Second, as Santos notes about China in this volume, 'If "friends" in general are similar to "affinal relatives through marriage" because both are outsiders and are not as obligated to us as local agnatic relatives, "friends" are also different from "affinal relatives through marriage" because they are even less obligated to an individual than the latter'. This emphasizes that even as friendship relations echo many aspects of kinship, often their most important characteristic is precisely that they stand outside of kinship relations.
5. Carrier demonstrates how 'ideal' the type is for the West, and what it masks about relations of power: the norms of friendship are shown to fit most closely with middle-class male concerns, making other groups who have internalized the norm feeling inadequate as social beings because their friendships do not conform to the ideal (1999: 35–6).
6. This 'mirror view' of friendship has been criticized by many (see in particular Cocking and Kennett 1998).
7. Here it is interesting to note Parry's argument of the importance of the Indian concept of *dana*, 'The Indian Gift' in Mauss's writings on the gift (Parry 1986: 459).

References

Adams, R. and G. Allan (eds). 1998. *Placing Friendship in Context*. Cambridge: Cambridge University Press.

Allan, G. 1989. *Friendship: Developing a Sociological Perspective*. London: Harvester Wheatsheaf.

———. 1996. *Kinship and Friendship in Modern Britain*. Oxford: Oxford University Press.

Bell, S. and S. Coleman (eds). 1999. *The Anthropology of Friendship*. Oxford: Berg.

Bouquet, M. 1993. *Reclaiming English kinship: Portuguese refractions on British kinship theory*. Manchester: Manchester University Press.

Brain, R. 1977. *Friends and Lovers*. London: Paladin.

Campbell, J. 1964. *Honour, Family and Patronage: A Study of Institutions and Moral Values in a Greek Mountain Community*. Oxford: Clarendon Press.

Carrier, J. 1999. 'People who can be friends: selves and social relationships', in Sandra Bell and Simon Coleman (eds), *The Anthropology of Friendship*. Oxford: Berg.

Carsten, J. 1997. *The Heat of the Hearth: the process of kinship in a Malay fishing community*. Oxford: Clarendon Press.

———. (ed.). 2000. *Cultures of Relatedness: New Approaches to the Study of Kinship*. Cambridge: Cambridge University Press.

———. 2004. *After Kinship*. Cambridge: Cambridge University Press.

Cocking, D. and J. Kennett. 1998. 'Friendship and the Self', *Ethics* 108(3): 502–27.

Craig, R. 1969. 'Marriage Among the Telefolmin', in R.M. Glasse and M.J. Meggitt (eds), *Pigs, Pearlshells and Women*. Englewood Cliffs, N.J.: Prentice-Hall.

Durham, D. 1995. 'Soliciting Gifts and Negotiating Agency: the spirit of asking in Botswana', *Journal of the Royal Anthropological Institute* 1(1): 111–28.

Firth, R. 1999. 'Preface', in Sandra Bell and Simon Coleman (eds), *The Anthropology of Friendship*. Oxford: Berg.

Giddens, A. 1992. *The Transformation of Intimacy: Sexuality, Love and Eroticism in Modern Societies*. Cambridge: Polity Press.

———. 1999. *Runaway World: How Globalisation is Reshaping Our Lives*. London: Profile Books.

Gudeman, S. 1972. 'The Compadrazgo as a Reflection of the Natural and Spiritual Person', *Proceedings of the Royal Anthropological Institute of Great Britain and Ireland for* 1971: 45–71.

———. 1975. 'Spiritual Relationships and Selecting a Godparent', *Man* 10(2): 221–37.

Hanawalt, B. A. 1986. *The Ties That Bound: Peasant Families in Medieval England*. New York: Oxford University Press.

Holy, L. 1996. *Anthropological Perspectives on Kinship*. London: Pluto Press.

Leach, E. 1968. *A Runaway World?* Oxford: Oxford University Press.

Loizos, P. and E. Papataxiarchis. 1991. 'Introduction: Gender and Kinship in Marriage and Alternative Contexts', in P. Loizos and E. Papataxiarchis (eds), *Contested Identities: Gender and Kinship in Modern Greece*. Princeton, NJ: Princeton University Press.

————. (eds). 1991. *Contested Identities: Gender and Kinship in Modern Greece.* Princeton, NJ: Princeton University Press.

Mauss, M. (translated by W.D. Halls). 1985 [1938]. 'A Category of the Human Mind: the Notion of Person; the Notion of Self', in Michael Carrithers, Steven Collins and Steven Lukes (eds), *The Category of the Person.* Cambridge: Cambridge University Press.

Oliker, S. J. 1998. 'The Modernisation of Friendship: individualism, intimacy, and gender in the nineteenth century', in Rebecca G. Adams and Graham Allen (eds), *Placing Friendship in Context.* Cambridge: Cambridge University Press.

Osella, C. and F. Osella. 1998. 'Friendship and Flirting: Micro-Politics in Kerala, South India', *The Journal of the Royal Anthropological Institute* 4(2): 189–206.

Paine, R. 1969. 'In Search of Friendship: An Exploratory Analysis in "Middle-Class" Culture', *Man* 4(4): 505–24.

Papataxiarchis, E. 1991. 'Friends of the Heart: Male Commensal Solidarity, Gender, and Kinship in Aegean Greece', in P. Loizos and E. Papataxiarchis (eds), *Contested Identities. Gender and Kinship in Modern Greece.* Princeton, NJ: Princeton University Press.

Parry, J. 1986. 'The Gift, the "Indian" Gift, and the "Indian Gift"', *Man* (n.s.) 21(3): 453–73.

Pitt-Rivers, J. 1973. 'The Kith and the Kin', in Jack Goody (ed.), *The Character of Kinship.* Cambridge: Cambridge University Press.

Rezende, C. B. 1999. 'Building Affinity through Friendship', in S. Bell and S. Coleman (eds), *The Anthropology of Friendship.* Oxford: Berg.

Santos-Granero, F. 2007. 'Of Fear and Friendship. Amazonian sociality beyond kinship and affinity', *Journal of the Royal Anthropological Institute* (n.s.) 13(1): 1–18.

Schneider, D. M. 1980 [1968]. *American Kinship: A cultural account.* Chicago: Chicago University Press.

————. 1984. *A Critique of the Study of Kinship.* Ann Arbor: University of Michigan Press.

Sherman, N. 1993. 'Aristotle and the Shared Life', in Neera Kapur Badhwar (ed.), *Friendship: A Philosophical Reader.* Ithaca, NY: Cornell University Press.

Silver, A. 1990. 'Friendship in Commercial Society: eighteenth-century social theory and modern sociology', *American Journal of Sociology* 95: 1474–1504.

Smart, A. 1999. 'Expressions of Interest. Friendship and *guanxi* in Chinese societies', in S. Bell and S. Coleman (eds), *The Anthropology of Friendship.* Oxford: Berg.

Spencer, L. and R. Pahl. 2006. *Rethinking Friendship: Hidden Solidarities Today.* Oxford: Princeton University Press.

Stafford, C. 2000. 'Chinese Patriliny and the Cycles of *yang* and *laiwang*', in J. Carsten (ed.), *Cultures of Relatedness.* Cambridge: Cambridge University Press.

Strathern, M. 1981. *Kinship at the Core: An Anthropology of Elmdon, Essex.* Cambridge: Cambridge University Press.

————. 1988. *The Gender of the Gift: problems with women and problems with society in Melanesia.* Berkeley: University of California Press.

————. 1992a. *After Nature: English Kinship in the Late Twentieth Century.* Cambridge: Cambridge University Press.

————. 1992b. 'Parts and Wholes: Refiguring relationships in a postplural world', in Adam Kuper (ed.), *Conceptualising Society.*London: Routledge.

————. 1992c. *Reproducing the Future: Essays on Anthropology, Kinship and the New Reproductive Technologies.* Manchester: Manchester University Press.

Viveiros de Castro, E. 1995. 'Pensando o Parentesco Ameríndio', in E. Viveiros de Castro (ed.), *Antropologia do Parentesco: Estudos Ameríndios.*Rio de Janeiro: Editora UFRJ.

Weston, K. 1997 [1991]. *Families We Choose: Lesbians, Gays, Kinship.* New York: Columbia University Press.

Yang, M. 1994. *Gifts, Favors and Banquets: the Art of Social Relationships in China.* Ithaca, NY: Cornell University Press.

Chapter 1

On 'Same-Year Siblings' in Rural South China[1]

GONÇALO D. SANTOS

This chapter draws attention to the little-known Southern Chinese idiom and institution of fictive/ritual kinship which I shall render in English as 'same-year siblingship'. 'Same-year siblings' are non-kin men or women born in the same year who found it necessary or desirable to formally reconfigure their relationship by means of a kinship metaphor of agnatic siblingship. This public idiom and institution of 'relatedness', to use a concept recently celebrated in the field of kinship studies (Carsten 2000b), is analogous to other well-known Chinese phenomena of fictive/ritual kinship, such as 'sworn siblinghood', but it has never been the object of systematic ethnographic attention. In this chapter, I shall try to correct this omission with data recently collected in the province of Guangdong. My ultimate analytical goal, in line with the spirit of this volume, will be to argue that the detailed ethnographic study of this phenomenon of fictive/ritual kinship suggests that 'friendship' is an important and highly productive subject of anthropological inquiry in its own right (see Killick and Desai in this volume).

Located in the coastal southern region near Hong Kong and Macao, the province of Guangdong is well known for its spectacular rates of economic growth and urbanization following the post-Mao reforms of the 1980s, but it first caught the attention of anthropologists back in the 1950s and 1960s due to the phenomenon of 'lineage-village organization'. As described in the 'classic' literature (see Freedman 1958, 1966), this is a 'traditional' form of agrarian ritual-social organization centred on patrilineal descent and territory that differs from similar modes of organization found, for example, in small-scale African societies because it is compatible with class stratification and state organization. Despite this comparative qualification, the 'classic' analytical emphasis on descent and territory was to have a strong influence on subsequent studies of kinship and sociality in the region, and these studies have in turn inspired the development of a powerful model of Chinese rural sociality in which friendship plays a very marginal role due to the dominance of agnatic kinship and locality (see Santos 2006).

The data presented in this chapter will both revise the original portrayal of rural South China given in this more general 'classic' model of Chinese rural sociality, and provide a post-Mao update. As in previous studies of Chinese sworn siblinghood (e.g. Gallin and Gallin 1977; Jordan 1985; Stockard 1992), my aim is to contribute to the widening of the study of relatedness in rural China beyond agnatic kinship and locality (see also Sangren 1984; Judd 1994; Yan 1996, 2003; Kipnis 1997; Stafford 2000a, 2000b; M.L. Cohen 2005). However, unlike most research on Chinese sworn siblinghood, the present discussion of 'same-year siblingship' will not take as its starting point the ideology of fictive/ritual kinship behind this idiom and institution, but rather the practical/affective phenomenon that leads to its strategic deployment in the first place. This is the phenomenon of friendship, or, as I will argue, a particularly well-matched form of friendship between same-sex persons of the same age/generation.

This focus on friendship via fictive/ritual kinship may seem somewhat novel within the field of China studies, but it is certainly not novel within the broader field of anthropology. As Robert Paine (1969) and more recently Sandra Bell and Simon Coleman (1999a) and Fernando Santos-Granero (2007) have pointed out, most classic discussions of friendship in 'non-modern', 'non-Euro-American' settings were notable for beginning and ending with phenomena of fictive/ritual kinship, such as the 'Mesoamerican bond of *compadrazgo*' or the 'tribal bond-friendship' (cf. Pitt-Rivers 1973). Unlike these discussions, however, I shall not assume *a priori* that the phenomenon of friendship has nothing to do with cross-cultural requirements for practical/affective well-being, nor that it represents an urban middle-class occurrence typical of 'modern' societies such as the 'Euro-American' where kinship no longer plays a prominent organizational role in wider society.

Building on this analytical caution, the data presented here on contemporary rural South China will show precisely that the fact that friendship is less visible and less formally valued than other forms of sociality (e.g. agnatic kinship) does not mean that it is less important to people or less ubiquitous in society. It only means that it often has to remain in the shadows or else be masked, as in the case of 'same-year siblings', with socially reassuring metaphoric clothing (cf. Uhl 1991). These data will lead me to suggest that friendship in rural South China has an expressive style of its own that does not entirely overlap with the modern Euro-American ideology of friendship (described, for example, by Paine 1969 and sociologically deconstructed by Allan 1979, 1989) as a highly autonomous, voluntary and affective personal relationship between particular individuals.

My aim is not to suggest that different socio-cultural contexts and structures are bound to engender different forms of friendship that are in turn indicative of friendship's varying degrees of prominence and centrality across cultures and social structures (see Y.A. Cohen 1961). Rather, my point will be to argue that the phenomenon of friendship is a key form of human relatedness in its own right despite significant historical, regional and cultural variations in the way in which it is represented in public discourses, rituals and practices (cf. Bell and Coleman 1999b; Santos-Granero 2007). This is a key form of human relatedness that is clearly separate from kinship and marriage in that it is directly associated neither with the question of sexuality and procreation nor with the question of the succession of generations and the appropriation of children. As defined in the present chapter, friendship constitutes a major form of individual and/or collective alliance which is marked by frequent, voluntary displays of mutual generosity and trust that can be more or less instrumental but that are always based on both affective and practical reasons. Towards the end of the chapter, I shall argue that the recognition of the centrality of friendship across cultures has important implications for recent debates about kinship and intimacy, and may lead ethnographers to make innovative contributions to the study of altruism and cooperation among humans.

The Contexts of Friendship in Contemporary Rural South China

Harmony Cave[2] is the pseudonym of the small Cantonese 'common-surname village' (*tuhng-sing-chyun*)[3] or 'single-lineage village' where I undertook fourteen months of intensive fieldwork between 1999 and 2001 and where I returned for additional field research in 2005, 2008 and 2009.[4] This village has a total population of about 700 individuals and is located in the 'hilly regions' of Northern Guangdong in the township of Brightpath, at about 250 km north of the provincial capital (Guangzhou). This is a relatively out-of-the-way rural township that is often praised by visiting urbanites for the beauty of its agrarian landscape of paddy-rice fields, figure-shaped limestone mountains, and small, compact 'lineage-villages'[5] still built for the most part with traditional clay bricks.

Agrarian as this landscape may seem, the Brightpath region is currently at the heart of a massive wave of 'temporary labour migration' to the wealthier southern urban cores of the province. This is part of a complex historical process that started to occur in the 1980s soon after the beginning of Deng's reform programme. Largely unable to change residence due to official restrictions on rural-to-urban migration, among other reasons, most local labour migrants invest their savings back home not just in personal projects like new 'modern' family houses, but also in collective projects like the reconstruction of old 'traditional' ancestral halls and temples which were destroyed or abandoned during the Maoist period. This widespread investment in pre-Communist forms of symbolic capital shows that the collectivist reforms of the Maoist period were not enough to eradicate people's sense of belonging to traditional corporate organizations, such as localized lineages or temple associations. Hence one of the major effects of Deng's reforms in the local society – and in much of rural South China (see for example Potter and Potter 1990; Siu 1990, 1993; Aijmer and Ho 2000; Ku 2003) – was the 'public revival' of many of the customs and traditions associated with these 'old' agrarian institutions of ritual-social organization.

Of course, these newly 'revived' old customs and traditions are only a poorly reproduced copy of their pre-Communist template. Particularly relevant to our discussion is the phenomenon of 'lineage-village organization' whose renewed vitality can be illustrated, for example, by the resurgence of the practice of communal ancestor worship or by the continuing adherence to the practice of village patrilocal exogamy. While these practices are clearly symptomatic of a return to past traditions, they are also at the heart of important socio-cultural metamorphoses which include the increasing monetarization and inflation of the local ritual economy. For example, although the 'traditional' system of marriage exchanges involving bridewealth and dowry is still in place, it is now almost exclusively centred on money, and the 'economic value' of these exchanges has already reached levels previously unknown to the local rural society.[6]

Brightpath's new 'old' lineage formations are also significantly weaker than their pre-Communist counterparts. This is because the local rural society has not remained static during the last five to six decades of socialist and post-socialist reforms. Rather, it has undergone a complex process of transformation whereby the 'old' lineage structures of social organization have lost much of their material power not just to the rising Communist state and its various 'modern' technologies of governance, but also to the rising younger generations (women included) and their equally 'modern' aspirations. As in much of rural China (Yan 2003), these individualistic aspirations were significantly empowered by the radical social reforms of the Maoist era, which were aimed at inter-generational and gender equality. More recently, the post-Mao institution of an increasingly liberal and market-oriented regime has further empowered the younger generations by giving them greater opportunities to move, spatially and economically. Today, this growing power of the younger generations is quite clear, for example, in their tendency to establish a separate family 'stove' and sometimes construct a separate family house immediately after marriage and regardless of parental opinion.

The relative weakness of Brightpath's new 'old' lineage formations notwithstanding, it is quite clear that agnatic kinship and locality still constitute key formal dimensions of the local dynamics of relatedness. People's affinal networks through marriage also play a fundamental structuring role in the local rural society, not least because after marriage women tend to maintain relations with their mothers, siblings and natal villages. Outside the realms of kinship and marriage, there are other equally important official and non-official, local and trans-local routes of relatedness such as administrative networks, marketing networks, popular religion networks and migration networks.

While most of these networks have already been the object of detailed ethnographic studies, the same cannot be said of friendship and friendship-based networks, as friendship is a largely neglected topic of research among sinological anthropologists. As Alan Smart (1999: 126–9) notes, it was only as recently as the 1990s that there was a relative upsurge of interest in the topic of friendship. On the one hand, scholars have drawn attention to friendship while making sense of the more general phenomenon of '*guanxi* [M]' or network building in the current market-oriented post-Mao period (see Yang 1994; Yan 1996; Kipnis 1997). On the other hand, scholars have looked at friendship while focusing on the prominence of the topic of separation and reunion in Chinese idioms of kinship and relatedness (see Stafford 2000b). The only problem with this literature, to come back to rural South China, is that it largely draws on data collected either in urban settings or else in rural settings (for example, in North China) not associated with lineage-village organization. As a result, this literature does not directly challenge the 'classic' lineage-centred picture of rural South China as a place in which friendship remains as marginal as the old Confucian moral orthodoxy depicts it: in other words, the least important of the 'five basic relationships' – the others being 'ruler and minister', 'father and son', 'husband and wife' and 'elder and younger brother' – seen to be at the heart of the world of humans (see Kutcher 2000).

Friendship among Agnatic Village Relatives

I shall first look at the interpersonal relations between residents of 'single-lineage villages' like Harmony Cave. The dominant view here is that kinship is of paramount importance because the closely-knit agnatic and territorial foundations of these villages imply that the residents are bound to be on intimate, amicable terms with one another. This view is probably derived from the impression that these villages are like 'big harmonious families', an impression that is encouraged by people's normative representations of these villages as 'big families' (*daaih-ga*).

This 'big family' picture is also supported by data such as the local practical kinship terminology, according to which all native village residents of ego's age-cohort (or of ego's formal lineage generation) are referred to as ego's brothers/sisters, those of younger generations as ego's nephews/nieces, grandsons/granddaughters, and so on, and those of older generations as ego's uncles/aunts, grandfathers/grandmothers, and so on.[7] It is far from being clear, however, whether when people refer, for example, to the eldest son of their father's brother (FBeS) as their 'eldest brother' (*daaih-go*), they are doing so in a metaphoric or literal sense.[8] My own field observations suggest that both hypotheses are equally valid because the meaning that people give to these kin terms changes according to the situation and context of usage. This means that the 'big family' picture of these villages is very misleading if taken in a strictly literal sense.

The same is true of the assumption that the residents of these 'big family' villages are bound to show to one another the kind of amicable behaviour that one sometimes finds in some particularly harmonious nuclear families. Although the closely-knit agnatic and territorial foundations of these villages provides a formal background of kin amity (which helps to reduce conflict and enhance cooperation), there is still a lot of competition at both the familial and the individual levels (see Watson 1985). As a result, people do not and cannot take active co-operation and support for granted, and, as such, they also have to work hard to make friends (i.e., their own, individual alliances) amongst their neighbours, usually persons of the same sex and of the same age-cohort. Early feminist scholars such as Margery Wolf (1972) have already drawn attention to the importance of this phenomenon of friendship among Taiwanese village women in the context of the Chinese patrilocal rural family and its customary rules of partible, patrilineal inheritance, but there is no reason to restrict this phenomenon to women.

Even in 'single-lineage villages' like Harmony Cave, where the practice of village patrilocal exogamy institutes remarkable sex/gender-based variations in social behaviour, it is quite clear that both men and women are affected by the phenomenon of intra-village friendship, which is described by them as a form of close voluntary association subject to the whims of history and dependent on various practical and affective factors. That this phenomenon is not always visible (in the case of both men and women) to the short-term visitor is because its unfolding does not imply that people will openly and normatively refer to their friendlier agnatic village relatives as their 'friends' or even as their 'kin-friends'. On the contrary, people simply refer to them as 'agnatic village relatives' or 'fellow villagers', and leave the friendship-like bonds in question unmentioned.[9] This is not because these bonds are trivial, but because, as we shall see, they are less formally valued than the bonds of localized agnatic kinship.

What if the person with whom one establishes a relationship of close relatedness does not live in one's village and is not a relative? Can this person be formally known as a 'friend'? Does this mean that we have to distinguish between formal and informal friendship?

The Circle of Relatives and Friends

Frequently differentiated in terms of their practical/affective degree of proximity, utility and/or loyalty, formally recognized 'friends' (*pahng-yauh*), including 'good friends' (*hou pahng-yauh* or *louh-yauh*), are usually persons of the same sex and of the same age-cohort living in neighbouring 'lineage-villages' within the township area or within neighbouring township marketing communities. The blossoming of this kind of formal friendship, as with informal friendship, usually requires some kind of shared context of activity (cf. Allan 1979, 1989; see also Froerer in this volume). Schools are quite important in this respect because they bring together boys and girls from different villages and agnatic backgrounds. Regardless, however, of how it may blossom or fade in time, this phenomenon is known to be as ubiquitous and as inevitable as the formation of informal friendship, but in contrast to the latter, it is explicitly recognized as a key part of people's networks of interpersonal relations.

This can be illustrated by its inclusion in what is arguably the most important higher-level category of practical/affective relatedness of every local family, the 'circle of relatives and friends' (*chan-chik pahng-yauh*). This is the relatively fluid network of close relatives, friends and other non-kin acquaintances, who are likely to be invited to major rituals of birth, marriage, and death, because they lie within the family's 'reliable zone', to use a term forged by Yan Yunxiang (1996: 99–100) in a detailed discussion of gift exchange and social networking in rural Northeastern China. To Yan, this 'reliable zone' is clearly set apart from the larger 'effective zone', where there is a greater emphasis on short-term reciprocity, and even more so from the wider 'impersonal society' both within and beyond the village community, where short-term instrumental gift-giving or bribes are often a way to get things done.

In 'single-lineage villages' like Harmony Cave, the representation of Yan's 'reliable zone' shares the dualistic ideology at the heart of the basic local unit of socialization: the patrilineal and patrilocal *'ga'* or 'family', whose actual size and structure are variable,[10] but which tends to be symbolically portrayed in terms of a series of operating dyads (e.g., father and son, husband and wife) as seemingly natural and harmonious as key cosmological/physiological dyads such as 'Heaven' and 'Earth' or 'Yang' and 'Yin'. From this dualistic perspective, Yan's 'reliable zone' resembles what Francesca Bray (2009) has recently called a 'double', that is, it includes two paired elements whose full character or meaning can only emerge through their shifting echoings, complementarities and contrasts.[11]

The first paired element of this 'double' is more masculine, more vertical, and more centred on ties of patrilineal descent customarily expressed through idioms of 'shared blood', 'shared territory' and above all 'shared ancestral breath'. This first paired element is the one that looks more formal, permanent and inflexible – and thus more given and ascribed – even though it often includes members who are recruited well outside the field of people's so-called 'blood relations'. In it, we find male and female descent relatives who belong to the families of a person's 'village brothers and uncles' (*hing-daih suk-baak*), that is, who belong to the families of a man's (or a woman's husband's) localized lineage. Although each family belongs at the same time to several agnatic branches and segments within this 'big family', people tend to draw particular attention to the agnatic group of village families that lies immediately above their extended family and that first became known in the literature as the *'wu-fu'* [M] or 'circle of mourning relatives' (Freedman 1958: 41–5). This 'close agnatic family grouping' (*chan-fo*), as I prefer to call it, includes the families which are most closely related to a person in terms of descent (no further than the fifth generation) and which are most heavily obligated in ritual and practical terms.

As for the second paired element of the 'double' under discussion, it is more feminine, more horizontal and more centred on affinal ties through marriage and friendship broadly defined. It also appears to be more informal, fluid and flexible – and thus more chosen and negotiated – even though it is often quite predictable and in many ways unchanging. In it, we find male and female relatives who belong to the families of a person's affinal relatives through marriage (*chan-ga*), including any unofficial extra-marital relations of concubinage.[12] In addition, we find close acquaintances – often generally known as 'friends' – who are clearly differentiated in various formal categories such as 'good friends' of several types, 'masters' (*si-fu*), 'teachers' (*louh-si*), 'colleagues' (*tuhng-sih*) and many others, including, as we shall later see, 'same-year siblings' (see Anonymous n.d.).

Seen as a whole, the major formal differences between the paired elements described above have to do with issues of locality and obligations. It is the first, agnatic element that includes people who live in one's own 'lineage-village' and who are most obligated in practical/ritual terms (e.g., they have to contribute with work and/or other resources to the family's major rituals). As to the second, affinal element, it includes people who are scattered in various localities outside the village, mostly within the neighbouring region (that today also includes key distant labour migration areas) where an individual is likely to find his or her spouse, unofficial concubines (if any), and friends. Perhaps not surprisingly, this second, affinal element is less obligated in practical/ritual terms, and this is why it is less formally valued in the local rural society, even though it can actually play a major role in people's well-being.

A similar hierarchical distinction in terms of obligations also lies at the heart of this second, affinal element. If 'friends' in general are similar to 'affinal relatives through marriage' because both are outsiders and are not as obligated to us as local agnatic relatives, 'friends' are also different from 'affinal relatives through marriage' because they are even less obligated to us than the latter. Whatever gifts 'friends' may give during a visit or a ritual celebration (e.g., bottles of rice wine, packs/boxes of cigarettes, old tea leaves), they are said to do it less out of obligation, like agnatic or affinal relatives, than out of sentiment. In other words, they are said to do it simply because they 'have a heart' (*yauh sam*) that tells them to do so. Note that this 'heart' pays attention not just to issues of emotional affection (*gam-chihng*), but also to practical considerations (*saht-jai*). This point emerges quite clearly in the villagers' descriptions of those 'good friendships' they had to stop stressing through visiting or gift-giving, not so much because of emotional reasons but because of practical issues such as lack of time or clashes with family interests. It is precisely this volatility (i.e. the sense that 'friends' may not be close to us in the future), together with their lack of strong obligations, that makes 'friends' even less formally valued than 'affinal relatives through marriage' in the local society. Does this mean that 'friends' are not important or cherished by people?

In what remains of this chapter, I shall show just how important people's 'friends' are and can be. However, instead of doing this by drawing attention to the instrumental efficacy of the metaphor of friendship in the villagers' increasingly market-oriented *guanxi*-building practices in the wider society (see E. Wolf 1966), I shall raise the question of what happens to two 'friends', or, better still, to two 'good friends', when they start to resemble the two paired elements of a family's reliable zone of interpersonal relations: an inseparable 'double'. We can now turn to what the local people call *'tuhng-nihn hing-daih'*, roughly 'same-year brothers', or *'tuhng-nihn je-muih'*, roughly 'same-year sisters'.

The Phenomenon of 'Same-Year Siblingship'

According to my informants, this phenomenon has been widespread in the region of Brightpath and surroundings at least since the late imperial period. I shall not speculate here on issues of historical origins and spatial distribution, which are beyond the scope of this chapter, but I would like to note that the phenomenon of 'same-year siblingship' is also known in other parts of rural South China. I had the opportunity to confirm this point empirically during a fieldtrip in the summer of 2005 to various Cantonese and non-Cantonese rural settings in Northern Guangdong and in the neighbouring coastal province of Guangxi.[13] Away from the field, I have also found explicit references to 'same-year siblings' in records of old extant Cantonese oral traditions such as children's songs (e.g. Kwok and Chan 1990: 72). Writing about the famous women's script (*nü-shu* [M]) discovered in the region of Southern Hunan (close to Northern Guangdong), the anthropologists William Chiang (1995) and Cathy Silber (1994) refer in passing to a form of 'ritual siblinghood' that presents striking resemblances with the one here described.

Like these two authors, I am convinced that the phenomenon of 'same-year siblingship' is a form of 'ritual siblinghood' that emerged during the long process of Han Chinese colonization of the region of South China from the second century BCE onwards, possibly through the merging of well-established features of ancient Han society with the traditions of former local indigenous populations such as the Yao, Thai and Yue. Obviously, further archival and field research is required to clarify this issue, but it may be worth pointing out in any case that the 'same-year siblingship' phenomenon is strongly evocative of the customs of ancient non-Han populations in South China concerning 'age-mate relationships' (Chiang 1995: 95–110). In addition, the idiom of 'same-year siblingship' also presents obvious formal resonances with ancient Han Chinese idioms of homosocial relatedness centred on age/generation. I have in mind here 'official' idioms of relatedness of the imperial period that formally acknowledge the existence of special bonds between friends who were born in the same year, or between students (men, by definition) who took, in the same year, the imperial examinations to gain entrance into the administrative ranks (see Liang and Zheng 1996: 140; Ciyuan 2006: vol. 1, 0475).

General Features and Gender Variations

People in contemporary Brightpath tend to explain 'same-year siblingship' to outsiders by comparing it to 'sworn siblinghood' (*git-baai hing-daih je-muih*) – another local phenomenon of fictive/ritual kinship that is widely noted for having existed among all elements of Chinese society for many centuries[14] (see Gallin and Gallin 1977; Jordan 1985; Ownby 1996; Chen 2003 for sworn brotherhood; and Honig 1985; Stockard 1992 for sworn sisterhood). The main reason for this comparison is that 'same-year siblingship' also entails a ritualized 'blood oath', together with a feast, to symbolize the adoption of binding terms of metaphoric agnatic siblingship between the persons involved. William Chiang (1995) and Cathy Silber (1994) also note this parallel in their writings on Southern Hunan, but they make it equally clear that these are two distinct forms of 'ritual siblinghood', as do the people of Brightpath.

Here are some of the differences between the two phenomena. Unlike 'sworn siblinghood', the local custom of 'same-year siblingship' designates the 'year of birth' as a key formal requirement of eligibility. Moreover, whereas the broader phenomenon of 'sworn siblinghood' can involve heterosocial relations and can be centred on large groups of persons, which may trigger the formation of complex corporate organizations as varied as political coalitions, secret societies, bandit groups or urban gangs, the local phenomenon of 'same-year siblingship' entails only homosocial relations and tends to be centred on dyadic relations, even if the consequences of these relations go well beyond the private lives of the dyads involved (see also Harrell 1982: 128–30 on the importance of dyadic relations in Taiwanese rural sworn brotherhoods).

Like much else in the local rural society, 'same-year siblingship' presents significant gender variations. In the village of Harmony Cave for example, around twenty to thirty per cent of the adult male population (above the age of sixteen) has at least one 'same-year brother' and a few even have two or three of these dyadic relations. By contrast, there are only a few cases of married and unmarried women with formal 'same-year sisters'. These numbers suggest that 'same-year sisterhood' is far less frequent than 'same-year brotherhood'. It is also much less stable and durable, and much less visible and celebrated (if celebrated at all) in the wider public sphere.

These gender differences are no doubt related to the combined effects of the local customary system of patrilineal inheritance and the local customary practice of village patrilocal exogamy, which place women in a marginal power position in the public sphere and institute a major structural rupture in the course of their lives (cf. Friedman 2006: 137–67).

More generally, these gender differences reflect the enduring influence in the local society of an old pre-Communist ethos linked to Han patriarchal culture that encourages the formal estrangement between the sexes in most interpersonal relations and that favours the association of women (and of the 'feminine') with activities related to the domestic sphere. However, while drawing attention to the importance of gender differences in 'same-year siblingship', both my male and female informants also insisted that this phenomenon, like the other forms of informal friendship discussed above, ultimately transcends the boundaries of gender (see also Uhl 1991). This point was most succinctly expressed when they noted, for example, that people only use one shortened term, *'a-tuhng'* (literally 'same', 'common', 'together'), *'louh-tuhng'* (literally 'old same') or even *'tuhng-nihn'* (literally 'same-year'), to refer to both 'same-year brothers' and 'same-year sisters'. The unspoken symbolic significance of these shortened terms of reference will become clearer later on.

The Restricted and the Extended Formats

If seen from the perspective of the subjects most directly involved, 'same-year siblingship' presents itself in two major formats that in fact constitute two extreme polar types of the same phenomenon. In its more restricted format, a siblingship-like relation is consecrated between two same-sex 'good friends' who were born in the same year and developed very close ties of affective and practical support for each other during their formative years.[15] For the two 'good friends' in question, the social institution of this siblingship-like relation, which usually happens immediately before their marriage, is a way of protecting and reinforcing their relation of close friendship and allowing it to last longer. This process may be self-initiated, but it may also be arranged (as in the pre-Communist era) or triggered by the concerns of their families (or even villages) that their close friendship is somewhat ambiguous and lies outside an adequate binding framework of formal obligations like the one between relatives. But 'same-year siblingship' can also present itself in a more extended format, whereby the siblingship-like relation is socially consecrated between two same-sex persons who have no close ties whatsoever with each other but who were born in the same year. It is in this far more instrumental manner – which, again, can be self-initiated or arranged/triggered by familial pressures – that people would often suggest during fieldwork that I could become their son's 'same-year brother' even though I had never met him before.

In both formats, the public institution of 'same-year siblingship' is made manifest by means of rituals, which tend to be more visible and noisy, as already noted, in the case of men. Not unlike marriage, these rituals are usually preceded by a process of negotiation in which the specific terms of the relationship in question (including the obligations it entails) have to be discussed by the two parties and may even be written down in the form of a contract-like document kept by the two sides. Obviously, the structure and shape of this process of negotiation (including the relative protagonism of individuals and collectives in it) are highly variable and have not been immune to the radical historical transformations that have recently occurred in the local society. The same is also true of the structure and shape of the local rites of 'same-year siblingship', although it seems to me that the basic point of these 'rites of institution', as Pierre Bourdieu (1982) would call them, is still the same: the formal consecration and announcement of the relation in question both to the world of the dead and to the world of the living.

To the world of the dead, this announcement ideally involves a ritualized oath in the temples and ancestral halls linked to the 'localized lineages' of the two participants. This oath is intended as the official registration of this relation in 'heaven', making it known to the local gods (whose protection is sought) and also, at least in the case of 'same-year brothers', to the ancestors of the 'localized lineages' of the two sides. In many ways, one of the key points of this cosmological registration – which is analogous to the one that occurs in the rituals of marriage – is precisely the metaphoric affiliation of the two 'same-year brothers' in the patriline of the other's family and 'localized lineage'. Unlike marriage however, the ritual ideology behind this affiliation is not concerned with alliance but with suggesting that the two initiates will become akin to agnatic siblings, or, better still, to agnatic village relatives of the same sex and age/generation.

This is also one of the key messages at the heart of the ceremonies aimed at the world of the living, which basically involve commensal feasting or what the local people call 'drinking' (*yam*) because there will be many delicious food-toppings (meat and/or fish) on the table to accompany white rice (the basic staple food). In Brightpath, this feasting usually involves a double banquet in the houses and villages of the two 'same-year siblings' in question and each side is expected to pay for the expenses of its own banquet. People say that it is during these banquets that the two sides will 'see each other's face' and 'eat together' for the first time as if they were one single, overarching 'agnatic family', although it is obvious to everyone that this public commensal institution of agnatic unity is only an ideological fantasy. This is because in practice the new 'same-year siblingship' relatives are bound to remain agnatic/local outsiders and will keep on being treated as such, despite the mutual adoption of colloquial family-like terms of reference by the two sides.[16] However, these are not just any outsiders. They are outsiders with whom a particular relation of affinity, or, better still, of individual/collective alliance has been ritually formalized: an alliance that, just like the one at stake in a formal marriage, is also patrilineally inheritable.[17]

This is no doubt the reason why Radcliffe-Brown (1952: 162) in his famous 1940 article on 'joking relationships' classified what he called 'blood-brotherhood' (i.e. 'ritual siblinghood'), together with marriage, as one of the key modes of 'alliance or consociation' in human societies. However, whereas Radcliffe-Brown was more concerned with the macro-historical and structural implications of this mode of alliance, I wish to pay more attention to the practical and affective phenomenon that inspires this alliance from the micro-historical point of view of the subjects more directly involved.

This question takes us back to our distinction between restricted and extended 'same-year siblingship' and to its relation with a distinction previously drawn by Bernard and Rita Gallin (1977) between two polar types of 'sworn brotherhood' in urban Taiwan. While 'affective sworn brotherhood' is characteristically undertaken by young or poor people seeking to reinforce close friendship ties and to expand their networks of relationships, 'instrumental sworn brotherhood' tends to be undertaken by older and higher class/status people and is often characterized by a more explicit goal of economic and socio-political gain through mutual aid.

David Jordan (1985) has already tried to soften this distinction by noting that his Taiwanese urban informants claimed that in 'affective sworn brotherhood' there is also mutual practical advantage involved. Jordan's position is closer to that of my informants who were certainly not shy about emphasizing the overall practical benefits of their 'same-year siblingship' associations. However, they also insisted that although these associations (like the ones of friendship) combine practical and affective elements, they vary in their degree of instrumentality, some of them being, at least initially, strictly instrumental. It seems to me therefore that Jordan's position ends up overlooking what is really at stake in the Gallins' typology or at least in my distinction between restricted and extended 'same-year siblingship'.

Whereas in the restricted format it is a strong 'good friendship' that triggers the self-initiated, pressured and/or arranged institution of 'same-year siblingship', in the extended format it is, by contrast, the self-initiated, pressured and/or arranged institution of this public status that will hopefully lead to a strong 'good friendship', or at least will cash in on the ensuing benefits of appearing to be one. This suggests that it is the social recognition of the importance of such strong 'good friendships' that explains – practically and affectively speaking – the existence of the institution of 'same-year siblingship' in the first place. The fact that what is instituted – metaphoric agnatic siblingship – is different from what leads to its institution – a strong 'good friendship' or the desire for it – brings to mind the previous discussion of the relative formal value of agnates, marriage relatives and friends in the local society.

A-Huhng and A-Yuhng

'Tomorrow morning you'll come to my house to drink. Distinguished guests will be coming'. This was how A-Huhng,[18] a young male friend and teacher from Harmony Cave, first invited me to his 'same-year siblingship' celebrations in early 2000, soon after Chinese New Year. A-Yuhng, his 'same-year brother', is also a young teacher at Brightpath middle school. At the time, both A-Huhng and A-Yuhng were still unmarried and in their early twenties. Moreover, neither of them had yet officially separated from their parents' families, although they already had their own earnings, ate mostly by themselves, and resided for the most part away from their villages in the lodging facilities of their work unit in the market town. A-Yuhng's family comes from a 'single-lineage village' that has a different patronymic from A-Huhng's and is located outside Harmony Cave's vicinity and rural administrative area, even if still inside the township and marketing area of Brightpath. In short, the two families share local ties, but they are not closely related through kinship and marriage. They do belong, however, to the same class, both being economically successful by local standards.

The distinguished guests mentioned by A-Huhng were the delegates of A-Yuhng's family and village. I knew that the banquet would be modest and small in size because, as is usually the case when the budget is low, only the male representatives of the two families and respective 'close agnatic family-groupings' had been invited (about twelve persons altogether). Nevertheless, this banquet represented a significant investment to A-Huhng's family, as it would cost more than RMB300 (c. €27) in food, wine and other expensive gifts like 'boxes of cigarettes' and 'red envelopes (with money)', representing almost half of A-Huhng's official monthly salary as a middle school teacher. Despite this heavy expenditure (which itself is insignificant if compared to an average marriage banquet), A-Huhng and A-Yuhng would later tell me in private that they had only agreed to these customary ceremonies to please their families. Both sides had long insisted that the two ought to undertake the ceremonies of 'same-year siblingship' so that their relationship of 'good friendship' could be properly framed in a binding structure of formal obligations like the one between relatives – this in spite of the boys' insistence that those ceremonies were unnecessary (not to mention expensive and old-fashioned) because they would have no direct bearing on the content of their relationship.

The case of A-Huhng and A-Yuhng reminds us first of all that although the days of forced arranged 'same-year siblingship', like those of forced marriage, are already in the past, the dynamics of social and economic emancipation of the local younger generations are not as straightforward as the increasing levels of socio-economic and geographical mobility may suggest. The fact, however, that both A-Huhng and A-Yuhng so openly resisted the ceremonies of 'same-year siblingship' is a clear-cut illustration of the growing power of the younger generations in the local society. More importantly perhaps, their views on the matter remind us of an often forgotten dimension of 'same-year siblingship', if not of 'sworn siblinghood' more generally. This is that the sense of closeness and mutual obligation between 'same-year siblings' is as much the product of the ceremonies that publicly institute it, as it can be the product of the practical/affective relation of friendship that triggered its public institution. Other 'same-year siblings' confided similar opinions to me.

As for the particular story of A-Huhng and A-Yuhng, it all began in the middle school where they are currently working and, according to them, it was all a question of what people call '*yuhn-fan*', usually translated as 'the fate that brings people together'. The story goes that although A-Huhng came to have a fantastic educational CV by local standards, he was not a very bright student in his early primary school years. Known for his strictness and firm belief in education, A-Huhng's father once forced him to repeat one year simply because he was getting relatively bad grades. If it were not for this repeated year, the two friends would probably have never met later on in Brightpath middle school, because A-Huhng is one year older than A-Yuhng and was one school year ahead of him. However, there are a few other signs suggesting that fate brought them together.

When A-Huhng and A-Yuhng enrolled in middle school in the late 1980s, chance assigned them not just to the same class but also to the same classroom table. It was by sharing that table – well beyond the world of their families and villages – that their friendship first started to blossom. At first they were simply '*tuhng-toih tuhng-hohk*', roughly 'same-table classmates', but they soon became 'good friends'. They were, as they themselves put it, making use of a very powerful local idiom of close relatedness (see Santos 2009), eating together on a quasi-daily basis in the school canteen (something that they had done before only with close family members). In the second year, they started to share the same room in the school's dormitory, and this gradually contributed to the development of a very strong sense of affection and mutual support between them. By being engaged in many kinds of shared activities in school (a kind of second 'lineage-village' for them), they soon developed the ability to help each other and to share and read each other's thoughts, secrets and experiences.

It is quite likely, however, that they would have never gone as far as pledging mutual loyalty to each other as 'same-year siblings' if they had not pursued a similar educational and career path; this was yet another way in which fate brought them together. After graduating from middle school in 1992, they convinced their families to enrol them in a senior middle school located in a neighbouring township (Brightpath still has no senior middle school at present). Two years later, they went on together to a teachers' training college in the county capital. They both graduated in 1997 and have since returned as teachers to Brightpath middle school. In order to do this, they told me, they relied heavily on their families' support and *guanxi* networks – and this was another reason why they agreed to go through with the customary 'same-year siblingship' ceremonies.

In the summer of 1999, A-Huhng, the elder of the two, was promoted to the pedagogical committee of Brightpath middle school, and, soon after, they decided to make a personal oath of 'same-year brotherhood', though it was only in the winter of 2000 that the public ceremonies took place in their villages. When I met them in the summer of 2005, they were both preparing to marry (they actually helped each other to find a match). A few years later, in January 2008, I learned that A-Huhng was the first to marry despite the fact that he is much more shy with girls. I also learned that A-Huhng's wife gave birth to a baby daughter in 2007, and that A-Yuhng's wife was about to deliver. In many respects, the interests, characters and personalities of these two 'same-year brothers' could not be more dissimilar, but they are also well known locally for being good at doing things together (*hou ngaam-baahn*) – an aspect of their relationship that I had the opportunity to observe at close range by joining their middle school teachers' basketball team during the local Lunar New Year tournament of 2000. How do they themselves explain this empathy?

Affinal Doubles Through Friendship

There are no easy answers here but if they had to choose one, A-Huhng and A-Yuhng once told me after a key basketball match in the market town, they would say that it is a question of mutual compatibility (a frequent explanation given by other 'same-year siblings'). As the old local saying has it, *'sahp jek yahn, sahp jek ban, ban ban dou mh-tuhng ge'*, roughly translated as 'ten different persons, ten different characters or qualities, each one being different from the other'. In this world of differences and uncertainty, people simply do not get along with everyone with the same degree of mutual affection and practical benefit, and it is not always easy to find someone who fully matches one's personality, interests or desires. In the case of A-Huhng and A-Yuhng, one such 'perfect' match occurred and has perpetuated itself over a significant period, something that does not always happen in such harmonious fashion.

These matches between 'same-year siblings' present some similarities with the matches between prospective married couples – a parallel also noted by Cathy Silber (1994: 50–8) and William Chiang (1995: 19–20) in their brief descriptions of 'same-year siblings' in Southern Hunan. As A-Huhng and A-Yuhng once sharply reminded me, just as brides and grooms seek traditional calendar experts before marriage to check their horoscopic degree of mutual compatibility as 'spouses', so prospective 'same-year siblings' often seek these calendar experts to do the same. Older informants also told me that back in the pre-Communist period, when the interests of familial collectives often had clear-cut precedence over the interests of individuals, this horoscopic checking used to be a formal requirement, or, better still, a formal procedure of diplomatic communication between the two parties during the process of negotiation preceding the ceremonies of 'same-year siblingship'.

That this parallel between 'same-year siblingship' and marriage is not more explicit in the representational efforts of my informants is because the relation that is ritually instituted (i.e. siblingship) is not symbolically associated in this part of China, as it is, for example, in much of Island Southeast Asia (Kipp 1986), with the relationship between spouses or lovers – an ethnographic fact that is no doubt related to the strong emphasis on patrilineality and patrilocal exogamy in Han Chinese society. However, what I want to suggest here is that despite the powerful reality-producing effects of the local ideology of agnatic kinship, the more practical and affective realities leading to the public institution of 'same-year siblingship' are indeed quite similar to the ones leading to the rites of marriage: 'friendly love' (in both a practical and affective sense) being to 'same-year siblingship' and alliance, what 'conjugal love' (in both a practical and affective sense) is to marriage and alliance. Quite clearly, these are practical and affective realities that, regardless of their degree of instrumentality, are more chosen than given, more on the side of affinity than of consanguinity and more focused on the present and future than the past.

My hypothesis then is that what triggers in practice the strategic deployment of 'same-year siblingship' is simply an extreme form of 'good friendship' or the desire to develop one. This is a mode of homosocial friendship in which people's practical and affective sense of mutual compatibility is so strong and so enduring that the two non-kin related persons in question may truly come to feel and/or resemble what I shall here call an 'affinal double', that is, paired affinal figures whose full character or meaning can only emerge through their shifting echoings, complementarities and contrasts. Because they have to be 'read' in pairs, these 'doubles' echo the traditional antithetical couplets that are customarily hung side by side on the doors and walls of most local houses, temples or ancestral halls during important ritual celebrations.

I call them 'affinal' because these 'allied doubles' evoke the Yin-Yang conjugal pairs depicted in popular items of material culture, such as painted mirrors with dragons and phoenixes, double happiness characters, and other common symbols of conjugal harmony. Unlike these conjugal pairs, however, 'same-year siblings' are not affinal doubles out of a relation of 'conjugal love' that is formally celebrated in the rituals of marriage, but are affinal doubles out of a relation of well-paired 'friendly love' that is formally celebrated in transfigured form in the rituals of 'same-year siblingship'. The fact that these rituals portray 'good friends' like A-Huhng and A-Yuhng as 'agnatic siblings' does not mean that to them siblings are better than friends, only that this is the expressive form through which their relation of 'good friendship' can be strategically reproduced in practice.

In all likelihood, this point is becoming more visible in the current post-Mao period than it was in the pre-Communist period or even in the Maoist era. This is because the desire for 'friendly love' – as for 'conjugal love' (Yan 2003) – is now being increasingly expressed in public with the individualistic terms used by young successful 'same-year siblings' like A-Huhng and A-Yuhng. Nevertheless, this should not lead us to think that this individualistic desire did not exist in the past, nor that it is only a post-Mao artefact largely restricted to members of the local rural elite. Quite the contrary, the impression I got from talking to older 'same-year siblings' was that this desire also existed in the past, even if its manifestation was overshadowed by a far less individualistic mode of expression – one that clearly reflected the power of the collective formations of the agrarian social order of the time.

Friendship, Kinship and Relatedness

In the wake of several decades of radical critiques of the discipline's 'grand kinship theories', recent developments in the field of kinship studies (e.g. Carsten 2000b, 2004; Franklin and McKinnon 2001) suggest that the cross-cultural study of kinship would be better grounded analytically if placed under the liberating shadow of more fluid and all-inclusive concepts such as 'relatedness'. The main advantage of such concepts, it is argued (Carsten 2000a: 4–5; 2004: 188–9), is that they allow one to move away from the assumption that the comparative study of kinship must rest on a supposedly universal analytic distinction between the biological and the social, and to pay more attention to people's own 'cultures of relatedness'. It is hoped that this shift of focus will lead not only to a better ethnographic understanding of the cross-cultural diversity of the human kinship experience, but also to the realization that the study of kinship cannot be separated from the more general phenomenon of intimacy and its wider effects in the public sphere.

In many respects, the present discussion of 'same-year siblingship' clearly suggests that the broadness and fluidity of concepts like 'relatedness' can be very helpful in countering the 'classic' tendency to overstate the centrality of agnatic kinship and locality in rural South China and in framing the question of intimacy outside this bounded realm in a more positive manner (see Stafford 2000a). However, the same discussion also suggests that the usage of such concepts must not entail the abandonment of 'classic' analytic distinctions such as those between kinship and friendship, consanguinity and affinity, filiation and descent, or marriage and alliance. The reason for this is that concepts like 'relatedness' do not help us make sense of the differentiations that 'real people' make between different kinds of relations and their varying degrees of importance, volatility and instrumentality. Perhaps more significantly, given the principal concerns of this chapter (and of this volume), concepts such as 'relatedness' are not very helpful when it comes to countering the old habit in the discipline, and in the social sciences more generally, of downplaying the cross-cultural importance of friendship.

It was only because the present discussion benefited from the universalistic spirit of the discipline's 'classic' analytical legacy in comparative sociology that I was able to realize that the data here presented are not just talking about the changing specificities of the expressive style of friendship in contemporary rural South China. They are also giving support to recent anthropological claims that friendship is a key form of human relatedness in its own right (see Bell and Coleman 1999b; Santos-Granero 2007; see also Viveiros de Castro 1992: 96–112).

My data also suggest that although this key form of human relatedness is clearly separate from kinship and marriage, as Santos-Granero (2007) has recently shown with Amazonian material, it also stands – sociologically speaking – more on the side of 'marriage and affinity' than on the side of 'consanguinity'. What makes it closer to 'marriage and affinity', despite not being associated with sexuality, procreation, generational succession, or the appropriation of children, is that it also constitutes – to expand Radcliffe Brown's (1952) original analysis – a key mode of individual and/or collective alliance.

I am convinced that the analytical recognition of the cross-cultural centrality of this largely neglected form of alliance will prompt innovative ethnographic contributions to the study of human intimacy and relatedness in general. It may also lead anthropologists to move beyond the recent efforts of disciplines like evolutionary psychology (see e.g. Tooby and Cosmides 1996) to find alternative evolutionary pathways, besides genetic relatedness and direct/delayed reciprocity, to the more general phenomenon of human altruism and cooperation. What this chapter suggests in this respect is that the micro-historical issue of affective as well as practical echoings, complementarities and contrasts between individuals/collectives is a promising avenue of research.

Notes

1. This chapter is a slightly modified version of an article with the same title previously published in the *Journal of the Royal Anthropological Institute*, 2008, Volume 14, Issue 3, pp.535–53. I would like to thank Blackwell Publishing for permission to reprint this material. The text was written while on a post-doctoral fellowship from the *Fundação para a Ciência e Tecnologia* (SFRH/BPD/20489/2004/1I9K). I gratefully acknowledge this foundation's support. I would also like to thank the organizers, speakers and discussants of the workshop on which this volume is based for their insightful comments and suggestions.
2. I use English pseudonyms to refer to all places located in my fieldwork area in order to facilitate the reading and safeguard the privacy of my informants.
3. Except where indicated with an [M], which indicates Mandarin (the official language), all Chinese words or expressions quoted in the text refer to the Cantonese language spoken in the village area. The system of Cantonese Romanization used in this chapter is the Yale system with minor modifications due to local variations. All words and expressions quoted in Mandarin follow the standard Pinyin system.
4. The fieldwork in Harmony Cave followed a three-year period of language training in the cities of Macao, Hong Kong and Guangzhou. My initial stay in the village between 1999 and 2001 was only possible due to the on-going support of the local population, whom I want to thank. During this period, I had the opportunity to live in three different village households and had the freedom to accompany the villagers in their daily activities. My field data was collected primarily through this participant observation, but I also used other more formal methodologies such as surveys and semi-structured interviews.
5. Most villages in Brightpath and surroundings are 'single-lineage villages'. There are also a few 'multi-lineage villages' (usually with no more than three localized lineages), but there are no villages with an entirely 'mixed' population in terms of surname and agnatic origins. This latter type of 'multi-surname village' can be found in some parts of South China, but is more

strongly associated with North China. The only places in Brightpath that look 'mixed' in this latter sense are market towns.

6. In the pre-Communist era, the economic value of bridewealth and dowry was modestly calculated in terms of 'bamboo-poles' – a local measure equivalent to about 50kg – of unhusked rice grain. Today, the value of bridewealth and dowry is calculated in terms of money, and in 2005 the standard value of bridewealth had already mounted to more than 10.000RMB (c. €900), an amount of money that is beyond the reach of many local families, especially if their primary economic activity is farming.

7. I only have in mind terms of reference used in ordinary conversations. The more ceremonious terms of reference used, for example, in written marriage invitations are far more complex and involve a much higher degree of formal differentiation (see Anonymous n.d. for an illustration).

8. This question is much less problematic when raised in the context of a 'multi-surname village' – the more 'mixed' type of village more commonly associated with North China. Typically, the resident families of these villages have very different agnatic origins, do not organize themselves in descent-based neighbourhoods, and do not share strong taboos on village endogamy. Hence they tend to acknowledge much more readily that when they refer to non-kin fellow villagers as 'kin', they do so only in a metaphoric sense (see Yan 1996; Kipnis 1997; see also Fei 1939).

9. This phenomenon is not entirely different from what happens in the highly mixed 'multi-surname villages' more strongly associated with North China. In these villages, a friend-like villager is also not a 'friend', but remains categorized as a 'fellow villager' or else as a 'metaphoric agnatic relative' (see Yan 1996; Kipnis 1997; see also Fei 1939).

10. The size/structure of the Chinese rural *ga* (or *jia* [M]) is a subject of immense controversy, not least because the term *ga* itself – like the English 'family' – is very elastic and ambiguous. In the Harmony Cave region, the 'traditional' ideal model is that of a classic patrilineal joint family system – one that necessarily provides for family division. If two conjugal units are formed in the junior generation, the family eventually fissions into two independent families; if three conjugal units are formed, the family eventually separates into three independent families. This normative model has undergone dramatic transformations during the last five decades of socialist and post-socialist reforms. For example, while in the pre-Communist era family partition was expected to occur only after all sons/daughters were married, today most sons are likely to start claiming their share of family property and to establish their own separate family 'stoves' (if not 'houses') immediately after marriage.

11. Originally developed in the context of a discussion of 'maternal doubling' in late imperial China (Bray 1997: 343–58), this notion of 'double' was inspired by the contrast between two kinds of doubling procedures in literary creations; for example, one in which a character or form of expression is to be perceived as two (as in Dr Jekyll and Mr. Hyde), and another in which two characters or forms of expression come to be perceived as one (as in classic

Chinese novels). For Bray (2009), this latter 'bipolar logic' is not just typical of Chinese classic literary creations, but echoes the predominance of relational, dualistic thinking in Chinese philosophical and medical discourses (e.g. the theory of *yin* and *yang*). I would like to add here that the prominence of 'dualistic representations' in China presents striking points of intersection with the prominence of phenomena such as 'ritual parallelism', 'dualistic symbolism' and 'gender dualism' in the neighbouring region of Southeast Asia (see, for example, Fox 1988).

12. Polygyny has a long and prominent history in China. This practice was legally abolished in the Communist era with the Marriage Law of 1950, which explicitly prohibited all forms of polygamy. Despite the official reiteration of this prohibition in 1981 and 2001, the phenomenon of extra-marital concubinage (with multiple residence) remains an unofficial marginal reality in China, one that often triggers intense public debate in many parts of the country, including Hong Kong and Macao.

13. This fieldtrip would have not been possible without the support of Professor Li Xiyuan, an anthropologist from Zhongshan University.

14. The longstanding popularity of this highly flexible custom can easily be illustrated by its frequent usage as a literary device in works of classic and modern literature (see Jordan 1985; Ownby 1996; Chen 2003). The two most popular examples are probably the sworn-brotherhoods depicted in two famous novels of the Yuan (1271–1368) and Ming (1368–1644) dynasties, usually known in English as *Romance of the Three Kingdoms* and *All Men are Brothers*.

15. Of course, sexual intimacy can occur (I heard some rumours about at least one case), but it is not socially regarded as a defining element of these ties (see also Stockard 1992: 40–1, 71).

16. This point can be further illustrated by the role of the incest taboo in this institution. Although people say that an incest prohibition must be extended to the family of one's 'same-year sibling', there are in practice many cases of 'same-year siblings' who end up getting married with the other's actual sister or brother. What is most revealing about these 'incestuous' cases is the fact that people do not make a big fuss about them, as they certainly would if they were confronted with a real case of incest in a village family. I should add here that people do make a big fuss when they are confronted with cases of agnatic incest at the village level – a major violation of the local taboo against village endogamy that is still not common in the township.

17. For example, just as one is bound to remain formally related to the patrilineal son of one's father's brother-in-law, so one is bound to remain formally related to the patrilineal son of one's father's 'same-year brother' (see Anonymous n.d.: 65).

18. In what follows, the names of all local interlocutors are Cantonese pseudonyms.

References

Aijmer, G. and V.K.Y. Ho. 2000. *Cantonese Society at a Time of Change*. Hong Kong: Chinese University Press.

Allan, G.A. 1979. *A Sociology of Friendship and Kinship*. London: George Allen & Unwin.

———. 1989. *Friendship. Developing a Sociological Perspective*. Boulder: Westview Press.

Anonymous. n.d. *Nannu zhengqin zaqin chenghu (Forms of address of male and female relatives)*. Handwritten manuscript obtained during fieldwork in rural Northern Guangdong between 1999 and 2001.

Bell, S. and S. Coleman. 1999a. 'The Anthropology of Friendship: Enduring Themes and Future Possibilities', in S. Bell and S. Coleman (eds), *The Anthropology of Friendship*. Oxford: Berg.

———. (eds). 1999b. *The Anthropology of Friendship*. Oxford: Berg.

Bourdieu, P. 1982. 'Les Rites d'Institution', *Actes de la Recherche en Sciences Sociales* 43: 58–63.

Bray, F. 1997. *Technology and Gender. Fabrics of Power in Late Imperial China*. Berkeley: University of California Press.

———. 2009. 'Becoming a Mother in Late Imperial China. Maternal Doubles and the Ambiguities of Fertility', in S. Brandtstädter and G.D. Santos (eds), *Chinese Kinship. Contemporary Anthropological Perspectives*. London: Routledge.

Carsten, J. 2000a. 'Introduction. Cultures of Relatedness', in J. Carsten (ed.), *Cultures of Relatedness: New Approaches to the Study of Kinship*. Cambridge: Cambridge University Press.

———. (ed.). 2000b. *Cultures of Relatedness: New Approaches to the Study of Kinship*. Cambridge: Cambridge University Press.

———. 2004. *After Kinship*. Cambridge: Cambridge University Press.

Chen, S.R. 2003. 'Mengyue yu jieyi – cong chunqiu yu 'sanguo' tanqi. (Oaths of alliance and Sworn Brotherhoods – from the Chunqiu period to the Romance of the Three Kingdoms).' *Zhejiang Xuebao*, No. 1: 34–42.

Chiang, W.W. 1995. *'We Two Know the Script; We Have Become Good Friends.' Linguistic and Social Aspects of the Women's Script Literacy in Southern Hunan, China*. Lanham: University Press of America.

Ciyuan (Origins of Words). 2006. *Xiudingben (Revised edition, 2 volumes)*. Beijing: Shangwu yinshuguan.

Cohen, M.L. 2005. *Kinship, Contract, Community, and the State. Anthropological Perspectives on China*. Stanford: Stanford University Press.

Cohen, Y.A. 1961. 'Patterns of Friendship', in Y.A. Cohen (ed.), *Social Structure and Personality. A Casebook*. New York: Holt, Rinehart & Winston.

Fei, X.T. 1939. *Peasant Life in China. A Field Study of Country Life in the Yangtze Valley*. London: Routledge.

Fox, J.J. (ed.). 1988. *To Speak in Pairs. Essays on the Ritual Languages of Eastern Indonesia*. Cambridge: Cambridge University Press.

Franklin, S. and S. Mckinnon (eds). 2001. *Relative Values. Reconfiguring Kinship Studies*. Durham: Duke University Press.

Freedman, M. 1958. *Lineage Organization in Southeastern China*. London: Athlone Press.

———. 1966. *Chinese Lineage and Society: Fukien and Kwangtung*. London: Athlone Press.

Friedman, S.L. 2006. *Intimate Politics: Marriage, the Market, and State Power in Southeastern China*. Cambridge, MA: Harvard University Press.

Gallin, B. and R.S. Gallin. 1977. 'Sociopolitical Power and Sworn Brother Groups in Chinese Society. A Taiwanese Case', in R.D. Fogelson and R.N. Adams (eds), *The Anthropology of Power*. New York: Academic Press.

Harrell, S. 1982. *Ploughshare Village. Culture and Context in Taiwan*. Seattle: University of Washington Press.

Honig, E. 1985. 'Burning Incense, Pledging Sisterhood: Communities of Women Workers in the Shanghai Cotton Mills, 1919–1949', *Signs: Journal of Women in Culture and Society* 10(4), 700–14.

Jordan, D. 1985. 'Sworn Brothers. A Study in Ritual Kinship', in J.C. Hsieh and Y.C. Chuang (eds), *The Chinese Family and its Ritual Behavior*. Taipei: Academia Sinica.

Judd, E. 1994. *Gender and Power in Rural North China*. Stanford: Stanford University Press.

Kipnis, A. 1997. *Producing Guanxi. Sentiment, Self and Subculture in a North China Village*. Durham: Duke University Press.

Kipp, R.S. 1986. 'Terms of Endearment. Karo Batak Lovers as Siblings', *American Ethnologist* 13(4): 632–45.

Ku, H.B. 2003. *Moral Politics in a South Chinese Village*. New York: Rowman & Littlefield.

Kutcher, N. 2000. 'The Fifth Relationship. Dangerous Friendships in the Confucian Context', *The American Historical Review* 105(5): 1615–30.

Kwok, H. and M. Chan. 1990. *Fossils from a Rural Past. A Study of Extant Cantonese Children's Songs*. Hong Kong: Hong Kong University Press.

Liang, Z.J. and Z. Zheng. 1996. *Chengwei lu. Qinshu ji*. (Record of forms of address. Record of the addressing forms of the relatives). Beijing: Zhonghua shuju.

Ownby, D. 1996. *Brotherhoods and Secret Societies in Early and Mid-Qing China: The Formation of a Tradition*. Stanford: Stanford University Press.

Paine, R. 1969. 'In Search of Friendship: An Exploratory Analysis in "Middle-Class" culture', *Man* (NS) 4(4): 505–24.

Pitt-Rivers, J. 1973. 'The Kith and the Kin', in J. Goody (ed.), *The Character of Kinship*. Cambridge: Cambridge University Press.

Potter, J. and S. Potter. 1990. *China's Peasants: The Anthropology of a Revolution*. Cambridge: Cambridge University Press.

Radcliffe-Brown, A.R. 1952 (1940). 'On Joking Relationships', *Structure and Function in Primitive Society. Essays and Addressess*. London: Cohen & West Ltd.

Sangren, P.S. 1984. 'Traditional Chinese corporations: beyond kinship', *Journal of Asian Studies* 43(3): 391–415.

Santos, G.D. 2006. 'The Anthropology of Chinese Kinship. A Critical Overview', *EJEAS* 5(2): 275–333.

———. 2009. 'The "Stove-Family" and the Process of Kinship in Rural South China', in S. Brandtstädter and G.D. Santos (eds), *Chinese Kinship. Contemporary Anthropological Perspectives*. London: Routledge.

Santos-Granero, F. 2007. 'Of Fear and Friendship. Amazonian Sociality beyond Kinship and Affinity', *J.R.A.I.* (NS) 13(1): 1–18.

Silber, C. 1994. 'From Daughter to Daughter-in-law in the Women's Script of Southern Hunan', in C.K. Gilmartin, G. Hershatter, L. Rofel and T. White (eds), *Engendering China: Women, Culture, and the State*. Cambridge, MA: Harvard University Press.

Siu, H. 1990. 'Recycling Tradition: Culture, History, and Political Economy in the Chrysanthemum Festivals of South China', *Comparative Studies in Society and History* 32(4): 765–94.

———. 1993. 'Reconstituting Dowry and Brideprice in South China', in D. David and S. Harrell (eds), *Chinese Families in the Post-Mao Era*. Berkeley: University of California Press.

Smart, A. 1999. 'Expressions of Interest. Friendship and *guanxi* in Chinese Societies', in S. Bell and S. Coleman (eds), *The Anthropology of Friendship*. Oxford: Berg.

Stafford, C. 2000a. 'Chinese Patriliny and the Cycles of *yang* and *laiwang*', in J. Carsten (ed.), *Cultures of Relatedness*. Cambridge: Cambridge University Press.

———. 2000b. *Separation and Reunion in Modern China*. Cambridge: Cambridge University Press.

Stockard, J.E. 1992 (1989). *Daughters of the Canton Delta. Marriage Patterns and Economic Strategies in South China, 1860–1930*. Stanford: Stanford University Press.

Tooby, J. and L. Cosmides. 1996. 'Friendship and the Banker's Paradox: Other Pathways to the Evolution of Adaptations for Altruism', *Proceedings of the British Academy* 88: 119–43.

Uhl, S. 1991. 'Forbidden Friends: Cultural Veils of Female Friendship in Andalusia', *American Ethnologist* 18(1): 90–105.

Viveiros de Castro, E. 1992. *Araweté. O povo do Ipixuna*. São Paulo: CEDI.

Watson, R.S. 1985. *Inequality among Brothers: Class and Kinship in South China*. Cambridge: Cambridge University Press.

Wolf, E. 1966. 'Kinship, Friendship, and Patron-Client Relations in Complex Societies', in M. Banton (ed.), *The Social Anthropology of Complex Societies*. London: Tavistock Publications.

Wolf, M. 1972. *Women and the Family in Rural Taiwan*. Stanford: Stanford University Press.

Yan, Y.X. 1996. *The Flow of Gifts: Reciprocity and Social Networks in a Chinese Village*. Stanford: Stanford University Press.

———. 2003. *Private Life under Socialism: Love, Intimacy and Family Change in a Chinese Village, 1949–1999*. Stanford: Stanford University Press.

Yang, M.M.H. 1994. *Gifts, Favors and Banquets. The Art of Social Relationships in China*. Ithaca, NY: Cornell University Press.

Chapter 2

Ayompari, Compadre, Amigo:
Forms of Fellowship
in Peruvian Amazonia

EVAN KILLICK

This chapter examines indigenous–*mestizo*[1] social relations in Peruvian Amazonia, considering the different ways in which individuals from the two groups conceptualize their relationships with each other. While individuals from the Ashéninka indigenous group characterize their relationships with *mestizos* in terms of *ayompari* formal friendships, their *mestizo* companions use the idiom of *compadrazgo* (co-parenthood). The chapter considers various features of these relationships, including their economic, religious and political aspects, and looks at the ways in which they have been dealt with in previous literature. It suggests that, in contrast to previous approaches which have characterized these relationships in terms of kinship, viewing them as 'para-', 'pseudo-' or 'fictive' kinship relations (Viveiros de Castro 1995: 14; Pitt-Rivers 1973: 95–6), these relationships are better conceptualized in terms of friendship. Such an approach emphasizes that even as these relationships are used to connect individuals by drawing them into bonds that have particular moral and social implications, part of their importance rests precisely on the fact that they are not relations of kinship.

Since Schneider (1980, 1984) anthropological considerations of kinship have critiqued the discipline's traditional emphasis on the biological underpinnings of kinship systems. This discussion has led to an explicit awareness that kinship 'does not simply mirror physical kinship' but rather is socially created in specific cultural contexts (Holy 1996: 153). One response to this realization has been to attempt to move beyond ideas of kinship based on reproduction and genealogical connections and instead to use more general terms such as 'relatedness' (Carsten 2000, 2004). While such approaches have made important advances for the anthropological study of kinship, as has been noted in the introduction and other chapters of this volume, their disadvantage is that they tend to subsume all forms of relationships under one all-encompassing notion; this masks distinctions that may remain important in people's everyday lives. According to such views it might be argued that the relationships studied in this chapter could be understood within a wider sphere that includes all social relations, but I contend that to do so would be to obscure key aspects of the relationships for those involved. For both *mestizos* and Ashéninka individuals it is significant that the relationship terms and forms that they use are distinct from those of kinship.

The trend of linking friendship relationships to other ways of relating can also be discerned in the literature on Amazonian societies. 'Formal' friendships and trading partnerships, such as the Ashéninka *ayompari* relationship, have been noted in a number of Amazonian societies. One approach has been to compare them to consanguineal relations, in that the giving and receiving of gifts is seen to make people into kin (McCallum 2001: 96). For example, Overing Kaplan describes how the Piaroa term *chuwaruwang*, which refers to a general kinship relation, is also a status conferred on foreign trading partners. She notes that it carries connotations of 'friendship' but that, in the Piaroa case, friendship and kinship are effectively synonymous: the Piaroa say that 'to be a kinsman (*chuwaruwang*) is to be a friend' and also that 'To be a friend is to be a *chuwaruwang*' (Overing Kaplan 1975: 71). In this view, exchange and trade are just another way of forming close relations with others with the ultimate aim of turning those relations into close bonds of kinship. In contrast, Viveiros de Castro suggests that in Amazonia, relations of 'formal or ceremonial friendship' should be considered as 'para-kinship' relationships, using as they do the 'conceptual and practical symbols of affinity' (1995: 14). According to this position, such friendships are part of wider processes of symbolic exchange (including war, cannibalism, hunting, shamanism, funerary rites and trade) that cross socio-political, cosmological, and ontological boundaries (Viveiros de Castro 1996: 188–9).

The differences between these approaches reflect distinctions not only between the people studied but also between the writers themselves (cf. Viveiros de Castro 1996). While, in the Ashéninka case, the *ayompari* relationship echoes aspects of both consanguineous and affinal relations, I contend that focusing too narrowly on its parallels with kinship relations masks the fact that, for its participants, its most important characteristic is that it stands outside of kinship relations. It might be argued that Viveiros de Castro's line of reasoning is removed from everyday considerations of these relationships and that the *ayompari* relation, based as it is on a relationship with an outsider, is still using the 'conceptual and practical symbols of affinity' (1995: 14). Here affinity, or rather 'potential affinity', is understood in its widest sense to include all 'others' (Viveiros de Castro 2001: 22; 1993). While I do not contest the logical formulation of this interpretation, I believe that its use of kinship terms to describe essentially ontological considerations prohibits, or at least complicates, attempts to understand local relationship ideologies that may include a range of distinct relationships. As such I reject both of these approaches as hindering a clear understanding of the practice and associations of these relationships.

Instead, I contend that the *ayompari* relation is best understood as separate from kinship relations. The *ayompari* relation allows individuals to form relationships with strangers where none previously existed. It is not a precursor to the formation of relationships based on affinity or consanguinity (cf. Santos-Granero 2007); instead, as I will show, it can be maintained deliberately even in situations where kinship connections could be invoked. *Mestizos* use of the institution of *compadrazgo* follows a similar logic, but differs from the *ayompari* relation, as we shall see, in being based on an underlying logic of hierarchical difference rather than the equality that characterizes the ideal for *ayompari* relations. For both *mestizos* and Ashéninka individuals, these types of relationships are associated with particular behaviour that they consider appropriate for forming relations with outsiders. Furthermore, while thinking of the relationships in these terms gives each individual a guide for how to behave, each individual also hopes that their partner will also come to understand the moral and social implications of the bond. Before going into greater detail about these relationships, I will give a brief introduction to the region in which my research was conducted.

The Ucayali River and the Ashéninka

The fieldwork for this chapter was undertaken in Ashéninka settlements along the Ucayali River in central, eastern Peru at various times between 2001 and 2007. The Ashéninka are part of a larger ethnic group now known as the Asháninka, and previously referred to as the Campa. This group, in turn, is part of the greater pre-Andean Arawakan linguistic group that includes the Yanesha, Matsiguenga, Nomatsiguenga and Piro (Yiné).

In common with many other Amazonian peoples, the Ashéninka's primary concern is with 'living well' (see Overing and Passes 2000). This notion encompasses their desire for peace between individuals as well as a general sense of tranquillity in which people are able to live and act as they wish. Amongst many Amazonian peoples, this desire leads them to live in integrated communities that contain numerous families bound by ties of kinship or organized according to particular principles. However, the same notion leads the Ashéninka to live apart, in relatively isolated and independent households based around nuclear families. They contend that to live in larger groups or in closer proximity for any duration leads to quarrels and even violence. Yet, even as they downplay interaction with their immediate neighbours, households retain an openness towards others, including strangers, that allows them to maintain their independence while being connected to others. I suggest that the main mechanism that allows for a family's independence, even as it connects people, is the Ashéninka's emphasis on downplaying kinship relationships while accentuating those based on what might be characterized as friendship. Instead of attempting to pull all others into specific, defined and permanent relationships, individuals prefer all ties to remain voluntary, limited and flexible (see also Killick 2009). The key to the maintenance of this system is the Ashéninka's notion of generosity. Their emphasis on unilateral giving, as opposed to reciprocity or unilateral taking (predation), allows them to open out their social relations to include, potentially, all others, even as it does not bind them to any individuals.

To the observer, the Ashéninka way of living thus appears remarkably atomized. Men and women generally form isolated and independent households centred on a single conjugal pair. Each household lives in its own cultivated land some distance through the forest from other households. The ideal is self-sufficiency and families can spend periods of days and weeks in isolation from others. Against this backdrop of autonomous nuclear families, however, there are two cultural institutions that facilitate social interaction. One is the practice of holding periodic gatherings in which one household invites others to come and join them in drinking freshly prepared manioc beer (*masato*). The other is the practice of forming enduring, formal relationships with trading partners (*ayompari*) from distant areas. These two practices work at the local and distant level respectively to draw individuals and families into wider networks while allowing them to maintain their autonomy and independence. The *ayompari* networks also provide practical access to scarce goods and potential marriage partners. It is this institution that is of particular interest in terms of the Ashéninka's contemporary relationships with non-Ashéninka and that is the focus of this chapter.

The Ashéninka's main interaction with outsiders takes place in the context of the local timber industry. This industry, the latest in a long line of extractive industries in the region, now encompasses a wide variety of timbers found throughout the region. The rugged terrain and lack of local roads has meant that throughout the area timberwork continues to rely on the use of manual labour to find, fell, shape and transport timber. The local centre of the industry is the city of Pucallpa, which has a road connection to Lima. *Mestizo* men, either working individually or in relatively small groups, spread out from the city along the Ucayali River in search of timber to bring back. They generally rely on local indigenous groups to provide labour to remove the trees, paying them with goods brought from the city, in an economic system known as *habilitación*.[2] This system (which is also referred to as debt peonage or, particularly in relation to agricultural labour, as *enganche*) has long been used in the region (Varese 2002: 125). While in the past it has been associated with extreme forms of coercion (Santos-Granero and Barclay 2000: 34; Brown and Fernández 1991: 59), the current relative lack of labour in the region, together with national laws giving rights to indigenous groups, have curbed its worst excesses (Killick 2008). In parallel with the Ashéninka's use of the idiom of *ayompari* trading relations, I will show how *mestizos* are keen to frame what can be characterized as patron-client relations in social terms using their own local institution of *compadrazgo*.

Before dealing with these two local relationships, I will begin with a description of one particular, enduring relationship that I encountered between a *mestizo* and an Ashéninka man. This specific example will be used to analyse the different expectations that each man brings to the relationship.

Nelson and Melvin

Nelson and his wife, Margarita, live an hour and a half's walk or canoe ride up-stream from the centre of the Ashéninka community of Pijuayal in which much of my fieldwork was centred. Of their nine children only their penultimate son, the sixteen-year-old Percy, still lives with them, along with their six-year-old granddaughter, Nancy. Their other children and grandchildren, as is common amongst the Ashéninka, have all moved away over the years. One daughter now lives with her husband within the vicinity of Pijuayal but the rest have moved to more distant communities, including their youngest son, who is attending school. Nelson and Margarita are still self-sufficient, cutting and planting their own gardens and depending on fish caught in the river. They seldom visit other Ashéninka in the area nor hold their own beer parties, only occasionally attending those held by others. Like many Ashéninka couples, they seem to value their independence and autonomy and show little desire for more company.

Melvin is a *mestizo* man from Pucallpa, the only city in the region. He is one of only a few *mestizos* who have worked continuously in and around Pijuayal for many years. He first came twelve years ago with his brother-in-law to grow coca. After his brother-in-law's death, and given the difficulties involved in coca production, he returned by himself to begin logging. Starting with only basic tools, he steadily used his earnings to buy boats, motors and chainsaws until he started employing other *mestizos* from Pucallpa to act as his foremen, enabling him to work a number of different sites simultaneously. He comes to Pijuayal every year for up to six months, felling, preparing and then rolling timber logs to the river before floating them downstream to Pucallpa during the rainy season. He has a wife and two sons in Pucallpa and uses his profits to improve his house and stock a shop run by his wife. Over the years Melvin has built up close relationships with some of the Ashéninka in the area and he is still keen to maintain these links. He would often describe to me how the first time he came alone to Pijuayal he had only a canoe and one chainsaw and depended upon the Ashéninka in the area for everything else. It was at this time that he and Nelson cemented their close relationship. Nelson had let Melvin stay in his house and together they had gone out to find suitable trees to cut. Then, together with Nelson's sons and other Ashéninka men, they had felled the trees and rolled the logs to the river, always depending on Nelson's gardens for food and his wife to prepare their meals and *masato* (manioc beer). Melvin was very aware of how crucial Nelson had been in those early years and how, even now, Nelson was a useful ally to have in the area.

Nelson told me numerous times about the various things that Melvin had done for him over the years: helping him take his children to a health post when they were sick, providing clothes, books and pens for their schooling and always willing to put him and his family up on the occasions when they went to Pucallpa. He also told me how Melvin had been instrumental in helping to get a government-paid teacher for Pijuayal and then helped to buy and bring the materials needed for building a school. Melvin also said that he felt responsible for helping Nelson and particularly his children. When he gave things to Nelson, he always couched them in terms of gifts for his children and grandchildren, and many of the gifts were specifically linked to the children's education. He gave Nelson these things even though the ageing Ashéninka man no longer actually worked for him. Nelson, meanwhile, now depended upon Melvin to bring him those things that he had no other means of acquiring. Sometimes he would specifically ask Melvin to bring new things from Pucallpa, such as a machete or an axe but often, usually as Melvin was heading downstream with his timber, Nelson would ask for some of the things that Melvin no longer needed, such as his cooking pots, mosquito nets or old clothes. Occasionally they would argue over particular things or Melvin would barter his old pots for a chicken or bananas; but more often they would give each other things as 'gifts', either noting that this was 'for nothing' or specifically linking it to something that had been given in the past or would be returned in the future. In general it was the latter form of transaction that seemed to be preferred by both men.

Beyond the economic transactions that occurred between them, however, they also shared a deeper sense of camaraderie. Whenever I visited Nelson he would ask for news of Melvin. Then he would reminisce about their various adventures over the years, recounting how they had tracked and killed a particularly large animal together, how a hunting expedition had been ruined by torrential rain, or how they had lost their belongings when a canoe capsized in rain-swollen rapids. Similarly, when I visited Melvin in Pucallpa during the dry months when he stayed at home, he would ask after Nelson, telling his own version of their exploits and of Nelson's skills as a tracker and woodsman. As I left he would give me some medicine or a gift to take back for Nelson. If they talked of each other in complimentary terms when apart, when they were together they would joke and tease each other and tell stories denigrating each other. Usually these stories would involve drunken antics or mistakes that they had made while floating timber down the river or while in the forest. The enjoyment came in the telling of these stories and the other's reactions to them and in each denying and qualifying them or telling their own tale in response. This interaction and the lengthy endurance of their relationship stood out from other relationships between Ashéninka and timbermen which tended to be marked by their transitory nature and by the levels of mutual suspicion on both sides.

As is clear from my brief description, there are many aspects to the relationship between Nelson and Melvin. There are, consequently, many ways in which one might approach this relationship. However, as I noted in the introduction to this chapter and consistent with the wider aim of this volume as a whole, my analysis is underpinned by local people's own feelings about their friendship relationships. There are many ways in which an Ashéninka individual might conceptualize their relationships to an outsider. Here I follow Carsten (2000: 1) in arguing that it is only through an examination of local views and lived experience that the salient characteristics, associations and implications of these relationships are likely to emerge. The first important observation in this mode is that each man had his own term of reference for the other. While Melvin referred to Nelson as his *compadre*, Nelson called Melvin his *ayompari*. I will first focus on the Ashéninka institution of *ayompari*.

Ayompari

During my fieldwork, I was often astonished by the distances travelled by seemingly random visitors. A number of people made the three-day trek from the Pachitea valley over the inhospitable Shira hills and many more arrived having canoed and walked down from the upper reaches and side tributaries of the Ucayali. People of all ages and both genders, both alone and in small groups, would make these visits. They would spend a few days or weeks staying with one family, bringing things with them and taking other objects from their host family or foraging in the forest for certain plants or animals. This system of travelling and trade has long been noted in the literature on the Ashéninka (Varese 2002; Renard-Casevitz 1993) as well as on other Arawakan societies (Hill and Santos-Granero 2002: 17). In the past the system specifically involved two men from geographically distant areas forming an alliance based on the trading of scarce goods.

> In what may be called the *ayompari* system, an individual agrees to trade on a regular basis with another individual … a man will give his *ayompari* a set of arrows thereby establishing a debt relationship, and ask him to give a steel knife in return. The second man will have an *ayompari* in another region who is perhaps in contact with white patrons or traders and from whom he can trade for a knife. Eventually the first man will get the knife he requested and the debt will be paid. (Bodley 1971: 51)

The Franciscan missionary Biedma (1989 [1682]) noted this form of trading system in the seventeenth century, centred on the movement of salt from *tsiviari* ('the mountain of salt') in the Chanchamayo valley, and it appears to have been active long before this. The basic articles for exchange seem to have been *cushmas* (woven cotton robes), animals and their pelts, and other jungle and garden produce. However, the most important goods were those that were not available locally, most notably bronze axes from the Andes and ceramics produced by other ethnic groups (Johnson 2003: 28–9). With the arrival of Europeans iron tools were quickly incorporated into the system and those with access to missionary forges formed new foci within the system (Santos-Granero 1988). The *ayompari* system can also be seen to have maintained a degree of social cohesion among the geographically disparate Asháninka and allowed young men access to distant, unrelated brides, thus maintaining a degree of cultural homogeneity throughout the population (cf. Renard-Casevitz 1993; Schäfer 1988).

Beyond its specific links to trade, the status of *ayompari* can also be seen to work more widely to give individuals a recognized status beyond their ordinary kinship networks; according to Bodley, this facilitates individuals' passage and acceptance in distant regions, particularly in 'potentially hostile regions' (1971: 51). More generally I would argue that the notion of *ayompari* has now become a category that allows individuals to form relationships with unknown others. In my own experience, while individuals would play with the various categories that I could be fitted into, most obviously that of brother-in-law based on my potential relationships with various young women in the area, they usually quickly settled for addressing me as *ayompari*. This was not specific to me, but indicative of a general avoidance by the Ashéninka of using kin terms when referring to unrelated and especially non-Ashéninka outsiders. Furthermore, while individuals still form these relationships with other Ashéninka in the present context, where timbermen have become the main sources of goods, formal *ayompari* relationships between Ashéninka men have been replaced by the relationships formed with *mestizo* timbermen. Timbermen have come to fulfil many of the economic and social functions once fulfilled by Ashéninka *ayompari*, particularly in becoming the main source of scarce goods, which are now represented by manufactured items.

This development – viewing timbermen as *ayompari* – is suggested by certain clear parallels between older descriptions of *ayompari* partners and the current interactions between Ashéninka men and timbermen. At its heart the *ayompari* relation is centred on delayed reciprocity and is associated with ideas of trust and loyalty (Schäfer 1991; Santos-Granero 2007). It is a relationship that emphasizes the debts that exist between individuals and uses them as a means of strengthening and prolonging the bond between them. In everyday situations the Ashéninka are noted for their generous hospitality; furthermore, as Hvalkof and Veber (2005) have noted, this generosity is not based on ideas of reciprocity but rather on the idea that everyday essential items and, most importantly, food and drink, must be unilaterally given by all to all (cf. Weiss 2005; Santos-Granero and Barclay 2005).[3] As I have argued elsewhere (Killick 2009), this obligation to give is paralleled by a cultural emphasis on not relying on others, so that Ashéninka individuals can be seen as striving to avoid situations in which such giving or receiving is necessary, and indeed, this seems, in part, to underlie their desire to live apart. The *ayompari* relationship, for the Ashéninka, thus stands in distinct contrast to everyday relations and is, as we shall see, based on particular ideas about the bond and obligations that the delayed and reciprocal exchange of goods places on the two individuals involved. It also stands in contrast to the immediate reciprocity of everyday economic transactions as they are carried out in local shops and markets.

Another central aspect of the *ayompari* relationship is that it occurs between equals. Elsewhere I have argued that the concept of egalitarianism lies at the heart of Ashéninka society (Killick 2007). Independence and personal autonomy are inculcated in children from a young age and by the time young couples marry and form their own households they have both the ability and the self-belief to care for themselves and their families with no outside assistance. All individuals thus come to place a high value on their own autonomy and act in everyday situations to discourage hierarchy and to prevent differentiation. This is also carried into their relationships with outsiders who they do not see as superior to themselves (cf. Veber 2000: 18), *Ayompari* relations are envisaged as reciprocal relations between equals who both give and demand respect of their partners.

In drawing outsiders into this form of relationship, Ashéninka individuals thus attempt to make them feel the same social and moral obligations that they feel themselves. In my fieldwork the first evidence of this came from the way in which the Ashéninka talked about timbermen, *mestizo* men who came to the area to fell timber to take and sell in the local city of Pucallpa. While the Spanish term used, *patrón*, can generally be understood as 'boss' or 'employer', the Ashéninka instead used it almost interchangeably with the word *amigo* (friend). This seemed a slightly strange equation given the undoubtedly exploitative nature that these relationships could entail. But the link was made clearer when Jorge, the man in whose house I lived, told me the story of 'mosquito'. The story recounted how, in the mythic 'before time', mosquitoes were 'people' and they used to trade with their *ayompari*. The only goods they wanted, however, were bamboo sticks full of the red achiote dye, used by the Ashéninka to paint their faces.[4] Because of this failure to accept other goods, and thus their failure to exchange any goods at all, the mosquitoes' *ayompari* grew angry with them and decided to kill them. Before they could act, however, the mosquitoes started dancing in a circle, humming loudly and turning faster and faster until, finally, they all flew away. This story clearly emphasized the importance of *ayompari* being generous with each other and of their obligations to trade with each other. What also caught my attention were the words that Jorge used to describe the men who had come to the mosquitoes' village with goods. At first he called them '*Ashéninka patrones*', saying that they brought goods, pots, machetes and *cushmas* to trade. Later he used the term *ayompari* and then interchanged this with the word *amigo*. This suggested that the correlation was between *ayompari* and *patrones*, via the equation of *ayomparis* with the Spanish term *amigo*, and emphasized that such people were viewed in primarily social and equal terms.[5] Having gained this insight, I slowly realized that it was a common perception and that people used the terms interchangeably in everyday speech.[6]

Further aspects of these relationships attested to the link between *patrones* and *ayomparis* in the minds of my informants. People always associated *patrones* with individual men. They would ask another man when 'his' *patrón* was arriving and complain about their own lack of a *patrón*, or compare their own unfavourably with another man's. In a context in which many of the men were working for the same person – and Ashéninka men would often seem to move quickly from working with one *patrón* to working for another – such talk seemed slightly odd. Yet, in relation to Bodley's description of the *ayompari* system, in which one man forms a particular bond with one other, the view of these relationships as being between individuals makes sense.

As I noted above, other Amazonian groups use ideas of consanguinity or affinity to relate to others. Ashéninka individuals are also open to the possibility of fitting outsiders into the categories of brother (*yeeye* in Ashéninka or *hermano* in Spanish) or brother-in-law (*ñani* in Ashéninka or *cuñado* in Spanish). However, they show a marked preference for using the term *ayompari*.[8] Indeed, as Santos-Granero notes, even between Ashéninka men who may in fact be related, 'when two men decide to establish a trading friendship, they stop addressing each other by the corresponding kinship or affinal term – if they are related in such a way – replacing it with the term ayompari or friend' (2007: 4). This emphasis on the *ayompari* relation as not being one of kinship is stressed in the case of Nelson and Melvin by the fact that the two of them recognize that they are now actually related through kinship. Specifically, neither man ever made claims on the other based on the fact that Melvin was the father of Nelson's granddaughter, Nancy.

The fact of Melvin's paternity was told to me separately by Nelson and Melvin, as well as by other people in the area. Yet, in their relationship with each other it was never mentioned. The girl, Nancy, was fathered in one of Melvin's camps when her mother, Juana, had been acting as cook for Melvin's timber-working party. While there never seems to have been any form of enduring relationship, and Nancy's birth might therefore be considered illicit, such relationships and resulting children are accepted in both Ashéninka and *mestizo* society. Throughout the area there were a number of both men and women who had had a number of children by different partners. These children were always accepted by whichever partner one of their parents finally settled with, even though their original parent was remembered. Thus, while Melvin did not explicitly treat Nancy as his daughter, he recognized a certain responsibility for her. This sense of duty may in part explain his generosity towards Nelson, in whose house she lived. Yet, it is noteworthy that neither he nor Nelson made anything of this link. In practice, the in-law relationship could have been used to make demands for respect and material assistance from each other. However, neither man, and in particular Nelson, who from his position as 'wife-giver' might be considered as being in the superior position, chose to enact this connection. I contend that this shows that the relationship of *ayompari* is seen in terms of friendship: as a relationship outside of and beyond kinship relations.

In another work (Killick 2009) I have argued that the Ashéninka attempt to play down all kinship relations, even those with their closest kin. Thus children, as they marry and form their own self-sufficient households, tend to move away from their parents and siblings and lead autonomous existences. Couples, like Nelson and Margarita, deal with all aspects of life without consulting others. A man can build a house, cut his garden, make a canoe and hunt and fish alone. Equally, a woman can tend to the garden, look after her children and even give birth on her own. Similarly, in spiritual and medical matters, while some might be respected as knowing more than others, individuals usually begin by attending to matters themselves. Women produce herbal remedies on their own, and I watched men perform simple healing acts on their families. This self-sufficiency is linked to the Ashéninka's desire, of which they often talk, to live apart from others, peaceably and well. Furthermore, they often commented on how they were unable to live in more settled and tight-knit communities, finding them oppressive and uncomfortable. They resent the obligations and power that are associated with kin relations, particularly to parents and parents-in-law and to living in tighter-knit settlements. They recognize that they must be generous to their kin and co-residents in particular and that, if they wish, such people can call on their allegiance. In all but a few cases couples are keen to avoid these potential obligations. In this cultural setting, in which individuals deliberately attempt to downplay and minimize close connections, it is unsurprising that the Ashéninka should emphasize other forms of relationship in their dealings with outsiders.

This aversion to kinship can also be linked to the Ashéninka's emphasis on egalitarianism. Not only do they want to be able to maintain their autonomy from their kin but neither do they want any individual to have power over them. Again this idea appears to be carried into *ayompari* relations, particularly with outsiders. Patron-client relations have an implicit hierarchical character with the patron's relative economic and political power putting him above his client. In the Ucayali case this difference is clear with Nelson relying on Melvin for otherwise unobtainable goods. Yet Nelson, in his relationship with Melvin, was at pains to emphasize their equality. This was true not only in the manner in which they talked and interacted but also in Nelson's emphasis on reciprocity between them, so that he generally repaid Melvin for his gifts. In this way while their mutual debts continued their connection, the gifts did not underpin a hierarchical difference between them.

Unfortunately for the Ashéninka, the social and moral prescriptions that they feel accompany the exchange of goods are not always shared by visiting outsiders. However, the possible power of this strategy was shown to me by the fact that *mestizos* like Melvin who interacted with Ashéninka often seemed to have relationships that were based on more than just economic ties. Yet while Melvin willingly participated in their everyday relations on a relatively egalitarian basis with Nelson, his own characterization of the relationship as one of *compadrazgo*, as I will now show, held certain hierarchical ideas.

Compadrazgo

If Nelson's understanding of his relationship with Melvin was based on Ashéninka ideas of an *ayompari* partner, then Melvin modelled and talked of his relationship with Nelson in terms of *compadrazgo* (co-parenthood). *Compadrazgo* is a common feature of Catholic countries, particularly in the Mediterranean and Latin America regions. It is based on the Catholic doctrine of infant baptism and at its core consists of three roles – parent, child and godparent – and three relationships – parent-child, child-godparent and parent-godparent (Gudeman 1972: 45). Beyond this core structure however, the literature attests to the diversity of forms and modifications that different groups have brought to the institution (Mintz and Wolf 1968; Chevalier 1982: 307). The number of people involved and the importance of each relationship can vary greatly, while the associated religious connections, secular duties and behavioural prohibitions can range from being of central importance to non-existent.

In the Ucayali case, the idea of *compadrazgo* has been reduced to its simplest elements. Rather than being between the godparent and child, the most important relationship is instead between the parent and godparent. Furthermore, any formal ceremony of baptism, blessing or of ritual connection has been dispensed with in the vast majority of cases. In this way the parallel with the *ayompari* relationship, as a relationship formed between two men, is clear. Yet, differences are still evident, not least in the fact that the bond still relies on children and appears to be based on hierarchical difference rather than the inherent equality of *ayompari*. This inequality appears to be founded on the underlying symbolic system and religious ideology of the *compadrazgo*, as suggested by Gudeman's work (1972, 1975).

Following Catholic ideology, Gudeman argues that 'all forms of the institution are based on the conceptual opposition of the natural and spiritual being and comprise a system of diachronic and synchronic permutations' (Gudeman 1972: 67). He thus examines the institution in terms of kinship and affinity and its physical and spiritual components and sees it as a solution 'to the problem inherent in man's existence as both a natural and spiritual being' (Gudeman 1972: 54). The key idea to Catholic baptism is the washing away of 'original sin' and thus the rebirth of a person to Christ (Gudeman 1972: 47). In this ritual Gudeman argues that it is the godparent who stands in the 'spiritual' position, representing the child's spiritual birth and his connection to the holy family and, ultimately, to God. The godparent thus stands in a superior position to both the child and his parents. Gudeman suggests that the widespread characteristic of godparents coming from higher social classes and of *compadrazgo* being unreciprocated is explained by this superior, 'spiritual' position of the godparent. He notes that while the church has never prohibited reciprocal roles nor promoted the idea that godparents should come from a distinct social position to the child and its parents, 'the ecclesiastical idea that the spiritual is higher than the natural seems to have had a profound impact upon folk practices: reciprocal selection is uncommon and when parent and godparent occupy unequal social statuses, the latter normally holds the higher position' (Gudeman 1975: 235).

This differentiation of status between the parent and godparent is apparent in the Ucayali case. The Ashéninka do not form co-parent ties with each other and *mestizos* would never ask Ashéninka to be godparents to their own children. While the Ashéninka do not give much thought to the relationship, *mestizos* do have particular ideas about what it means and how it should be conducted. They seek out important people in their society to become godparents to their own children. The godfather of one of Melvin's sons in Pucallpa was the head of the local *barrio* (town district), while that of the other was a timber merchant. In the same way that Melvin seemed to think it right for such powerful and wealthy men to help him and his children, Melvin also considered that he had some kind of 'duty' to help Ashéninka individuals. He made no reference to ideas of spirituality and religious purity, but the same structural hierarchy is apparent.

If historical approaches that focus on underlying religious ideas are useful in explaining the hierarchical structures of *compadrazgo*, as with studies of indigenous trading partnerships, the predominant mode of analysis has still been to compare *compadre* relations to kinship. Thus Coy, following Lévi-Strauss' ideas of kinship 'structures', compares the *compadrazgo* to affinal relations and argues that the *compadrazgo* is also an 'encounter between nature and culture, between alliance and kinship' (Coy 1974: 470). According to this view, *compadrazgo* is used in the same manner as marriage to form alliances; here, however, 'spiritual procreation' is used instead of 'natural procreation' to form bonds between people (Coy 1974: 470; Gudeman 1972: 64). Lévi-Strauss makes this argument in the Latin American case when he compares the settling French people's custom of *compérage* with the indigenous Tupi group's *chetouasap* (brother-in-law) complex (Lévi-Strauss 1943: 406). Lévi-Strauss then considered the European evolution of *compérage* from a religious connection to a secular one and as 'an artificial link of kinship' (Lévi-Strauss 1943: 408). He argues that the terms *compère* and *commère* were used as a means of 'adopting' newcomers into a community, an arrangement that was later made more permanent by their marriage to a resident. This leads him to argue that 'in all small communities of Mediterranean Europe and of Latin America, the *compère* or *compadre* is an actual or a potential brother-in-law' (Lévi-Strauss 1943: 408). The parallels to Viveiros de Castro's arguments about ceremonial friendship, cited above, are clear.

Another approach is to compare *compadrazgo* to ties of consanguinity. One foundation for this view is that the terms used in the *compadrazgo* so clearly echo those of consanguinity: *padrino* (godfather), *madrina* (godmother), *compadre* (co-father), *comadre* (co-mother) and *ahijado/a* (godson/daughter), which all follow their familial equivalents of *padre*, *madre* and *hijo/a* (father, mother and son/daughter). Jack Goody, in tracing the historical evolution of *compadrazgo* in Europe, shows how in the twelfth century godparenthood replaced adoption as the preferred way of creating legitimate ties for the inheritance of property (1983: 73–5), thus mirroring ties of consanguinity (1983: 196). However, he shows how, over the centuries, the emphasis shifted from the tie between godparent and child to the relationship between parent and godparent, thus from consanguinity to affinity. Yet even though the parallels between *compadrazgo* and kinship are clear, I contend that to understand the institution in this manner is to miss other important aspects of how it is experienced and used, particularly in the Ucayali case.

Brain argues that the original form of *compadrazgo* in Europe, 'despite [the] exogamic restrictions and the use of kin terms … was no more a kinship one than that between a priest and his flock – "father and children"' (Brain 1977: 93). He suggests that it is better to understand the relationship as one between friends and close neighbours who then used a Christian ritual to add an extra dimension to their friendship. He argues that this is shown linguistically in the manner in which the English word 'godsib', which was used to refer to co-parents, came to be used more generally for neighbours before gaining its modern connotations as 'gossip' (Brain 1977: 93).[8] Similarly, Brain notes that in Andalusia 'a *compadre* becomes an honorary member of the elementary family, but not a kinsman as such since the relationship is seen as one free of the trammels which may bring dissension among kinsfolk' (Brain 1977: 99–100). To understand *compadrazgo* in terms of kinship is to obscure the important fact that for its practitioners its distinguishing characteristic is often precisely that it is not a kinship relation.

With this conclusion we can return to the example of Nelson and Melvin and to the observation that, from their perspective, part of the importance of their relationship lies in the very fact of it not being a kinship connection. This is most clearly shown by the fact that both could have activated what they each independently recognize as a kinship tie between them, but choose not to. If, as I argued above, Nelson's desire to limit this relationship stemmed from a deeper cultural emphasis on independence and autonomy then Melvin's can be seen to stem from a more hierarchical view of the difference between him and Nelson and a desire to remain at some remove from indigenous people. As I showed at the start, Melvin considered his relationships with Ashéninka people in Pijuayal to be important economically, socially and morally. Yet, there were also limits to how close he wanted these relationships to become. While Melvin did recognize a connection to the young Nancy, it seems that he wished to avoid the threat of the limitless demands that could be made by a child of its parent. It is for these reasons, I contend, that Melvin was keen to downplay this connection not only to the child but also to her recognized consanguines, his possible affines. If Nelson's desire to downplay kinship was linked to an Ashéninka desire for autonomy, Melvin's was linked to more pragmatic concerns. As with the *ayompari* relation for Nelson, the *compadrazgo* idiom allowed Melvin to recognize a connection and profess his care for Nelson's children, while still maintaining limits on what was required of him and preventing the potential limitless demands of 'true' kin.

Another case emphasizes the hierarchical aspect of the *compadre* relationship. In this case it involves Don Fernando, the grandson of a *'gringo cauchero'* (white rubber boss) who came to the mouth of the Amaquaria and set up a large cattle ranch there. With the death of the latter and the early death of Fernando's father when Fernando was only a baby, the fortunes of the family had foundered. Fernando, however, still has reasonably extensive agricultural land by the river and attempts to work as a timberman as well. His mother, still living, is in fact of Ashéninka descent, and Fernando therefore has kinship connections to a number of Ashéninka in the area. Yet rather than attempting to use these connections, Don Fernando instead places great emphasis on his identity as a *mestizo* and, as with Melvin, portrays his relationships with Ashéninka in terms of *compadrazgo*. In this case I would argue that the hierarchical aspects of the *compadrazgo* relationship are of even more importance and that he uses it to emphasize his relative separation from and superiority to Ashéninka men. Again his own children, all four properly baptised in the Catholic Church, have *padrinos* from Pucallpa.

In making this point I am not arguing that all relationships of *compadrazgo* should be seen as distinct from kinship. As Mintz and Wolf note, the outstanding characteristic of *compadrazgo* is its adaptiveness (1968: 343) and there are certainly cases where the relationship between *compadrazgo* and kinship is clear (for example Osborn's work on the Kwaiker Indians, 1968). My point is therefore not to argue that *compadrazgo* need always be a limited relationship that is deliberately contrasted to kinship, but rather that in order to gain a full understanding of the way in which *compadrazgo* works in a particular situation, it is useful to regard it in the first instance as a separate and distinct relation of its own.

Friendship and Politics

As I noted earlier, inter-Ashéninka *ayompari* formal friendships, can be seen to have had an underlying function: to allow individuals access to otherwise scarce goods and therefore to act as a means of economic redistribution. The formality of ceremonial friendship can therefore be seen as ensuring the security and continuation of exchanges, especially in areas of potential hostility (Descola 1996: 155). Descola similarly describes the *compadre* relationship as 'an association more political than religious', arguing that Quichuas in Ecuador enter into such relationships with outsiders 'to win the protection of a powerful man' who, in turn, gains a client who will provide him with local goods and 'unprotestingly accept the systematically unfavourable rate of exchange that he will impose' (Descola 1996: 11). According to this view, both formal friends and *compadres* are useful political relations that give individuals access to goods and influence.

In the case of *compadrazgo* relations formed between indigenous and *mestizo* peoples, the political nature of the relationship can become particularly apparent when the indigenous person tries to withdraw. As Osborn notes, in such situations 'the relationship may emerge as a pure form of 'enforced clientship', an observation which leads her to conclude that 'compadrazgo ties between mestizos and Kwaiker constitute, in fact, little more than a patron-client relationship' (Osborn 1968: 604–5). Van Den Berghe and van Den Berghe also argue that 'vertical compadrazgo typically falls in the patron-client or paternalistic model of social relations' and should be seen as 'a mechanism whereby lower status persons enter, or, more often, reinforce, a client relationship' (1966: 1238–9). As the case of Don Fernando shows, the hierarchical element of the relationship can be used to reinforce and emphasize differences of status between people who are of relatively equal economic status. In the context of Pijuayal, however, I believe that both sides are keen to downplay these separations.

For *mestizos* the *compadrazgo* is precisely a means of forming connections with Ashéninka individuals that are based on more than their political and economic power. It was noticeable that those timbermen who did rely purely on the respect that was granted to them as outsiders and their promise of goods rarely managed to work in the region for more than a single season. If they did not take time to form relations with their workers, then the Ashéninka that they worked with were likely to desert them. In the past under the system of *habilitación*, powerful *mestizos* were able to keep indigenous peoples virtually enslaved by debt. However, such monopolies of power depend upon two factors that no longer existed: first, that the outsider is his workers' only reliable source of desired items; and second, that no one is in competition with him for the goods being extracted. In the past, particular *mestizos* had complete control of large swathes of jungle and its residents and thus gained a high degree of power over those natives within their network (Santos-Granero and Barclay 2000). In modern day Peru such a monopoly is seldom possible. The closeness of my fieldsites to Pucallpa, together with my informants' relatively good knowledge of the outside world and the presence of a number of different timbermen and the occasional trader, made it impossible for any individual to wield so much power. In this new situation, the balance of power may still be with the relatively richer *mestizos* who have access to the money and timbermills of Pucallpa, but their complete dominance is no longer assured. Instead they depend on the cooperation of their workers, relying on their goodwill to continue working, particularly after the goods originally given to them at the start of the season have run out. It was noticeable that when timbermen arrived at the start of each season to recruit labour, as well as offering goods they used their prior connections of friendship and *compadrazgo* to call on the help of the Ashéninka men.

The Ashéninka's idea of *ayompari* can be seen to be working in the same way as *compadrazgo* to create an enduring relation and a sense of obligation between partners. If the timbermen's greatest fear is that after having taken initial payments their workers will disappear into the forest, an Ashéninka man worries that after having worked for a season a *mestizo* may take his timber to Pucallpa and never return. Varese, in the first major anthropological work on the Ashéninka, argued that the *ayompari* relation was 'an eminently religious feature' (Varese 2002: 33). He seems to have had in mind Mauss's discussion of the *hau* ('spirit') of the gift among the Maori (Mauss 1990[1950]: 12), which while compelling, as Lévi-Strauss suggested, carries a danger of 'the ethnologist allow[ing] himself to be mystified by the native' (1966: xxxviii). Yet Varese's discussion points to a definite sense that, for the Ashéninka, this trade carries a moral obligation to the other and is more than 'just' trade. Firth, in a rejection of the more spiritual Maussian explanation of reciprocity, outlines more secular ways in which individuals can claim substantive help, one of which is to attempt to transform it into a moral obligation (1967: 13). This is what, I contend, the Ashéninka are trying to do with their *mestizo ayompari*. They want their partner to feel the 'power' of the link between them as they do, and thus to feel a moral obligation to treat and recompense them fairly.[9] In this way, they recognize that the important thing is to try to impose some social hold on the timbermen. This is why Nelson preferred the objects he received from Melvin to be in a system of delayed, rather than immediate, reciprocity. For if he still owed Melvin things, and Melvin was aware of his own debts, the relationship was more likely to continue.

Conclusion

In the above discussion the basic similarities and differences between *ayompari* and *compadre* relations have become apparent. Whereas the *ayompari* relation revolves around horizontal ties based on an ideology of individuals' independence and equality, the *compadre* tie can be seen as hierarchical. Both institutions have also shown a degree of flexibility and have been adapted over time to fit the current social situation, particularly in dealing with outsiders from different cultural/ethnic backgrounds. Finally, they are both based on ties of reciprocity and by ideas of mutual obligation, whilst being held to be distinct from ties of kinship that are seen as more binding. My argument is therefore that *ayompari* and *compadre* are similar yet distinct local relationship forms that, while linked to specific cultural ideas – of trade and religion respectively – and while bearing comparison with kinship systems, remain distinct in the minds of their practitioners. This example is useful in showing the similarities and connections between these types of relationship and other forms, such as those of a kin, economic or political nature. However, as I have shown, the essential utility and power of these relationships stems from the fact that they are distinct from other relationships.

Acknowledgments

This chapter is based on full-time fieldwork conducted in 2000–2003 and subsequent visits in August 2006 and May 2007 supported by the Central Research Fund (University of London), the London School of Economics and the Royal Anthropological Institute. The final trip and the writing of this article were supported by an ESRC Postdoctoral Research Fellowship (PTA-026-27-1354). I am grateful to Peter Loizos for his astute comments as well as to the other participants at the workshop on which this volume is based.

Notes

1. This term is used locally both descriptively and self-referentially to refer to people of mixed heritage, involving any mixture of European, indigenous Andean or Amazonian ancestry.
2. *Habilitación* directly translates as 'fitting out', as in 'fitting out an expedition' – the way in which it was referred to in North America.
3. This generosity stands in contrast to the giving that has been observed in other societies, particularly hunter-gatherer societies such as the Hadza of whom Woodburn writes 'We often think of sharing as deriving from generosity. The emphasis in these societies is quite different. Shares are asked for, even demanded. We have what can appropriately be called demand sharing. People believe that they are entitled to their share and are not slow to make their claims. The whole emphasis is on donor obligation and recipient entitlement' (1998: 49).
4. Jorge explicitly linked the redness of the achiote to that of blood.
5. All of these terms have undoubtedly gone through various semantic shifts through history. This is attested to in the first instance by the fact that the term *ayompari* itself appears to be derived from the Spanish word *compadre* (Schäfer 1991: 50).
6. This connection also occurs amongst the Achuar whose current term for their trading partners is *amik*, a term that, as Descola notes, is clearly derived from *amigo*, even as the institution is almost certainly of autochthonous origin (Descola 1996: 154).
7. Obviously the use, or non-use, of a kinship term does not in itself express a different kind of relationship; however, the Ashéninka's deliberate use of different terms to refer to distinct people seems to emphasize the categories into which they were attempting to put them.
8. A similar connection is made in French where the term *commère* also has connotations of being a gossip. Brain also notes that Shakespeare's play *The Merry Wives of Windsor* is translated into Italian as *Le Allegre Commari* (Brain 1977: 97).
9. There is a parallel here to Rezende's study of middle-class women's relationships with their maids in Rio de Janeiro when she argues that maids in particular were emphasizing their common humanity and gender with their employers in order to promote a relationship of care and consideration (Rezende 1999: 92).

References

Biedma, M. (ed. Antonio Tibesar) 1989 [1682]. *La conquista Franciscana del Alto Ucayali*. Lima: Editorial Milla Batres.

Bodley, J. H. 1971. *Campa Socio-economic Adaptation*. PhD thesis, University of Oregon, University Microfilms, Ann Arbor.

Brain, R. 1977. *Friends and Lovers*. London: Paladin.

Brown, M. F. and E. Fernández. 1991. *War of Shadows: The Struggle for Utopia in the Peruvian Amazon*. Berkeley: University of California Press.

Carsten, J. (ed.). 2000. *Cultures of Relatedness: New Approaches to the Study of Kinship*. Cambridge: Cambridge University Press.

———. 2004. *After Kinship*. Cambridge: Cambridge University Press.

Chevalier, J. M. 1982. *Civilization and the Stolen Gift: Capital, Kin, and Cult in Eastern Peru*. Toronto: University of Toronto Press.

Coy, P. 1974. 'An Elementary Structure of Ritual Kinship: a case of prescription in the compadrazgo', *Man* 9(3): 470–9.

Descola, P. 1996. *The Spears of Twilight: Life and Death in Amazon Jungle*. London: Harper Collins.

Firth, R. 1967. *Themes in Economic Anthropology*. London: Tavistock Publications.

Goody, J. 1983. *The Development of the Family and Marriage in Europe*. Cambridge: Cambridge University Press.

Gudeman, S. 1972. 'The Compadrazgo as a Reflection of the Natural and Spiritual Person' *Proceedings of the Royal Anthropological Institute of Great Britain and Ireland for* 1971: 45–71.

———. 1975. 'Spiritual Relationships and Selecting a Godparent', *Man* 10(2): 221–37.

Hill, J.D. and F. Santos-Granero. 2002. 'Introduction', in J.D. Hill and F. Santos-Granero (eds), *Comparative Arawakan Histories*. Urbana: University of Illinois Press.

Holy, L. 1996. *Anthropological Perspectives on Kinship*. London: Pluto Press.

Hvalkof, S. and H. Veber. 2005. 'Ashéninka del Gran Pajonal' ,in F. Santos-Granero and F. Barclay (eds), *Guía Etnográfica de la Alta Amazonía, Vol. V*. Panama and Lima: Smithsonian Tropical Research Institute and IFEA.

Johnson, A. 2003. *Families of the Forest: The Matsigenka Indians of the Peruvian Amazon*. Berkeley: University of California Press.

Killick, E. 2007. 'Autonomy and Leadership: Political Formations among the Ashéninka of Peruvian Amazonia', *Ethnos* 72(4): 461–82.

———. 2008. 'Creating Community: Land titling, education and settlement formation amongst the Ashéninka of Peruvian Amazonia', *Journal of Latin American and Caribbean Anthropology* 13(1): 22–47.

———. 2009. 'Ashéninka Amity: A Study of Social Relations in an Amazonian Society', *Journal of the Royal Anthropological Institute* 15(4): 701–718.

Lévi-Strauss, C. 1943. 'The Social Use of Kinship Terms among Brazilian Indians', *American Anthropologist* 45(3): 398–409.

———. 1966. 'Introduction à l'œuvre de Marcel Mauss', in M. Mauss, *Sociologie et anthropologie*. Paris: Presses Universitaires de France.

Mauss, M. (translated by W.D. Halls). 1990 [1950]. *The Gift: the Form and Reason for Exchange in Archaic Societies*. London: Routledge.

McCallum, C. 2001. *Gender and Sociality in Amazonia. How real people are made.* Oxford and New York: Berg.

Mintz, S.W. and E.R. Wolf. 1968. 'An Analysis of Ritual Co-Parenthood (Compadrazgo)', in P. Bohannon and J. Middleton (eds), *Marriage, Family and Residence*. Garden City, New York: Natural History Press.

Osborn, A. 1968. 'Compadrazgo and Patronage: A Colombian Case', *Man* 3(4): 593–608.

Overing Kaplan, J. 1975. *The Piaroa: A People of the Orinoco Basin*. Oxford: Clarendon Press.

Overing, J. and Alan P. (eds). 2000. *The Anthropology of Love and Anger: The aesthetics of conviviality in native Amazonia*. London: Routledge.

Pitt-Rivers, J. 1973. 'The Kith and the Kin', in Jack Goody (ed.), *The Character of Kinship*. Cambridge: Cambridge University Press.

Renard-Casevitz, F-M. 1993. 'Guerriers du sel, sauniers de la paix', *L'Homme* 126(8): 25–43.

Rezende, C. B. 1999. 'Building Affinity through Friendship', in S. Bell and S. Coleman (eds), *The Anthropology of Friendship*. Oxford: Berg.

Santos-Granero, F. 1988. 'Templos y Herrerías: Utopía y Recreación Cultural en la Amazonía Peruana', *Bulletin de l'Institut Français d'Etudes Andines* XVII(2): 1–22.

———. 2007. 'Of Fear and Friendship: Amazonian sociality beyond kinship and affinity', *Journal of the Royal Anthropological Institute* 13(1): 1–18.

Santos-Granero, F. and F. Barclay Rey de Castro. 2000. *Tamed Frontiers: Economy, Society, and Civil Rights in Upper Amazonia*. Boulder, Colorado: Westview Press.

———. 2005. 'Introducción, Campa ribereños', in F. Santos-Granero and F. Barclay (eds), *Guía Etnográfica de la Alta Amazonía, Vol. V*. Panama and Lima: Smithsonian Tropical Research Institute and IFEA.

Schäfer, M. 1988. *Ayompari, Amigos und die Peirsche: Die Verflechtung der ökonomischen Tauschbeziehungen der Ashéninga in der Gesellschaft des Gran Pajonal/Ostperu*. PhD dissertation, University of München, Germany.

———. 1991. 'Ayompari "El que me de las Cosas": El intercambio entre los Ashéninga y Asháninca de la Selva central Peruana en perspectiva histórica', in P. Jorna, L. Malaver and M. Oostra (eds), *Etnohistoria del Amazonas*. Ecuador: Abya-Yala.

Schneider, D. M. 1980 [1968]. *American Kinship: A cultural account*. Chicago: Chicago University Press.

———. 1984. *A Critique of the Study of Kinship*. Ann Arbor: University of Michigan Press.

Van Den Berghe, G. and P.L. van Den Berghe. 1966. 'Compadrazgo and Class in Southeastern Mexico', *American Anthropologist* 68(5): 1236–44.

Varese, S. 2002 [1968]. *Salt of the Mountain* (Fourth Edition). Norman: University of Oklahoma Press.

Veber, H. 2000. *Gendered Spaces and Interethnic Politics: The Pajonal Ashéninka case.* Copenhagen: University of Copenhagen Press.

Viveiros de Castro, E. 1993. 'Alguns aspectos de afinidade no dravidianato Amazónico', in E. Viveiros de Castro and M. Carneiro de Cunha (eds), *Amazónia: enologia e história.* São Paulo: NHII/Universidade de São Paulo and FAPESP.

———. 1995. 'Pensando o Parentesco Ameríndio', in E. Viveiros de Castro (ed.), *Antropologia do Parentesco: Estudos Ameríndios.* Rio de Janeiro: Editora UFRJ.

———. 1996. 'Images of Nature and Society in Amazonian Ethnology', *Annual Review of Anthropology* 25: 179–200.

———. 2001. 'GUT Feelings about Amazonia: Potential Affinity and the Construction of Sociality', in L.M. Rival and N.L. Whitehead (eds), *Beyond the Visible and the Material: The Amerindianization of society in the work of Peter Rivière.* Oxford: Oxford University Press.

Weiss, G. 2005. '*Campa ribereños*', in F. Santos-Granero and F. Barclay (eds), in *Guía Etnográfica de la Alta Amazonía, Vol. V.* Panama and Lima: Smithsonian Tropical Research Institute and IFEA.

Woodburn, J. 1998. '"Sharing is not a form of exchange": an analysis of property-sharing in immediate-return hunter-gatherer societies', in C.M. Hann (ed.), *Property Relations: Renewing the Anthropological Tradition.*

Chapter 3

Friendship, Distance and Kinship-Talk Amongst Mozambican Refugees in South Africa

GRAEME RODGERS

Between the mid-1980s and the early 1990s an estimated 250,000 Mozambicans crossed the border into South Africa in search of refuge from civil war. The majority were Tsonga speakers from remote rural villages in the southern provinces of Gaza, Inhambane and Maputo and took refuge from the RENAMO rebel movement's campaign of destruction in the rural southern hinterland (Roesch 1992; Vines 1991). Throughout the war, which ended in 1992, the South African government refused to consider granting international refugee status to Mozambicans, insisting that such large-scale undocumented migration was economically motivated and therefore illegal. When arrested, Mozambican refugees were deported summarily without any legal recourse or effective right of appeal.

But despite receiving such an unwelcoming official reception, many refugees were able to settle successfully in South Africa, mostly within the homeland territories of Gazankulu and KaNgwane, situated relatively close to the border. Local authorities and chiefs in these ethnically defined 'self-governing' territories permitted and sometimes even encouraged Mozambicans to settle informally on the peripheries of villages. Significantly, the Mozambicans were incorporated, not on the basis of a recognized status as international refugees, but as co-ethnics or 'relatives' (*maxaka*). Beaten by the logic of its own system of separate development, the apartheid government had little choice but to tolerate a large undocumented Mozambican refugee population, as long as it remained 'contained' within the homeland territories.

Following the achievement of peace in Mozambique and the dismantling of apartheid in South Africa, Mozambicans were finally granted refugee status for a limited period. This was essentially to facilitate their repatriation. However, only about thirteen per cent of the total estimated refugee population opted for formal voluntary repatriation with assistance from the office of the United Nations High Commissioner for Refugees (UNHCR) (Rodgers 2001). For the majority that remained, the question of return to a post-war Mozambique was far more complex than simply loading possessions and family members onto a truck bound for home. To confront the social and economic challenges of the post-war period, many refugees pursued varied strategies of transnational settlement, exchange and communication between home villages in Mozambique and refugee settlements in South Africa. Ongoing state policies that sought to prevent or control such movement had limited effect, testifying to the power of everyday social practices in overcoming official attempts to limit transnational settlement.

This chapter considers the contributions that relationships of friendship made towards enabling and facilitating ongoing transnational Mozambican refugee settlement in South Africa. I explore these relationships ethnographically, in situations where they have often found expression with reference to kinship. I argue that kinship and friendship were intersecting social forms that established relatedness through everyday practice (Carsten 2000: 17–8). In the aftermath of war, such relatedness was not always predictable or controllable and experiences of friendship and kinship took various forms, such as dilemmas over betrayal, anxieties over abandonment, and longing for familiar patterns of interaction. Commentaries on friendship and amicability sometimes affirmed the resilience of kinship but were also indicative of its declining value in a rapidly changing social context. So, whilst Bell and Coleman (1999) warn anthropologists about the dangers of analysing friendship as kinship, or approaching friendship in terms of kinship, Mozambican refugees made these suggestions and linkages routinely in the course of addressing the disruptions of displacement. Caught up in situations where contact – suggested by Erwin (1993) as a prerequisite to friendship relationships – could be neither predicted nor taken for granted, both friendship and kinship became sites of social anxiety and existential insecurity (Jackson 1998). As other papers in this collection note, Pitt-Rivers' (1973) claim that friendship is conceptually distinct from kinship, and even absent from the realm of the social, is not borne out in this case. Just as friendships are observed to play a significant role in establishing and sustaining networks in corporate environments (Krackhardt and Kilduff 1990) and migrant communities (see, for example, Gardner 1995; Bretell 2007), so they were drawn into strategies for confronting social disorder in this context. As Mozambican refugees struggled to re-establish and reconcile patterns of interactivity, friendships achieved wider resonance and significance through being recognized, performed and talked about; they were often judged against the constraints and possibilities of kinship. In this context, the appearance of friendship symbolized the pressures on tradition and its modern replacements.[1]

My argument starts from the observation that local cultural notions of friendship resonated strongly with discourses on kinship. The value of relationships between persons presented as friends was frequently expressed as reflective of a social tie that was ultimately rooted in kinship. This was even evident amongst friends who, at least structurally, did not appear to be particularly close kin. The corollary was also true, where a positive state of kin relations was partly measured and recognized by the extent to which kinship took on the form of friendship. With this in mind, the chapter demonstrates how the social and spatial changes brought about by refuge not only placed strains on existing friendship/kinship relationships and possibilities, but also realized new potentials for friendships that could not be recast so easily or comfortably as kinship. The dilemmas and tensions brought about by such a change in the patterns and proximities of everyday social interaction led to friendship relationships being experienced ambiguously, as both a public marker of the cohesiveness of kinship and also as potentially threatening that very cohesiveness.

My argument is drawn from a broader ethnographic study of the impacts that refuge and return had on the social production and reproduction of everyday life. Initial ethnographic research, conducted in 1998 in a refugee community in Timbavati,[2] was augmented by additional 'multi-sited' research carried out across various socially connected sites on either side of the border. The research data that I draw on here was generated primarily through audio and video messages that I recorded and delivered between individuals and families on either side of the border. Although the socially connected places that I examine were no more than 120 kilometres apart, the many practical, legal and economic constraints on Mozambican communication and movement across the border meant that cross-border messaging was a particularly effective and appropriate research tool for generating data on the nature of complex cross-border relationships, including friendships.

Tsonga Friendship/Kinship in Theory and Practice

The Tsonga term 'friendship' (*xinghana*) was used on both sides of the border to describe a broad range of relationships characterized by mutual affection, lack of formal constraint (c.f. Carrier 1999: 21) and forged on the basis of some 'common ground' (c.f. Bell and Coleman 1999: 15). Furthermore, friendships also often incorporated expectations of social and material obligation and, contrary to the Aristotelian virtue of perfect friendship, seemed to include the overtly self-serving elements of utility, pleasure and companionship. Indeed, people who described one another as 'friend' (*munghana*) were inevitably linked in multiple ways that could be disguised by the overt overtones of their friendship. Those linked through debt, for example, could reasonably see the respective acts of lending and borrowing as both indicative and constitutive of a friendship, although the borrower and lender might be inclined to emphasize the friendship aspect of the relationship differently in different contexts. Whilst friends were generally distinguished from lovers (*xigangu*), these terms were often interchanged in ways that could be deployed both playfully and tactically. When I worked with a female field assistant, for example, men would enquire from me if she were my lover. When I replied that she was my 'friend', they often responded in a 'nudge-nudge-wink-wink' kind of way. Whilst men and women could be friends, it was expected that close everyday contact on the basis of affection would, in all likelihood, lead them to become lovers.

In common with other contexts, any attempt to understand friendship across this border region compels some consideration of the rhetorical domain of kinship.[3] As illustrated by Obeid (this volume), the analysis of friendship can be approached usefully without separating it analytically from kinship. Friendship can be experienced as growing out of kinship, as undermining kinship obligations, or even as having nothing to do with kinship; but to talk of friendship in this disrupted borderland compels us to at least think about kinship. To configure friendship in terms of kinship enables, as Jackson (1998: 155) notes with reference to Australian Aboriginal communities, 'a way of safeguarding oneself, of soliciting respect, of avoiding humiliation. Kinship implies knownness'. Indeed, the language of kinship or 'relatedness' (*vuxaka*) provided the primary imagery that was cultivated around the experience of friendship. For Mozambicans and South African Tsonga speakers alike, relationships characterized by affection were frequently portrayed as an inevitable product of strong bonds of kinship. Good friendship and good kinship existed in a kind of dialectical arrangement. In some instances, kinship even appeared to me to be invented or exaggerated in the course of enthusiastic efforts to establish or develop friendships.

A proliferation of kinship-talk, as a defining aspect of friendship, arose partly from the fact that relatedness was highlighted explicitly and repeatedly through the rhythms and rhetoric of everyday life. Informal uses of kinship terms, even when technically incorrect or difficult to justify, denoted an intent to engage socially. Persons of the same generational status would refer casually to one another using slang terms, such as for 'brother' ('*bhuti*', '*broer*') or 'sister' ('*sesi*') or the more formal 'sibling' (*'makwenu'*). Persons of differing generational status would also use appropriate fictive terminology, such as 'in-law' (*'mukhonwana'*), to initiate or perpetuate light-hearted conversation and banter. Deliberate inversions or overstatements of kinship sometimes acknowledged a joking relationship. For example the children of a mother's siblings may refer to each other as 'grandparent' (*'kokwana'*), recognizing a casual interaction. Similarly a grandparent might express affection for a grandchild by referring to them as grandparent (*'kokwana'*). Whilst such playful usage of kinship terminology acknowledged affection, it could also refer to status or power. For example, a person may refer to someone to whom they were especially grateful as a 'father' (*'bava'*) or even 'grandparent' (*'kokwana'*). Such references were also sometimes invoked as a means of injecting humour into an awkward moment.

Kinship-talk therefore played an important role in initiating, signifying and enhancing relationships that people considered as friendships. I observed on many occasions how people who, upon meeting for the first time, justified their mutual desire to pursue closer social contact on the basis of a newly discovered kinship tie that they simply could not ignore. Any possible objection that such a tie might be too distant or complicated to work out seemed irrelevant and could be overcome by a less precise acceptance of each other as 'close relatives' (*'maxaka ngopfu'*). Whilst the details of relatedness did not always matter, the fact of kinship remained an important moral basis for friendship. Discourses on ideal friendships were therefore embedded deeply within the broad experience of kinship. This should not, however, be taken to suggest an unqualified endorsement of earlier anthropological claims of friendship being contingent or dependent on kinship (for example, Paine 1969; Schwimmer 1974). Whilst kinship certainly played a structuring role in enabling friendships, good friendships also produced good kin relations. Rather than simply appearing as an extension or elaboration of kinship, friendship relationships contributed actively towards establishing and sustaining a 'culture of relatedness' (Carsten 2000) across this border zone. In the wake of refuge and post-war transnationalism, the social tensions that resulted from such profound disruptions of people's everyday lives challenged the viability of this folk model, forcing people to re-evaluate the meaning and significance of friendship.

Experiencing the intensity of friendship as a function of the closeness of kinship ties was dependent on a system of broad kinship possibilities. Kinship, or relatedness (*vuxaka*), amongst Tsonga speakers constituted a widespread potential that could be activated in flexible ways, depending on the intentions of those involved. Relatedness was imagined around the idea of a relatively few territorially-based patrilineal clans (*swivongo*).[4] These clans often took the name of the founding ancestor and provided a corporate identity for both men and women. In theory, marriage was exogamous and virilocal with respect to clan. However, over time, as clan populations increased in size and blood ties became more distant, pressure towards intra-clan marriage forced clans to split. Effectively therefore, clans became comprised of different branches or exogamous sub-clans and individuals from different sub-clans who were once regarded as being related by blood were now related by marriage.[5]

The possibilities of kinship recognition were enhanced further through polygynous marriage, bilateral kin recognition and a highly inclusive extension of the categories 'mother', 'father', 'sibling' and 'cousin'. The term 'father' was applied routinely, not only to one's biological father, but also his brothers.[6] The children of one's father and his (social and biological) brothers were recognized as 'siblings', as were the children of one's mother and her sisters. The co-wives of one's mother were also recognized within the category of 'mother', since their children would be one's siblings, by virtue of having the same father. The term 'uncle' (*malume*) was used most directly with reference to one's mother's brothers but its application was extended beyond this direct relationship to his family members. The term 'aunt', reserved formally for one's father's sisters, was used in practice in similar ways. Such a highly elaborated social landscape of kin recognition sustained the possibility for everyday interactions to be framed by the lens of kinship, but elaborated selectively through the intentions of friendship.

The broad basis for potential ties of kinship between Tsonga speakers across the border landscape enabled a wide (but not open-ended) opportunity for exploring friendship relationships. When it seemed appropriate, people identified and agreed upon quite specific kinship ties without knowing the complicated genealogical basis of them. For example, age mates that were also good friends might refer affectionately and casually to each other as 'grandparent' and 'grandchild'. My questioning of this elicited comments such as, 'I just call them that because I was told by the elders that that's how they were related to me. I don't know exactly why'. Importantly, the expressions of close kinship that indicated friendship were not always consistent or expressed in quite the same way by all parties. Deteriorating friendships, for example, were often explained in terms of failed kinship obligations, or a new revelation that the kinship basis of the relationship was not that strong to begin with. Whilst widespread kinship ties between Tsonga speakers were frequently undeniable, they were also highly malleable and were somewhat open to revision and reinterpretation in the wake of sudden social change.

Unsurprisingly, following the large-scale movement of Mozambicans into South Africa as refugees, kinship comprised a vital form of social and cultural capital that informed everyday strategies of survival and social incorporation. Kinship discourses underpinned negotiated arrangements for ongoing Mozambican settlement in South Africa, local tolerance of refugee settlement as well as claims for direct support and assistance, either between refugees or between Mozambicans and South Africans. After the war and organized repatriation, the primacy of kinship between locals and refugees persisted as an important rationale for justifying ongoing settlement in South Africa. However, the new social and economic conditions of life in refuge created greater opportunity for friendships to develop beyond the framework of kinship. Transformations in the meanings and morality of institutions like work, schools and churches, for example, were precipitated by profound changes in the practices and patterns of everyday life. In the context of these changes, friendship had a morally ambiguous character, comprising at the same time the necessary 'glue' that linked people together through kinship, as well as the corrosion that weakened such links.

Traditional Kin, Modern Friends

Scholars examining the social and economic impacts of population displacement have noted that such displacement not only disrupts existing patterns of social life but also often compels people to enter into new social relationships, opened up by new social possibilities. This observation was first elaborated by Elizabeth Colson (1971) in her famous study of the social impacts of resettlement amongst the Gwembe Tonga of Zambia, but has been expanded on by researchers, including de Wet (1995, 2001), Sørenson (1996) and Oliver-Smith (1996). Applying this insight to understand the dynamics and social significance of friendship in Timbavati, the discussion below reveals how friendships established on the basis of kinship enjoyed the authority and security of being represented as 'tradition' (*xintu*) reconstituted in the face of dramatic social and spatial change. Friendships that were facilitated by the condition of refuge, yet unable to be configured as kinship, were treated with suspicion, as an acceptance of modernity in South Africa, or the 'ways of whites' (*xilungu*). When pursued beyond the domain of kinship, friendships also ran the risk of appearing morally ambiguous and threatening to the controls of kinship.

Relatives as Friends, Friends as Relatives

In the late 1990s Philemon Mongoe, an elderly man, probably in his late seventies, would sit under a large wild fig tree weaving reeds into mats using discarded plastic wrapping. Philemon's seemingly constant presence under the fig tree, a strong 'peasant intellectualism' (c.f. Feierman 1991) and a friendly and talkative disposition made him an ideal informant. We met almost daily and became good friends throughout the course of my research. Over time I learned how, amidst the chaos and the constraints of life in a refugee settlement, he remained steadfastly committed to what he considered to be a traditional lifestyle. Despite having his world being turned upside down by war, Philemon attributed problems in his life to the intrusive and debilitating impacts of modernity in South Africa. This worldview probably helped him to respond to the inherent vulnerability in being elderly, ill and unemployable in a modern cash-based economy with few formal social safety nets. At various times he would claim status as a chief (*hosi*) in Mozambique, a powerful traditional healer (*inyanga*) and, on the odd occasion when he was angry, drunk or desperate, he even alluded to knowledge of witchcraft (*loyi*). He would sometimes claim, rather dramatically, that he feared that he would be unable to prevent himself from 'raping' a woman if he saw her dressed in (modern) trousers as opposed to a (traditional) wrap-around skirt. Those around him would laugh, casually dismissing Philemon's determination to live in another time and another place as age-related eccentricity.

Although Philemon lived a precarious life on the social and geographical edges of Timbavati village, he felt relatively secure in the knowledge that his adult sons lived around him.[7] They supported the household and when they went off in search of work as labourers either locally or in the urban centres of South Africa, he would keep an eye on the *va-makoti*, his son's wives, making sure that they did the work that was expected of them and that they did not go off in search of lovers.[8] As my own friendship with Philemon developed out of our mutual interest in his history and culture, he began to refer to me as his 'child' ('*n'wana wa minha*'). Whilst this should have been an ecstatic moment for me, as an ethnographer, I was always conscious that it reflected his way of acknowledging our growing friendship, rather than any ethnographic breakthrough on my part. The language of kinship was drawn into his expression of our friendship even though, in this case, it was fictive.

Once I started transporting messages between Mozambique and South Africa, Philemon's participation was unavoidable. He could not pass up the chance to engage directly with the places and people in Mozambique that were at the same time both far away and central to his everyday life.

He sent many long and very public messages that emphasized his continued relevance to the lives of those around him as well as those on the other side of the border. In remote areas in rural Mozambique, where villagers would crowd around a cassette player or video monitor, paying careful attention to both the foreground and background, Philemon expressed frustration at not being where he felt he belonged. He explored these frustrations, sometimes through friendly banter and innocuous exchange and other times through anger, demands and direct instruction. Comparing the conversations that evolved between Philemon and two of his brothers-in-law (*mukhonwana*) reveals how the qualities of friendship, including affection and companionship, affected the men's respective abilities to meet wider obligations. More interestingly, it also reveals how the social and geographic distances set up between those who sought refuge and those who stayed behind affected such friendship/kinship relationships.

One of the first people in Mozambique that I was asked to contact on Philemon's behalf was Omar Ndlovu. Omar was married to Philemon's sister, Rosia, who was the eldest of Omar's three wives. Omar and Rosia seemed to get on well together and projected a fairly easy-going relationship in the video and audio messages that they sent to South Africa. Rosia would reassure Philemon that he still had a place in Mozambique and urge him to return, before changing the subject and complaining about a shortage of things in Mozambique, such as plastic buckets. Philemon would nod and respond directly to the messages as I presented them to him. In one instance, Omar asked Philemon to send a pair of gumboots as a present, 'size ten and a half', he specified. On my next trip to Mozambique I presented Omar with a pair that were size eleven. He responded bitterly yet affectionately to Philemon, complaining about him sending shoes that were far too big. Philemon smiled in response at Omar's performance.

In contrast to the tone of his interactions with Omar, video and audio messages between Philemon and another brother-in-law, Xikwamba Ngobeni, were formal, serious and occasionally confrontational. Philemon was married to Xikwamba's sister. The marriage was not a happy one and had been arranged as part of an elaborate 'revenge' over many generations, for the killing of one of Philemon's ancestors by Xikwamba and Cecilia's forefathers. According to Philemon, neither he nor Cecilia were happy to bear this ancestral burden. Between 1998 and 2000 their relationship had deteriorated so badly that Philemon had banished Cecilia from his homestead. She continued, however, to live on the periphery of the homestead under increasingly desperate circumstances. Cecilia sent messages to Xikwamba in Mozambique, bemoaning her fate and pleading for his help. In 2001 she sent a video message, which included the following:

> 'When we left Mozambique, you knew that we were in love. We had children together. I used up all my fertility with him. So when he gets sick [now], he says it is me who bewitches him. Who am I going to tell? I don't have any siblings around here to tell about this.'

But whilst Xikwamba expressed some concern over his sister's well-being, his real issue with Philemon related to cattle – the traditional property of bridewealth exchange. Through taped messages that I transported between Xikwamba, Philemon and Omar, it appeared that five of Philemon's cattle had survived the war in Mozambique and were being cared for by Xikwamba. At Philemon's request, I accompanied Omar to Xikwamba's village to confirm this. Quite coincidentally, we arrived in time to find one of Philemon's bulls lying on its side, with Xikwamba and his family gathered around to hear its death rattle. In a very abrupt message, Xikwamba informed Philemon of this and also informed Philemon that he was giving away one of the four remaining cattle, as payment to the boy who had been looking after the cattle. The boy happened to be the son of Xikwamba's mistress (*mbuzi*).

After observing this event, Omar sent additional messages to Philemon, expressing his concern and unhappiness over Xikwamba's decision. Given the context of the long-standing, ancestrally sanctioned relationship of 'revenge' and ongoing debt between Philemon and Xikwamba's respective families, Philemon was predictably outraged when I returned with the messages that cattle from his family, belonging to his ancestors, were being given away by Xikwamba.

Apart from brief discussions over serious matters, such as the cattle, Philemon and Omar's cross-border messages generally comprised amusing dramatizations of self-importance, comically ironic acknowledgements of affection, occasional lapses into nostalgia and playful banter. Omar constantly asked for 'things' from South Africa and Philemon repeatedly announced his imminent return to Mozambique, demanding that the way be prepared. Their relationship was built explicitly on a mutual appreciation of their obligations to each other as in-laws. However, they had few compelling reasons to send messages across the border, apart from the fact that they missed one another's company. At one point Omar noted: 'I feel I might see someone like you when I walk around the ruins of your house. I look around thinking that I see you, but I see nothing, and I end up only seeing the wind blow.' Philemon's many responses to Omar were similarly wistful and suggested strongly that he simply missed Omar's company.

In contrast, Philemon's video and audio exchanges with Xikwamba reflected a long-standing conflict of interest over the well-being of

Xikwamba's sister and Philemon's cattle and the difficulties in overcoming the distance required to address these issues. Messages were aggressively short and formal. Unsurprisingly, these family issues inhibited any possible friendship between the two men. Philemon interpreted this absence of any warmth in his relationship with Xikwamba as resulting directly from a failure of the latter's kinship obligations. For Philemon, good friends were first and foremost good kinsmen. I never discussed this with Xikwamba, but it is possible that he felt the same about Philemon. Philemon's contrasting relationship with each brother-in-law reveals how the possibilities of friendship were enmeshed, almost inevitably, in the extent to which kinship could be experienced in positive terms. This supports Carsten's (2000) argument that kinship or relatedness cannot be taken for granted but is constituted through practice. In the case above, kinship was won and lost at least partly over the qualities normally associated with friendship.

In the context of refuge, relationships, even when they were built on the recognition of kinship, were at risk of deteriorating over distances and the morality of kinship was often drawn upon to comment on such decline. Joyce Ngobene was the daughter of Jane Nyathi's maternal uncle (*malume*) and the two young women were therefore 'cousins' (*mzala*). They were also firm friends in South Africa. In 1998 Joyce attended a female initiation (*khoba*) that was organized by Jane's 'younger mother'[9] and the two spent a lot of time together. Joyce returned to Mozambique in 1999, and shortly afterwards, I transported the following message to her, from Jane:

> To you, my young mother. I would like to tell you that your money will be coming with my brother Nelson Nyathi. I am greeting my grandparent Nyankwavi and my grandparent Talia… You, my young mother Joyce Ngobeni, Mathabela[10] says he loves you. You must come back with Graeme when he returns… Keep well. I am Jane Nyathi.

To Rameka, the wife of her maternal uncle and the mother of Joyce, Jane sent the following additional message, which appears to be fulfilling a classic joking relationship:

> To you Rameka Ngobeni. I am asking for a printed cloth and a scarf. And fish. Send it to me by giving it to Graeme Rodgers. Here at our place it is a good place. Here at Acornhoek, we are buying bread. In the morning we wake up and drink tea. We want you to tell us what you are eating on that side. Here at our place there are beautiful schools. Our children are going to school very well. They learn *xilungu* (the language and ways of the whites). They also learn Afrikaans. They learn everything. And xi-Tsonga, they learn. I also want you to write Portuguese on that side, so that we can hear it. Here at our place, we are eating oranges and bananas. We get everything. This

place is called *Majisa* and *Makhoma*.[11] We eat at Spar, at Makhoma. We eat at Score.[12] We dress in fashionable clothes. We want you to visit us so that we can give some of the clothes to you. Ta Ta.

Whilst listening to this message Rameka commented that whilst Jane was praising the things in South Africa, she was also asking for things from Mozambique.

A year later, I returned with video messages of Jane being similarly boastful of the things that they enjoyed in the refugee settlements of South Africa, compared to the backwardness and presumed suffering of Mozambique. Unbeknown to Jane, Joyce's father, Nyankwavi, was very ill and a few days away from death, as it turned out. Under these circumstances, Jane's recital of abundance in South Africa seemed particularly inappropriate, despite the acceptable basis for a joking relationship. On this occasion, Joyce responded strongly, recalling that Jane had still not returned her money.

> I just want to talk to you Jane, about what you told me about giving me my money... This year is now 2000. Does that mean that you have used the money you owe me to buy the clothes you are wearing now because you are looking more beautiful than before? Use my money if you want to buy the paint for the houses that you are very proud to be showing us. I also have a beautiful yard but I can't jump up and down because there isn't anything going well with my family. My family are not well. You can jump around your yard because all your family and your parents are very happy. So you can carry on spending my money. Do whatever you want. I was just working for you because you are my aunt's child. So I was contributing to your life. I will finish here.

The physical distance between Jane and Joyce, brought about by Joyce's return to Mozambique, clearly affected their friendship (see chapters by Desai and Froerer in this volume for a fuller discussion of the significance of proximity). Unlike Philemon, Jane embraced and celebrated the modern lifestyle of South Africa. Joyce, on the other hand presented her situation in terms of a reverence for, and responsibility towards, tradition. Whilst the unpaid loan remained at the centre of Joyce's irritation with Jane, Joyce framed this sense of betrayal of their friendship in terms of a failed responsibility towards kinship, reducing any affection between them to the bare-bone fact of her 'working' for her 'aunt's child'. The imagery of this resonated with people working for whites in South Africa under conditions that were highly alienating, exploitative and impersonal.

Bloch (1973) has demonstrated how 'short term' efforts to promote good relations with affines could be necessary in sustaining the 'long term' structure and coherency of the kinship system. Similarly, in the wake of being settled on both sides of a hard border, Mozambican refugees placed considerable value on the qualities of friendship, such as greeting or sending news (*'ku rungula'*), as building on or cementing positive kinship relations across the border. Philemon and Omar's obvious affection for each other, even after so many years of being out of touch, seemed remarkable and exceptional. However, it is important to bear in mind that not much was at stake in their relationship. Beyond the performances of kinship, their relationship as 'in-laws' provided the imagery, the language and the opportunity for exploring, developing and acknowledging a friendship that, in fact, had rather little to do with how they were related. Philemon's structurally similar relationship with Xikwamba, which was much more tense and conflict ridden, yielded comparatively little kinship-talk. The tension that developed in Jane and Joyce's relationship became so problematic that Joyce suggested that their relationship was now defined purely through the most formal kinship obligations. Friendship had been squeezed out of the dispute over the unpaid loan through a failure to meet the expectations of kinship.

These vignettes of Mozambican refugee expressions of friendship, caught up in the opportunities and frustrations offered by my cross-border messaging methodology, confirm Bell and Coleman's (1999: 6) observation that in practice it is sometimes difficult to sustain a clear analytical distinction between friendship and kinship (see also Obeid, this volume). However, the distance between kinship and friendship becomes clearer in the next section through more focused attention on the potential for friendships to develop beyond an imagined moral world bound together, even across a modern border, by kinship.

Friendship without Kinship

The case studies above show how the emergence, persistence and decline of friendships were experienced as fairly localized commentaries on the state of kinship. But in the aftermath of refuge and subsequent regional and global transformations,[13] friendship relationships were certainly also recognized as possible beyond the logic of kinship. Throughout much of the twentieth century South Africa (*Jhoni*) represented a stomping ground for male migrant labourers, mainly working in the mining industry (First 1983). The risks of men getting 'lost' amidst the social chaos of the urban industrial landscape were mitigated to some extent by strong kinship and locality-based 'home boy networks', which sought to extend the logic of patriarchal kinship into the workplace (McNamara 1985). Large-scale refuge in the 1980s and 1990s exposed women, children and the elderly to the attractions and dangers of life in South Africa on an unprecedented scale. Refugees were thrust into new social relationships in what was previously the work-world of men, compelling their participation in broader social institutions and networks. Unsurprisingly, this generated new opportunities for friendships to evolve. New friendships, with strangers, could not be framed easily or convincingly in terms of kinship and appeared as ambiguous: they were necessary and inevitable but also potentially threatening to a lifestyle that was, or was imagined to be, spatially rooted in Mozambique and structurally bound by kinship. This was particularly evident amongst women that had left their rural homesteads in the Mozambican hinterland and amongst Mozambican children that had grown up in South Africa.

For children and adolescents, life in the refugee settlements of South Africa opened up opportunities for education that were considered better than in Mozambique. In Timbavati, Mozambican children were able to attend local schools and, according to teachers, attendance rates of refugees regularized over time. Many Mozambican children, as well as their (mostly uneducated) parents, placed a high value on education in South Africa. They regarded it as an important signifier of social and economic integration into South Africa and a means to escape the impoverished conditions that most refugees lived in. Some people even stated the education of their children as the primary reason why they had delayed their repatriation to Mozambique. In the early years of refuge it was relatively easy for teachers to identify refugee children through accents, clothing and other markers of difference. Some refugees reported being victimized by teachers on the basis of their national identity, especially when they excelled. However, over time these differences became far less marked and seemingly less significant to everyday interactions at school. By the late 1990s, even though it was difficult to identify the national identity of school children, teachers were adamant that children of refugee parentage dominated the top positions of each class. They explained this apparent situation as a consequence of the traditional forms of discipline that characterized the governance of Mozambican households. Unlike South African children, who had become softened and spoiled by the luxury of a more modern lifestyle, Mozambican children purportedly still lived within a disciplined domestic environment that fostered a determination to be strong and alert and to perform well.

In rural southern Mozambique, where many schools were small and isolated (much like the communities they served), kinship would have been a common basis for the identification of playmates and social interaction. In South Africa, where population densities were much higher, school populations much larger and where traditional settlement arrangements had been transformed into large and impersonal government-designed 'villages', school children's friendships seemed to evolve in ways that deliberately played down both locality and kinship.[14]

Within the refugee settlements, Mozambican children would talk of their networks of 'buddies' (*tjomies*) that grew out of their school experience, which extended beyond the worlds and experience of their parents, grandparents and relatives. Sports and various informal 'street corner' gathering opportunities, made possible by the modern cosmopolitan lifestyle of South Africa, represented important contexts where children and young people's friendships could be formed without reference to the organizing effect of Mozambique-based kinship identities.

Football was a particularly popular leisure activity for both those who played as well as for the many who gathered around as spectators. Many of the skilled and enthusiastic football players in Timbavati played for a local team called 'Dragon'. Dragon played within a loosely organized local league, against other villages and village sections around Timbavati. Whenever I asked about the national composition of the team, perhaps unconsciously hoping to identify a 'Mozambican team', I was always told that no one really paid any attention to national identity, even though most of the players were indeed of Mozambican origin. In 1998, whilst on a research trip to Decada Vittoria, a village in the remote Massingir District of Mozambique, I met up with a young man who revealed to me that he had only recently returned to Mozambique, from the Timbavati area. After we had exchanged pleasantries and identified a set of mutual contacts (through kinship-talk), he recorded the following message that I transported back to South Africa:

> I am Albert Makhuvele. I was a supporter of Maxakane Homeboys [football team]. So now it is called 'Dragon'. I greet that club, all of you at that club, especially you Andrea Ngoveni, and you Julio Ringane, I greet Sandros Ringane, I am Albert Makhuvele. I also greet Mr Mahlaule, I greet you, I am closer to you. And my cousin (*mzala*) Ngqove, greetings a lot. I am still living in Mozambique. Thank you.

Subsequent conversations revealed that Albert had returned to Mozambique reluctantly. His family had been the victim of repeated misfortune, which was eventually disclosed to be related to witchcraft. His return to Mozambique was at the request of his mother and was part of a consolidated family effort to confront the cause of this misfortune. But despite the circumstances that prompted his return, Albert longed to go back to South Africa and missed the football team around which so many of his friendships were structured. He complained that 'home' (i.e. Mozambique) was quiet, rather boring and lacking in the urban vibrancy of South Africa.

Whilst Albert's reverence of traditional power and the well-being of his family took precedence over his love of football, the socializing around football matches and practice sessions represented a strong interest for youngsters. This point was emphasized, almost ritualized, in early 1999 at an ancestral ceremony that was held at the home of Philemon Mongoe. At some point in the ritual, Philemon's grandson, Lucas, was supposed to be the first to taste the meat of the slaughtered ox. Philemon made a very public appeal to the participants to keep an eye on Lucas to ensure that he did not abandon the ritual before he had tasted the food in order to play football with his friends. If Lucas disappeared everybody else would go hungry, Philemon insisted. From the perspective of someone like Philemon, the magic of soccer and the lure of childhood friendships formed around soccer represented a constant distraction for children from their obligations towards tradition and kinship.

Friendships formed on the roughly hewn football fields of Timbavati did not explicitly counter or oppose the demands of tradition and kinship. Reflections of such friendships did however reveal some anxiety over new social opportunities for children that were beyond the comprehension and control of their parents. But such anxiety was not limited to the activities of children in South Africa. Prior to being displaced into South Africa, women were represented as being largely confined to peasant agricultural production within the realm in their husband's homestead.[15] Refuge both compelled and enabled many to socialize beyond the homestead, through the economic necessity of seeking out wage labour and creatively meeting the demands of life in a refugee settlement. In the course of doing so, many were able to participate in new social activities and arenas, leading to new social relationships.

The independent Christian churches that spread across the Timbavati region provided unique opportunities for refugees, particularly women, to socialize beyond their often-troubled domestic spheres. Although churches also proliferated across the Mozambican landscape, their organization within relatively small and isolated villages led them to remain largely embedded within other aspects of village life. By comparison, churches in South Africa were arguably better connected, served by better transport and communications infrastructures and with access to larger and more fluid populations. These comparatively greater cosmopolitan and 'modern' attributes allowed churches to offer greater social anonymity to the women that attended them. As the case of Alita Ngoveni illustrates below, some women regarded their church activities and associated friendships and relationships as providing an important sanctuary from the pressures and tensions of family life. This is not to suggest that church could not serve the same function in Mozambique but rather that the relative remoteness and isolation of rural Mozambique limited this possibility for many.

In 1999, Alita Ngoveni lived in Timbavati with her husband, children and recently arrived siblings from Mozambique. She was a passionate member of an evangelical church and represented herself as a devout Christian and active church member. Her messages to Mozambique suggested that she lived under desperate circumstances. To her mother-in-law, she reported the following:

> To you, my mother, Nositha Nyathi, I am your daughter-in-law. I am very well and the children are well. Isaka is around, but this week he is not here, he is in Johannesburg. Hey!! You mother, hey!! I am just criticizing myself because I have not got money to send to you that side. Your child is not behaving himself well any longer. He is working, but aysh!! He does not do well. He has got a lot of women. You know him. Truly, because he is your child. He has a lot of women. I have heard that he has a woman in Mugiana. He does not send money, so what am I going to give you? Don't criticize me my *mamazala* [mother-in-law], I do get some money from your child, but aysh!! it is very difficult to get it. As you know I have a lot of children and as you know in this country, you need money. Life is money. You, my mother. I am suffering a lot. I don't have anyone to look after the children. When I go to fetch money from him, he chases me with a *knopkerrie* [club]... I ran away with all the children. I just slipped them inside the taxi... Even if you don't have money, we will pay for you when you arrive with him. Come. Your grandchildren must not forget about you, especially Tertia, who is crying ... You will be eaten by dogs if you do not come!

By framing her message as a confession of her failings as a daughter-in-law, Alita also communicated her husband's abuse and neglect. But her problems did not end with her husband. Her mother had died and her father, who was a church leader in Mozambique, had remarried soon afterwards. Alita's younger siblings, living with their father, had crossed into South Africa unexpectedly and arrived on Alita's doorstep, telling of abuse from their new stepmother. They feared that she was trying to poison them. After complaining of the burden of having to look after her siblings, Alita expressed the following to her father:

> So, all of this, I am putting it in God's hands. We are just requesting your prayer. To you, our father, who brought us to this world. All I want to say is, is it true that you are leaving us, my father? Really? My father, please respond... You had better wash your hands of me, because I am nothing. Yes, we are nothing. All my mother's children, we are nothing to you. But you, my father, you must know that you have chosen between your children. You have separated us. So my father, I know that you were married in a western marriage ['*u chatile*']. So it means that we, as your children, will not have a share in what you are having with your wife on that side. So, it means that you have chased the children and said 'go to your sisters and brothers because all the belongings are for my children here in Mozambique'... We will see who is praying to God and who will enter the

kingdom of heaven. I am not saying that I am doing the best, but my spirit is painful. I was not remembering anything. I was just thinking that one of these years, I will be coming back home to visit you and to see you. The way that things are now, it does not encourage me to come back home. If this boy [her husband] can beat me until he kills me, I will be unable to come back. If I have a fight with my husband, I will have to look for where I can stay and linger around and get a place. I do not have a home anymore, since my in-laws here, where my marriage is, have heard my problem about my family. They will make me suffer, saying that I do not have a home. They will say that your father has even chased your mother's children away. Hey! That is what I am telling you my father, I do not have lots to say…

This rather lengthy extract from a much longer recorded message reveals a strong sense of social isolation and vulnerability brought about by Alita's physical distance from her natal family. She was also frustrated by the difficulties in addressing family issues, such as the conflict with her stepmother, across such a vast distance. Subsequent discussions with Alita suggest that she drew her strength and resolve to continue from her Christian beliefs and her involvement in the church. She took great pride in wearing her church uniform and spent much of her time devoted to church activities. Broader observations of church activities in the area suggest that they provided an important and desired site of social interaction between women who were friends, away from the domestic worlds of their husbands' homestead. Discussion with Alita suggested that church provided an important sanctuary for her and other women in similar predicaments, through forms of mutual support.

Significantly, involvement in church activities carried a strong moral authority within Timbavati, even amongst people who were not Christian. Given Alita's passionate commitment to the church, it would have taken a brave and foolish husband to try to prevent her from attending church. Because male priests and congregants were notorious for having affairs with women members of their congregation, husbands occasionally expressed suspicion over their wives' involvement in the church. However, they seemed unable to do much about it. Churches therefore represented spaces in South Africa where refugee women could socialize and interact with each other in ways that gave them some reprieve from the enormous social pressures that they were often subjected to in the refugee settlements. It is important to bear in mind that the friendships that emerged in these contexts did not explicitly counter the structuring authority of kinship and marriage, but appeared to provide some compensation for the failings of these institutions. However, the support represented by such friendships was not always regarded in positive terms and, viewed from certain quarters (e.g.

suspicious husbands), threatened to undermine the authority of more traditionally sanctioned social arrangements.

Anxieties over Mozambican women's friendships were certainly not limited to their attendance at church. Such concerns need to be seen in the context of a much longer history of predominantly male migrant labour to South Africa. Prompted by poverty, many refugee women desperately sought to participate in the South African labour market, seeking out niche opportunities that were often highly exploitative, low-paid, illegal and dangerous. This included commercial farm labour, domestic labour and production and sale of home-brewed alcohol. The often seductively dangerous environments that the women ventured into increased the possibility of them 'running away' or becoming 'lost' to their husbands and families. Many of the more serious messages that I transported from Mozambique to South Africa included enquiries as to the whereabouts of women who had disappeared from South African farms or urban areas. Some incorporated open-ended and desperate pleas for women to return to their families in Mozambique. Such abandonment was often blamed on the company they kept, the friends they made and the influence of a more modern lifestyle.

In places like Timbavati, women provided much of the seasonal labour force on commercial farms in the vicinity of the refugee settlements. The work was low-paid, insecure and often illegal. Celeste Zitha moved to Timbavati in the late 1990s specifically to work on the farms and to make money to support her family in Mozambique. By the time I met her in 1998, she had a well-earned local reputation as a drunkard (*dakwa*). On weekends and in between contracts Celeste spent her time drinking with a regular group of friends in Timbavati. As they wandered around the settlement to wherever cheap or (ideally) free alcohol was available, often causing arguments and fights, they were regarded as a nuisance by Timbavati's more sober-minded residents. In the course of my research, I tried to avoid them as far as possible because they would inevitably put a lot of pressure on me to purchase alcohol for them.

In Mozambique, drunkenness, especially when brought about by drinking home-brewed beer, was not necessarily considered problematic and was often spoken of as a highly desirable and sociable means of getting through the day. Drinking and drunkenness in South Africa was considered more problematic, primarily because it was expensive. Even home-brewed beer was bought and sold, with the result that many hard drinkers, like Celeste, squandered their limited resources. By all accounts, Celeste had accumulated very little during her time in South Africa. To make matters worse, she had also managed to spend the bridewealth of one of her daughters – a considerable sum of money that was passed on to her for safe-keeping. Her failure to account for the lost bridewealth made her even more reluctant to return to Mozambique and face the consequences. Celeste's husband and much of her immediate family remained in Mozambique. Her relationships with relatives in Timbavati, such as her 'son',[16] deteriorated, possibly as a result of her heavy drinking and confrontational manner. Messages recorded by her daughter, daughter-in-law and granddaughter comprised short and direct requests for her return, and for the presents of clothing that they expected from her but never received.

A year later, in 1999, nothing had changed and Celeste's daughter-in-law sent another recorded message urging her to come home. This time, she told Celeste of 'bad luck' in the family, suggesting miscarriage, illness and hunger. In early 2001, whilst I was away from Timbavati, Celeste suddenly returned to Mozambique. According to her neighbours, she returned specifically to assist her family to confront the problem that her daughter-in-law had alluded to a few months earlier. The source was identified as the revengeful spirit of a man who was killed accidentally by Celeste's son during the civil war in the course of a military training exercise. His angry spirit was wreaking havoc on the family and this required a concerted and united family effort of appeasement. Despite her failures in South Africa and the degenerative company that she was regarded as keeping, Celeste was 'forced' to return to help confront the demands of 'tradition'. For observers like Philemon Mongoe, this was an example of how powerful traditional forces could forcefully reclaim those women, like Celeste, who had strayed or become influenced by the 'wrong crowd' in South Africa. In other cases that I recorded in Mozambique, women could not always be reclaimed as effectively. Their refusal or inability to return was often blamed on the influence of the friends that they had made, especially 'boyfriends'.[17] Such friendships, represented as emanating from people's attraction and exposure to the modern, cash-based consumer-oriented lifestyle in South Africa, were presented as having the potential to dissolve the cohesiveness of kinship.

Refuge and the Proximities of Friendship

The case material considered above shows how social transformations brought about by war and refuge not only disrupted pre-existing patterns of friendship, they also generated new conditions and opportunities for friendships to develop and flourish. Importantly, these new bases for friendship were not always represented as socially productive and were sometimes experienced as morally ambiguous and socially threatening by those who observed them or were affected by them. Given the unavoidable overlaps between discourses of friendship and kinship, such ambiguities were often articulated or experienced as tension between the 'traditional' values of Mozambique and the 'modern' lifestyle of South Africa. The changing nature of the social mechanics and moralities of friendship cannot therefore be understood in isolation from a broader appreciation of social changes brought about by refuge in South Africa. Indeed, examining the changing proximities of friendship also permits new insight into the broader social and cultural experience of exile.

It seems that many Mozambican refugees who continued to live on the margins of rural South Africa in the post-war period could not separate their dilemmas of friendship from concerns over kinship. Some, like Philemon Mongoe, sought to resolve this by reconfiguring friendship as kinship. Whilst this may seem unsurprising coming from a man of his age and standing, other cross-border encounters examined suggest that an expected commitment to kinship could also be used by younger people as a language of judgement on the state of (particularly cross-border) friendships. But the possibilities for doing so also had its limits. Friendships that followed refuge in South Africa could not always be held accountable to kinship obligations. Schools, churches, towns and places of employment provided some of the sites of social interaction where refugees, particularly women and children, could explore new 'modern' bases for friendships. However dangerous and alienating, the possibilities for friendships in South Africa with strangers, or friendships that could not be experienced as kinship, permitted individuals to play down, ignore or even escape the 'localizing' effects and expectations of kinship.

In conclusion, by exploring how questions of friendship are confronted in particular social situations that arose in the wake of refuge, this chapter seeks to make a modest ethnographic contribution. By isolating particular relationships and focusing on situations where local concerns of 'friendship' (*xinghana*) became an issue, I have not sought to define the concept of friendship too precisely, or as analytically distinct and separable from kinship. By focusing on the social meanings and implications of relationships that were represented as 'friendships', my analysis makes the following more general points.

Firstly, it problematizes the creation of a clear separation between friendship and kinship that some writers have claimed. Whilst Mozambican refugees make some distinctions between friendship and kinship, their usages and invocations in real time and real contexts are often tied up in complex and ambiguous ways. It is precisely this ambiguous quality that people draw on creatively in their attempts to reconstruct their livelihoods and lifeworlds in new and challenging political and economic environments. Occasionally, kinship emerged as a measure or basis for judging a relationship that looked more like friendship or companionship, either affirming it or condemning it. Secondly, friendships, although defined through sentiment and amicability, may be experienced as socially negative or threatening relationships, particularly by observers that may be left out of the social loop. Whilst paying closer attention to these narratives might not reveal much of the essential quality of friendship relationships, they do provide an important insight into the social consequences of friendship. Finally, the chapter also suggests that a closer analytical focus on transformations in the meanings, practices and patterns of friendship that appear in contexts of displacement may enhance attempts to reveal aspects of the changing social worlds of refugees in ways that have not been explored fully. More focused attention on friendship relationships amongst displaced persons may lead to greater insight into, for example, the significance of territoriality, national identity, changing gender and generational relations, and debates over the meanings of modernity.

Acknowledgments

I would like to thank Evan Killick and Amit Desai for inviting me to participate in the workshop that resulted in this collection. I am grateful for their careful editing and thoughtful suggestions in the course of developing the paper.

Notes

1. I am aware of the risks of lapsing unreflectively into the anthropological habit of describing social change in terms of an uncertain present, poised between the purity of a traditional past and the dangers of a future modernity (see Gellner 1991:19; Fabian 2002). However, in this case, the spatial changes brought about by refuge were often expressed in terms of a temporal transformation from tradition to modernity.
2. A Mozambican refugee neighbourhood, located between rural villages, close to the town of Acornhoek, South Africa.
3. See Loizos and Papataxiarchis (1991) and Schwimmer (1974), for a broader discussion of this effect.
4. Junod's (1927) early exposition of this link between clan and territory has been undermined largely by the border and by subsequent colonial and post-colonial disruptions in Mozambique. However, this link still underpinned idealized representations of the social arrangement.
5. In this context, Tsonga speakers would use the term blood (*ngati*) in much the same way as I use it here.
6. That is, sons of the same man.

7. To remain living in the vicinity of his sons was one of the few reassuringly familiar aspects of Philemon's pre-war lifestyle that he was able to re-establish in the refugee settlement.
8. He, together with many other refugees who feared such illicit affairs, would often use the English term, 'boyfriend', when describing these inappropriate lovers.
9. Mother's younger sister.
10. She was teasing her cousin here. Freddy Mathabela, a rather comical character, was my local South African field assistant and accompanied me on this particular trip.
11. Suggesting a place of abundance.
12. Local supermarkets in South Africa.
13. Notably the end of apartheid in South Africa, the end of the Cold War and the intensification of what Ferguson (2006) describes as the 'neoliberal world order'.
14. I have not conducted detailed ethnographic research within schools. This interpretation is drawn from interviews and interactions with school children in their home contexts.
15. This is, of course, a strongly male–oriented perspective. Although their situation is not as institutionalized as male migrant labour, women have certainly ventured beyond their domestic spaces to find work throughout Mozambique's history (see for example, Penvenne 1997).
16. Her husband's son by another wife.
17. People would frequently use the English term 'boyfriend' to make such a point.

References

Bell, S. and S. Coleman. 1999. 'The Anthropology of Friendship: Enduring Themes and Future Possibilities', in S. Bell and S. Coleman (eds), *The Anthropology of Friendship*. Oxford: Berg.

Bloch, M. 1973. 'The Long Term and the Short Term: the Economics and Political Significance of the Morality of Kinship' in J. Goody (ed.), *The Character of Kinship*. Cambridge: Cambridge University Press.

Brettell, C.B. 2007. 'Theorizing Migration in Anthropology: The Social Construction of Networks, Identities, Communities and Globalscapes' in C. Brettell and J.F. Hollifield (eds), *Migration Theory: Talking Across Disciplines*. London: Routledge.

Carrier, J. 1999. 'People who can be friends: selves and social relationships', in S. Bell and S. Coleman (eds), *The Anthropology of Friendship*. Oxford: Berg.

Carsten, J. 2000. 'Introduction: Cultures of Relatedness', in J. Carsten (ed.), *Cultures of Relatedness: New Approaches to the Study of Kinship*. Cambridge: Cambridge University Press.

Colson, E. 1971. *The Social Consequences of Resettlement: The Impact of Kariba Resettlement upon the Gwembe Tonga*. Manchester: Manchester University Press.

de Wet, C. 1995. *Moving Together Drifting Apart: Betterment Planning and Villagisation in a South African Homeland*. Johnnesburg: Witwatersrand University Press.

———. 2001. 'Economic Displacement and Population Displacement: Can Everybody Win?', *Economic and Political Weekly*, 15 December 2001: 4637–46.

Erwin, P. 1993. *Friendship and Peer Relations in Children*. Chichester: John Wiley and Sons.

Fabian, J. 2002. *Time and the Other: How Anthropology Makes its Object*. New York: Columbia University Press.

Feierman, S. 1991. *Peasant Intellectuals: Anthropology and History in Tanzania*. Wisconsin: University of Wisconsin Press.

Ferguson, J. 2006. *Global Shadows: Africa in the Neoliberal World Order*. Durham, NC: Duke University Press.

First, R. 1983. *Black Gold: the Mozambican Miner, Proletarian and Peasant*. Sussex: The Harvester Press.

Gardner, K. 1995. *Global Migrants, Local Lives: Migration and Transformation in Rural Bangladesh*. Oxford: Oxford University Press.

Gellner E. 1991. *Plough, Sword and Book: The Structure of Human History*. London: Paladin.

Jackson, M. *Minima Ethnographica: Intersubjectivity and the Anthropological Project*. Chicago: University of Chicago Press.

Junod, H.A. 1927. *The Life of a South African Tribe*. New York: University Books Inc.

Krackhardt, D. and M. Kilduff. 1990. 'Friendship Patterns and Culture: The Control of Organisational Diversity', *American Anthropologist* 92(1): 142–54.

Loizos, P. and E. Papataxiarchis. 1991. 'Introduction: Gender and Kinship in Marriage and Alternative Contexts', in P. Loizos and E. Papataxiarchis (eds), *Contested Identities: Gender and Kinship in Modern Greece*. Princeton, NJ: Princeton University Press.

McNamara, K. 1985. 'Black Worker Conflicts on South African Gold Mines: 1973–1982', PhD thesis, University of the Witwatersrand, Johannesburg.

Oliver-Smith, A. 1996. 'Fighting for a Place: The Policy Implications of Resistance to Development-Induced Resettlement', in C. McDowell (ed.), *Understanding Impoverishment: The Consequences of Development-Induced Displacement*. Oxford: Berghahn Books.

Paine, R. 1969. 'In Search of Friendship: An Exploratory Analysis in "Middle-Class" Culture', *Man* 4(4_: 505–24.

Penvenne, J. 1997. 'Seeking the Factory for Women: Mozambican Urbanization in the Late Colonial Era', *Journal of Urban History* 23(3): 342–79.

Pitt-Rivers, J. 1973. 'The Kith and the Kin', in J. Goody (ed.), *The Character of Kinship*. Cambridge: Cambridge University Press.

Rodgers, G.E. 2001. 'Structuring the Demise of a Refugee Identity: The UNHCR's Voluntary Repatriation Programme for Mozambican Refugees in South Africa', in C. de Wet and R. Fox (eds), *Transforming Settlement in Southern Africa*. Edinburgh: Edinburgh University Press

Roesch, O. 1992. 'Renamo and the Peasantry in Mozambique – A View from Gaza Province', *Canadian Journal of African Studies* 26(3): 462–84.

Schwimmer, E. 1974. 'Friendship and Kinship: An Attempt to Relate Two Anthropological Concepts', in E. Leyton (ed.), *The Compact: Selected Dimensions of Friendship*. Newfoundland: Institute of Social and Economic Research.

Sørenson, B.R. 1996. *Relocated Lives: Displacement and Resettlement within the Mahaweli Project, Sri Lanka*. Amsterdam: VU University Press.

Vines, A. 1991. *Renamo: Terrorism in Mozambique*. London: James Currey.

Chapter 4

Friendship, Kinship and Sociality in a Lebanese Town

MICHELLE OBEID

A few weeks into my fieldwork year in the Lebanese town of Arsal, I was invited by one of the local NGOs to a ceremony for handing out certificates after the completion of a computer course. One young woman, whom I had not met before, curious to find out what an outsider was doing at the NGO, sat next to me and started a conversation. Intrigued by the fact that I was living in the town, she asked if I had any kin (*qaraybīn*). For her, as well as for the majority of people in Arsal, it was inconceivable to live alone, away from one's kin, especially for unmarried women. Having by then become accustomed to a range of reactions to my staying on my own in a room in the NGO's headquarters – alarm, pity, hints of admiration for my 'courage' mixed with general disapproval – I replied with what I felt was a reassuring response, to show her that I was not totally on my own: 'I don't have relatives in Arsal but I have lots of friends (*ashāb*)'. She nodded agreeably and replied '*ahla qurba*[1] *al-suhba*' (friendship is the best kinship). At the time, I had taken her statement as a polite end to an otherwise onerous discussion about the vices of living alone, particularly because I had not heard the term *qurba* being used for non-kin; nor did people talk afterwards about friendship and kinship in that manner, as a single form of social relationship. In retrospect, though, her description may well be a significant way to decipher sociality in this, descent-type, society.

This chapter will look at local understandings of friendship in a particular Arab setting where an ideology of patrilineal descent predominates and where agnatic relations are favoured over all others. The supremacy of the ties of kinship is propagated by a dominant political stereotype which portrays Arsal as a rigidly lineage-based society where lineage (*'ā'ila*) organizes every level of social and political life, to the extent that the town has often been cited in the national media and by its own residents as an exemplar of *'ā'iliyya* (extreme lineage loyalty, familism). The question of the place of relationships beyond agnation, such as everyday friendships, the rules that govern them and the shape they take, becomes all the more salient in such a context.

Literature on friendship as an analytical category, but also as an ethnographic subject in Arab contexts, is almost non-existent. The scant attention given to this topic, in favour of the 'anthropological romance of kinship' (Peletz 1995: 344), while typical of the discipline as a whole, is even more emblematic of the anthropology of the Arab world, which has long preoccupied itself with deciphering Arab social organization through the lenses of descent and segmentation theory.[2] This longstanding tradition was followed by the use of transactionalist concepts of 'closeness' (Eickelman 1981) and 'relatedness'[3] (Rosen 1979). These latter approaches brought to light the elasticity of relationships and Arab kinship categories by showing that, more often than not, they tend to include non-kin (Eickelman 2002; Geertz 1979). Despite such conclusions, however, these studies, and ones that followed, have not focused on friendship as an independent topic in Arab ethnography.

Recent attempts in anthropology have urged us to pay more attention to friendship, both as an analytical construct in its own right and as a social practice that is embedded in social and economic realities, which are themselves changeable (Allan 1996; Adams and Allan 1998; Bell and Coleman 1999). Much of the debate about friendship however, including chapters in this volume, has still had to frame itself in relation to kinship, partly due to the dominance of kinship in the general anthropological literature, but also due to the fact that, in many societies, as Bell and Coleman have concluded, we cannot deny 'the power of kinship as an idiom through which to express the power of all social relations considered to have binding qualities' (1999: 6). Having made this statement, Bell and Coleman warn that while there can be a relationship between friendship and kinship, we must not reduce friendship to kinship. Along similar lines, Allan agrees that kinship and friendship may be based on different principles. Nevertheless, he questions the need to treat them as 'totally discrete and separate' (1996: 94).

The data presented in this chapter will deal precisely with the power of kinship in providing an ideal for social relationships such as friendship. The objective is to show that in a society ruled by a strong ideology of kinship, Arsalis idolize friendship as a relationship that is 'free' of the oppressive obligations dictated by kinship, at a time when transformations in livelihoods and in production are having a tangible bearing on the social organization of households and hence on the discourses, values, and ideologies surrounding the family. Despite the perception of friendship as an autonomous and idealized social realm, when probing the features of friendship – the rules, obligations and maintenance of such relationships – I suggest that they are modelled on the same rules of reciprocity and exchange, sentiment and permanence that govern kinship relations. By no means am I advocating here that friendship is 'kinship in disguise' or that 'non-kin amity loves to masquerade as kinship' (Pitt-Rivers 1973: 90). Rather, I argue that friendship, even though considered a separate type of relationship constituting an autonomous realm, is part of an all encompassing ideology of sociality at the heart of which lies kinship.

In order to understand friendship, kinship and their relationship in Arsal, we must first address the general economic transformations that have been taking place over the last few decades. Social relations are embedded in economic realities. Therefore, economic change will have a bearing on both the ideology and the practice of sociality at large. The chapter begins by exploring sociological factors that have given rise to 'friendship', as it is currently constituted, and goes on to explore its ideology.

Socio-Economic Transformations and the Decline of the Collective

Arsal[4] is a border town that lies on the slopes of what is known as the Anti-Lebanon Mountains, southwest of Syria, away from the main road. Officially, Arsal is labelled as a town (*balda*) because of its large population, estimated at 32,000[5] and its vast area – about 1/22 of all Lebanese land. The Arsalis, however, still refer to it as *day`a* (a village).

According to older people, half a century ago Arsal was much smaller, both in terms of population size and residential area. They recount that in the 1940s the population was less than 4,000 people, who were concentrated in two neighbourhoods, the 'Upper' and the 'Lower', as they are still called, despite their considerable expansion. In this earlier period, the houses were surrounded by fields of grain and cereal. People had houses in the town but also moved around in the highlands: the predominant livelihood in the early twentieth century was agro-pastoralism, and seasonal transhumance accompanied cereal farming. Today, the town is expanding, both towards its neighbouring villages on the main road and inwards toward the highlands.

Population growth and town expansion are but one feature of the rapid changes that Arsal has undergone in the last few decades. The town has experienced considerable transformations in the livelihoods of its inhabitants, a process which started before the Lebanese Civil War

(1975–91). The Arsalis consider themselves to be descended from a system of herding, traditionally entailing seasonal transhumance between the highlands of Arsal in summer and the lowlands of Syria in winter. But since the 1970s, many residents gradually shifted to fruit production, a transition which allowed for the diversification of livelihoods. These shifts gave way, towards the end of the war, to informal (and illegal) livelihoods. In particular, there was an intensification of smuggling across the Lebanese-Syrian border. This brought in new capital to the town and resulted in investment in small private businesses (petrol stations, shops, trucking equipment, transport vehicles). Another major industry that emerged at that time was quarrying, much of it operating without licenses. This industry was brought to life by the process of reverse migration which took place at the beginning of the civil war when many Arsalis who had been living in the suburbs of the capital Beirut gradually returned to take refuge in Arsal – which was far from the main battle zones – and upon their return brought with them new ideas, values and experiences (Baalbaki 1997).

Today most Arsali households adopt a multiple livelihoods strategy. Almost all households, including herding households,[6] are internally diversified in terms of occupations and livelihoods. It is known to the residents that these new economic activities have brought in capital to the town and created a class of wealthier people with new trends in consumption. Off-farm occupations have become quite popular with the young generation, even those who are not capital owners, due to their stability and higher income as opposed to the seasonal returns from agriculture and herding.

What is relevant here is that these changes have had an impact on the moral economies of livelihoods and the choices people make in adopting one or another livelihood in a diversified system and, most importantly, a changing attitude towards the nature of social life. The tensions most apparent at the time of my research were those between older and younger generations and people of different economic groups, over the perceived relationship between production and sociality (Obeid 2006a). Herding and agriculture reinforce a collective sentiment and an ethos of cooperation no longer available in the growing occupations such as quarrying, which tend to be male-dominated and hence preclude the involvement of families or communities.

The increase in livelihoods built on individual as opposed to family labour – together with other forces of modernization – has pushed for a new model of a 'family' and family relations. The aspired for household model today is that of a nuclear family with two or three children and a routine rhythm that persists all year long. Such households have a very defined, inflexible sexual division of labour with the husband holding a wage-earning job while the wife 'sits for [tends] her house and children' (*qāʿda li bayt-ha wa awlad-ha*). There are two main aspects of this new model: the first is that it is located far away from the wilderness and the second is that its members, namely women, are *murtāhī n* (comfortable), both aspects that resonate with an urban modernity (*tamaddun*) sought by young Arsalis.

This trend in the organization of production has meant that for both men and women, these economic changes have liberated them from the complex web of kin relations that controls their life decisions – including education, marriage and occupation – in the herding system of production. I suggest here that it is because of these changes that more space has been created for forging friendship relationships, particularly through the move away from herding as a system of production. There are many sociological factors in the town that have allowed for, firstly, more intermixing between lineages and secondly, more mixing with outsiders.

New Spaces for New Relationships

Many developments at the local and national levels have given way to new spaces which had not existed before in Arsal. Under the herding system of production, sociality is generally reduced to relationships with kin. This is not to say that people had no friends or spoke of no other social categories when herding predominated. Indeed they were semi-nomadic, which evidently meant that they mixed with people across the Lebanese/Syrian border and in different villages. But daily interaction took place mainly within circles of kin. With the move away from herding and parallel transformations taking place in the town and the country, new social categories such as comradeship, colleagueship and friendship began to gain significance. Three main developments in Arsal are worth discussing here: the development of new neighbourhoods, the promulgation of political party and NGO activism, and increasing access to education.

In the older herding system of production, neighbours (*jīrān*) and kin (*qarāyib*) often coincided, whether in the highlands or the town. The spatial as well as the human organization of herders necessitates that members of a herding unit live in the highlands and lowlands surrounding the residential area all year long. When a large number of herds are reared, several households enter a form of partnership expressed in the *khalt* (mixing) of their flocks, with each household contributing an equal amount of labour. A herding unit comprises a cluster of households with each having defined tasks. The number of households usually ranges between two and eight. It is common for these partnerships to take place between brothers, and sometimes cousins. This means it is quite possible that on a daily basis throughout the year members of a herding unit socialize only with a few close kin members. While they will have visitors, sociality for them, including marriages and relations of production, takes place among kin.

This kin-centred sociality was also the case for people living in the residential areas of the town, where, as described earlier, the old neighbourhoods were built based on lineage – even though some people from different lineages were bound to have lived side by side. Up until the 1940s there were four main lineages[7] with a significant number of members. Generally, residents built houses on their own land. At a time when the population was expanding noticeably, one common strategy (which to some extent persists today) was to add an extra floor to the parental home for married children (usually sons) to occupy. Even today, one will find that in the central and older quarters of the town, neighbours are often themselves kin. But because of the density of houses in the centre of the town, newlyweds tend to move outwards, constructing houses on communal land and thereby creating new town neighbourhoods. It is in these new neighbourhoods, in which mixing takes place with people from different lineages, that neighbours are not by default kin.

Despite earlier spatial divisions, neighbourly relations did exist between different lineages. In the mid-1960s, however, inter-lineage tensions mounted and there were outbursts of violence and killings following the 1964 Municipality Council elections in which smaller lineages contested the traditionally leading lineage (Obeid 2006b). These events, people recount, have led to avoidance and long-term, sometimes generational, enmities. Today, there are thirty-two registered lineages. It is estimated that one of the largest lineages may have up to 10,000[8] people which makes it possible that, although considered relatives, members of the same lineage may never have met. Therefore, it is the new neighbourhoods which provide an opportunity for lineages to mix, where neighbours are not just kin but could also be 'friends'.

Paralleling these structural changes, other socio-economic and political developments provided spaces in which town dwellers mixed with non-kin and outsiders too. When the civil war broke out in 1975, the political landscape of Arsal began to change. Leftist political parties, that focused on recruiting members in rural areas, became quite active in the town. Many Arsalis joined and since parties operated at a national level, men moved around the country; for example, in the 1980s, many Arsali men fought the Israelis in southern Lebanon following the invasion of 1982. Many others volunteered or were reimbursed in return for jobs secured for them by their parties in the capital. Political parties provided a forum for meeting people from different religious sects and regions in Lebanon and for forging valuable comradeships and friendships. This is clear in one of my informant's comments, given below, about a friend who used to be a comrade (*rafīq*) in the Communist Party during the war.

Ali and Zuhayr fought together during the civil war. After the war, Ali became disenchanted with 'politics' and stopped renewing his membership in the Communist Party. His lot had changed considerably, thanks to his engagement in the quarrying industry and he was now one of the richest people in the town. Zuhayr, on the other hand, being an environmentalist, refused to engage in such a hazardous occupation and chose instead to work for a local NGO, despite the low salary that he received. With a family of eight children, he sometimes failed to make ends meet. But Ali was always there for him, offering moral and financial help. He even paid for Zuhayr's children's school fees, with no expectations of repayment. In describing their relationship, Zuhayr felt that his comrade, and friend, was much more reliable than his own brothers.

> I cannot depend on my brothers in the same way I could on Ali. My older brother is hopeless. He is hooked on gambling. Can you believe that he has wasted his pension? All that money that the government gave him ... wasted. He called to ask me for money. I should be asking *him*. And my younger brother, look at him. All he cares about is to dress well and he has no job. But Ali, he 'feels' (*yash`ur*) with me. Last Ramadan [the Muslim fasting month], he came over with two kilos of meat for our house and my father's. He has lent me money so many times. With my salary, you know I could not have paid the children's school fees.

This level of closeness, according to Zuhayr, was developed as a result of a common experience as comrades in the political party.

With the end of the civil war, Lebanon witnessed a decline in political party membership and action. In Arsal, political party activism was replaced by the establishment of a number of environment and development NGOs,[9] which pride themselves on cutting across lineage boundaries and in working for the benefit of the entire town. Their membership is, therefore, based on mixed kin and sometimes on outsiders. This has encouraged the development of friendships across kin and developed a relationship that had not existed before: *zamāla* (colleagueship). *Zamāla* also developed in new institutions such as schools[10] and quarries that provided employment at a scale larger than that provided by small businesses such as grocery or clothes shops. As mentioned earlier, these larger establishments only grew during or after the civil war.

Education institutions, to which the Arsalis increasingly have access, are one of the most important spaces for forging friendships. Today, friendship in Arsal begins mainly at school. In the past, men were taught the Qur'ān in the mosques but women received no education. Nowadays, it is a common expectation that children will complete secondary school, and education has gained significant value in the town for both women and men. As for higher education, the nearest university is in a city an hour and a half's drive away. In the mid-1990s, many university students found it impossible to complete their degrees mainly because transport was very expensive and students could not pass their exams without attending classes on a weekly basis (Obeid 1997). But since 2000 the transport business has flourished in Arsal and many drivers have started operating their cars, vans and buses on diesel. This has made journeys to nearby cities and to the capital, about eighty kilometres away, much cheaper. It has thus become easier to commute on a daily basis to university which, in common with other institutions, is a vibrant place for forging friendships.

Internal and external changes in Arsal have resulted in the creation of avenues for forging new relationships which had not existed before. Changes in livelihoods, particularly the move away from herding, population expansion and changes in living arrangements, urban and reverse migration during the civil war and the emergence of new institutions have all provided spaces for new social categories and ways of behaving in which friendship relations play a central role.

Gender and Friendship

Older anthropological studies of the Mediterranean have tended to question whether friendship exists at all in certain societies where it may be perceived to compete with domestic roles – especially for women – and kin loyalty. This view has been reconsidered by more recent work. Uhl, for example, contests literature which had previously assumed that friendship does not exist among Andalusian females or that 'friendship, which has no biological basis, has been conceptually genderised' (1991: 91). She argues that 'adult female friendship constitutes a hidden message in that it is subsumed into women's public expressions of domesticity and is thus practically imperceptible in public contexts' (Uhl 1991: 92). In Arsal, for both males and females,[11] friendship is an important social relationship that has gained even more value with the rapid social change in the town. This importance remains for both men and women despite the relative differences in their opportunities for friendship.

Arsal does not have any cafes, restaurants or entertainment outlets.[12] Friends, like neighbours and kin, visit each other's houses for leisure, especially in winter. It is, therefore, far more practical to maintain friendships with people who live nearby, considering the extent to which the town is expanding. The matter is somewhat different for boys and men. It is common for them to hang out in the town square, which often intimidates women who then try to avoid passing in front of them. Men can drive to any part of the town; women depend on kin or neighbours for a lift. Men also drive to neighbouring villages where there are more entertainment options and in summer they go to the highlands for picnics or hunting trips.

On the other hand, women, unless they have jobs, often visit each other at different times of the day for breaks. Although they do go out on visits in the evenings, they do not stay as late as men, unless they are with their husbands or sons. Married and older women generally have more independence of movement than younger unmarried ones. It must also be said that, despite the fact that residents consider themselves to be conservative (*muhāfiz*) Sunni Muslims, inter-gender friendships are allowed, as long as they abide by social restrictions. For example, many students form study groups and meet either in the youth club or at somebody's house. Male friends can visit a female friend, single or married, as long as they sit with the family and not alone.[13]

The importance of proximity as an essential factor for the maintenance of adult friendships has been highlighted by Froerer (this volume). Similarly, the principal barrier to maintaining friendship in Arsal, particularly among women, is place of residence, both before and after marriage. Once friends live far away, it becomes more difficult to maintain ties. Below is an example of how place of residence can be an obstacle for female friends.

Immediately following their marriage, Dunya's parents moved into one of the older neighbourhoods where the majority of residents belonged to a different lineage from theirs. They were on good terms with their next-door neighbours with whom they were separated by a wall. Their children grew up together. In the years before Dunya married, she would visit Sanā' and Hala, her unmarried neighbours, for a morning round of *matte* (Argentinean herbal drink) before they started cleaning their respective houses. She would often visit them in the evening too. They would chat, share secrets, gossip and sometimes play cards in winter. At the time of Dunya's marriage, Sanā' and Hala were heavily involved in organizing her wedding party and they helped out with the cooking and other preparations. Following her marriage, Dunya moved far away to the house her husband had built in one of the new distant neighbourhoods. Dunya fell pregnant shortly afterwards and her visits to her parents' house, and those of her old friends, became rare. Hala complained, 'We really miss her. But she lives far away and now she is married. We don't expect her to leave her child and husband and come over. And we have no one to take us there! So we haven't seen her in a long time.' The barrier here is distance rather than the new responsibilities imposed by marriage and having a child.

Thus far, the chapter has focused on sociological factors that have allowed friendship relationships to gain ground in a kinship-based setting which has been undergoing social and economic transformation. I have shown in particular how changes in livelihood, as well as increased access to education and the growing relative freedom of women, have allowed individuals to form relationships outside of kinship that would not have been possible in previous generations. In the remainder of the chapter, I will address the ideology that governs these kinds of 'friendship' relationships. Of particular importance is the way in which ideologies of friendship relate to the predominant and powerful ideology that constitutes kinship.

The Ideology of Friendship

In the first half of this chapter, I described the reasons behind the increasing significance of social relationships outside of kinship, and the ways in which these categories can and often do overlap: kin can be neighbours, colleagues, comrades and/or friends all at once. Compare this, for example, with Allan who argues that among British middle classes,

> The tendency has been more for non-kin relationships to remain bounded by the initial setting of interaction even when particular individuals are significant people in one another's personal networks. Thus, by and large, workmates are not seen elsewhere unless they share activities in common; people from a leisure or sporting club are not routinely invited home; neighbours are only rarely included in other sociable activities (1996: 87).

In this sense, people are bound by the activity and not the relationship itself. However, Arsalis mix their relationships and spend time with colleagues or comrades at their homes.

Yet despite this overlap in people's relationships, there is still a local discourse that separates friendship relations from all others, particularly in comparison to kinship. The case of Arsal shows that despite transformations in kinship structures, a dominant kinship ideology persists, while still leaving room for friendships to exist and to be highly valued as social relations. The material here therefore supports approaches, including those in this volume, that challenge the sharp dichotomy between the domains of friendship and kinship. The boundaries between the two are often blurred.

The experience of friendship is sometimes cast in the language of kinship, to the extent that 'good friendship and good kinship [can] exist in a kind of dialectical arrangement' (Rodgers, this volume). In the following section, I will discuss the values ascribed to friendship in Arsal and then move on to consider the relationship of friendship to kinship, which constitutes an ideal for sociality.

Voluntarism and Choice

In local discourse, the description of friendship is framed in a similar fashion to that found among Euro-American middle classes (Allan 1989; see also Killick and Desai, this volume). Friendship is valued precisely for those characteristics that place it in contrast to kinship: voluntarism, choice, egalitarianism, and the ability to end friendships, if need be. The following discussion about social relationships that took place in Arsal attests to this view.

In one of our usual late morning breaks at the local NGO, a few members sipped tea as they shifted from one conversation to another. The discussion led us to a debate about kinship and friendship. Khawla was complaining about the predicament of women in Arsal, whereby they are expected to relinquish all their jural rights to the benefit of their male kin, who indeed take advantage of the expected 'female altruism', even when they are conscious of its injustice. Husayn linked this to the oppressive nature of kinship. '*Ahl* (kin), for example brothers', he asserted, 'are *imposed* on you'. He then explained that, 'maybe, if you had a *choice* (*khayār*), you would never want to be around these people. You are obliged to them but you might not like them!' His statement about choice was then followed by a medley of examples from the others of how relationships of friendship, acquired by choice, are often 'closer', 'better' and 'more reliable' than those ascribed by kinship. Arsalis, like many others, perceive friendships to be characterized by personal autonomy, voluntarism and moral self-governance (Bell and Coleman 1999) as opposed to kinship, which is dominated by obligation (*wājib*).

The anthropological literature on friendship has explored extensively themes of voluntarism and choice in friendship as opposed to kinship. Pitt-Rivers (1973) argues that friendship is defined by its opposition to kinship and that it exists in societies that have abandoned kinship as an organizing principle. In a similar vein, Greek ethnography shows how 'emotional friendship is remarkably different from kinship in many respects: as a haven of egalitarianism, as an autonomous basis of personhood, and in effect, as a sentimental alternative to maternal love and the amity of kinship' (Papataxiarchis 1991: 158). According to this view, friendship 'opposes' kinship and cannot be said to be continuous with it. Hence, kin cannot be friends as they are bound by different types of material as well as hierarchical bonds; in contradiction to the nature of friendship which is based solely on emotional ties. Friendship is then based on 'sameness, marked off from contract, and increasingly freed from reciprocity' (Papataxiarchis 1991: 176). Along similar lines, the study of friendship in Western societies has tended to divorce friendship from institutions like kinship altogether (Pitt-Rivers 1973) to the extent that Paine, for example, considers friendship to be an 'institutional non-institution' (Paine 1969: 541).

More recently, the literature has sought to demystify the freedom perceived in friendship relations. Sociological realities (Allan 1989), such as class, race, ethnicity and gender, among others, play an important role in the maintenance of friendships and the changes in their networks. The ease with which friendships can be broken has also been contested by Cohen (1961), leading many to believe that perhaps voluntarism in friendship may have been exaggerated (Bell and Coleman 1999). Thus the idea that 'true' friendship is undermined by social rules and obligations has been contested. Killick (this volume) takes this argument further by contending that mutual obligations and even debt, in the form of reciprocal exchange, in fact lend 'power' to the bond between friends. In light of the new literature, I would like to argue that in spite of the fact that friendship in Arsal is idolized as being based on 'freedom of choice', as Husayn's comment suggests, it is not 'free from contract' or rules of sociality that govern other social relationships. To make this point, we need to understand idioms of sociality used for both kin and non-kin.

Sociality: Kin and Non-Kin

Friendship was identified by Andalucians as 'intimate relationships emerging from periods of intense social contact during which the sharing of experiences, attitudes, insecurities, successes, secrets, and values forge enduring trust and loyalty' (Uhl 1991: 99). This summary closely resembles the Arsali view of sociality which rests on the concept of `ishra. Literature on the Arab world has described `ishra as 'the bond of living together or sharing a life' (Abu-Lughod 1986: 63). Unlike the Egyptian case described by Abu-Lughod, where `ishra refers to either matrikin or co-residents, in the Arsali context, `ishra is used to describe bonds between both kin and non-kin.

Two particular idioms are central to this bond. The first is the idiom of 'seeing' (*n-shūf*). The closer people are, the more they 'see' – visit and interact with – each other; in fact, one could be an indicator of the other.

The more people 'see each other', the more they become involved in each other's lives, share similar experiences and most importantly 'ask (*yas'al*) about each other'. Note that in the example of Zuhayr and Ali above, Ali not only 'asked' about his friend but also 'felt' with him and offered help when needed. The importance of seeing is expressed in the consequences of its lack. People invoke the Arabic version of the proverb that says 'out of sight, out of heart'.[14] 'Seeing', in this context, refers to much more than the act of sight itself. It imparts the constellation of mutual transactions that allow a relation to be considered socially alive and the 'heart' to be nurtured, hence making sociality a base for emotional ties and amity. This principle applies to both kin and non-kin. When kin do not see each other on a regular basis, a tension is set up between the perceived obligations towards kin and the emotional distance that exists.

Another common idiom of sociality is one related to commensality, 'the sharing of bread and salt' (*khubz wa milh*). In Arab societies, as is common with others, people believe that when they share food, a bond is created and, with it, various mutual expectations, especially when the relationship extends over a period of time. Food is a central conveyor of hospitality and amity in Arsal. When guests visit, especially strangers, they are immediately offered a drink and a meal, even if it is not time for one. It is this gesture of offering and sharing food that removes barriers between people. `Ishra therefore requires that relationships are nurtured by becoming more involved in each other's lives and sharing similar experiences. But `ishra is never free of obligation.

Social obligations are epitomized in two basic life events: marriage and death.[15] Kin, neighbours and friends participate in both, for it is in happiness and sadness that people demonstrate closeness and care. In weddings, women gather to cook for the luncheon feast eaten before the groom picks up the bride and takes her to her new house. As soon as the news of a death spreads, crowds of people immediately go to the deceased's house even before the burial. Since the deceased's family is usually in shock, it is close ones (kin, neighbours and friends) who cook. The idea is to show the deceased's family that their grief is being shared. At funerals, men carry the coffin to the cemetery and help bury the body, an act which the Arsalis believe is religiously encouraged as *ajr* (religious recognition). Among the most important occasions are the two Islamic Ids, during which people visit family and friends to wish them well. Unlike daily visits, the above events are taken more seriously and are more formalized in the sense that offence is taken if, at a funeral for instance, an expected mourner fails to show up. This happened at the time of my stay when an NGO member passed away. One development researcher, who is from the capital but had worked with the NGO for over ten years, not only failed to show up to the funeral but neither offered his condolences to the family of the deceased nor even to his colleagues at the NGO. This created deep wounds as the mentioned researcher had failed the `ishra built up over years.

Having explored this general notion of sociality, I would like to go back to the two issues related to friendship mentioned in the previous section: firstly, the claim that there is no contract or reciprocity in friendship; and secondly, that relationships can end freely. The description of `ishra suggests that its obligations apply to all social relationships equally. There are clear rules and expectations of social exchange and reciprocity. Kin, neighbours, comrades and colleagues are all aware of them. Hence, even when Arsalis express their preference for 'free' choice-based relationships such as friendship, they are cognisant of the obligations that need to be observed. As for the second issue, while in principle any relationship (including kin relations) can be broken (e.g. one can stop talking to a brother), in reality, because of the ethic of sociality, it is not a course of action that is easily pursued. Let us take the following example.

The herders' summer camp consisted of three tent-houses. Two of these belonged to two brothers, and the third to a herder from another lineage who had been camping in the same spot for a couple of years. The latter's unmarried sister, Su`ād, visited Fātima, the wife of one of the brothers, more frequently than the other wife since Fātima had no help and was usually busier. But from time to time Fātima did manage to go to Su`ād's tent to return her visits and to drink *matte,* especially when Su`ād was left alone when her mother went back to the town and the shepherds were sleeping outdoors with their herds. At one point Fātima became annoyed because Su`ād was receiving a male visitor – and one who had a particularly bad reputation – when she was alone. Such an act is seen as immodest but Fātima decided to ignore the matter. However, matters came to a head on one occasion after Fātima went to Su`ād's tent to ask her to join them in watching a Syrian TV[16] series that they were following and found Su`ād with the dubious male guest.

> I acted normally. It's none of my business. But then, he said a word ... it offended me. I asked him whether it's true that his cousin was engaged to a girl I know. Guess what he said? He said, 'Herders lie'. How can he say this about us? Su`ād just listened and didn't say a word to defend me. I was in her house and she is my friend, like my sister, and she didn't say anything.

This incident irked Fātima for weeks and she stopped visiting Su`ād. When Su`ād came to visit her, Fātima now received her as a formal guest (*rasmi*), not as a friend and 'sister'. She stopped sharing stories and even avoided baking bread with her. But as the days went by, Fātima's anger subsided and Su`ād carried on visiting her. A year later, when I asked

Fātima about their relationship, she replied, 'we are friends. We've lived like sisters and *za`al* (anger) [or sadness] is not good between people.' Note here that even when she was upset, she still received her friend politely and met her social obligations.

In a similar example, a woman called Shifā' quarrelled with a neighbour who was visiting her because the neighbour mistook Shifā's daughter's jacket for her own child's, thus indirectly accusing her of stealing. Not long after, Shifā` asked the neighbour to leave. When Shifā's mother found out, she expressed disapproval of her daughter's behaviour, even though she believed the neighbour was at fault. She asked her daughter to visit the neighbour, taking her some freshly baked bread. '*Al jirān li ba`d*' (neighbours stand by each other), her mother reminded her.

From such cases it is clear that while one may 'choose' a friend out of one's own free will, friendship, like other relationships in Arsal, is governed by a set of social rules and obligations dictated by bonds of `*ishra*. Breaking away from these bonds contradicts a powerful social ethic and attracts public disapproval, as it is with kinship, such that friendship, though 'chosen', becomes just as inflexible as kinship when it is entered into seriously.

Kinship as a Model for Relationships

One of the main functions of `*ishra* is to create long-term relationships. Bonds of sharing produce proximity and shared values to the extent that town dwellers repeat the old Arab proverb that says 'one who lives with people for forty days becomes one of them' (*man `āshar*[17] *al qawm arba`īn yawm sār minhum*). 'Seeing', eating together, frequent visits and generally sharing life in its happy and sad moments are catalysts for not only proximity and sentiment but also inclusion. 'Becoming one of us', I suggest, is a statement of permanence and endurance that are believed to be characteristic of kin relations. I argue, therefore, that although friendship is framed in the language of choice, freedom, voluntarism and self-governance, it is modelled on the same ideals as those of kinship.

As I discuss elsewhere (Obeid 2006b), Arsalis express kinship in an idiom of patrilineal descent in which people construct a mental map of proximity where kin are arranged according to relations of blood (*qurbat damm*). People are also related by marriage in the sense that ego is related to a web of kin, both agnatically and cognatically. Affinal relations, however, do not make two groups of people kin, unless they were already related by descent prior to marriage (i.e. close kin marriage). When asked to explain how people are related to each other, Arsalis offer a classical account of patrilineal descent that parallels those found in earlier anthropological writings, where the largest unit on the map of kinship is the `ā'ila (lineage) and the smallest is the *bayt* (house). In between is the *jubb* (branch) which denotes the son of an ancestor and his descendents. Thus, members of a *bayt* are genealogically closer to those of a *jubb* who, in turn, are closer to those of an `ā'ila. This description, however, perhaps better depicts a standard formula of kinship rules rather than actual relationships. Arsalis have two ideals of kinship proximity that run simultaneously. One relates to a formal, fixed understanding of kinship, which is not inclusive, while the other is shaped by the performative elements of amity, sociality and the bonds of `ishra described above. While it is the latter that determines amity in kin relations, the former is what dictates obligations. A father remains one's father, even if he is unjust, oppressive or selfish, and therefore his children are obliged to obey and respect him and take care of him in his old age. This by no means implies that breaches of obligations do not take place. In fact, the ideology of kinship recognizes conflict as part and parcel of human relations and makes room for breaches, even though they are disapproved of.

The fixity that derives from an agnatic outlook on kinship is paralleled by the fixity in the perceived morality of kinship (Bloch 1973). The morality of kinship naturalizes kin relations. It postulates that kin are by definition reliable and trustworthy. Kin bonds are lasting and enduring and will survive any challenge. Kin relations are, as Bloch argues, long-term relations in which 'the actor sees himself as forced into imbalanced relationships by morality' (Bloch 1973: 76). The degree to which the imbalance is tolerated reflects the morality of relationships such that 'relationships classed by the actor as political, neighbourhood, or friendship have a shorter term than those classed as kinship and thus are less moral' (Bloch 1973: 77). In Arsal, moreover, the morality of kinship is reinforced by a religious ethic. Islam places particular importance on respecting both parents and also emphasizes the bond between siblings. In this sense, I suggest here that in Arsali local understandings, friendship, unlike kinship, is not permanent 'by nature', and as valued as friendship is, it ranks second best to kinship on a hierarchy of power and natural capacity for long-term endurance. I argue, therefore, that friendship in Arsal is modelled on kinship, and in discussing the strength of friendship, Arsalis use the language of kinship.

If we look back at the ethnographic examples presented above, we can see how both Zuhayr and Fātima, in describing their friends, placed them in an analytical comparison with kin. Zuhayr pointed out the failure of his brothers to observe kin obligations as opposed to the friend who played that role. On the other hand, Fātima emphasized how close she was to Su`ād, who was 'like my sister'. Good friends are as good as kin, without ever really becoming kin – since that is not possible in Arsali logic – but their relationship achieves a kin-like[18] status with equivalent value and prospects of permanence. Particular cases even suggest that friendship relationships can be more enduring than kinship ones.

This also explains the disappointment of the NGO members when the researcher failed to offer his condolences to them when their colleague passed away. As the deceased man's long-time friends, they felt as close as his kin and expected the researcher to respect that closeness. When he failed to do so, they were as disappointed as the deceased man's own kin might have been had condolences been withheld from them. One of them described their relationship: 'We have been together for such a long time. We have tasted the sweet and the bitter. He [the deceased] was like a brother to me. His children even called me "`ammati" (my father's sister). This is the extent of our friendship (*hal add kunna suhba*).' This may also explain the comment made by the woman quoted at the beginning of the chapter. Perhaps she was trying to convey to me that good friends are as good as kin in her town and that there was no need for me, or her, to worry about being on my own. Good friends, she might have thought, would treat me as if I was their own daughter or sister.

I have suggested here that according to local understandings in Arsal, kinship and friendship belong to two social domains, one governed by free choice and voluntarism and the other by obligation and fixity. But a closer examination of people's practices and expectations indicates that, in analytical terms, it makes more sense to understand the two as belonging to a single principle of sociality in which permanence is a virtue because it provides the endurance necessary for the survival of relationships. Kinship, therefore, becomes an ideal for friendships, even when the latter are idolized for their perceived freedom.

Conclusion

This chapter hopes to have contributed to an understanding of social relations in an Arab society. Friendship is a valued relation that is gaining more ground in a society that has been undergoing considerable transformations at the economic, social and political levels. In this sense, it is important to deconstruct the taken-for-granted supremacy of kinship in a 'kin-based society'. Arsal is notorious for its 'familistic' ties, a reputation gained from its political history, lineage factionalism and tensions dating in particular from the 1960s. But this obscures the day to day exchanges, the manner in which people relate to each other and the extent to which social relationships, including networks of kin, are embedded in larger changes taking place at the local but also national levels. I have thus shown how production regimes have played an integral role in enabling people to break away from the webs of kin dictated by the spatial and human organization of the previously predominant herding system of production. New occupations that emerged during and after the war have contributed to structural as well as symbolic changes to households, the sexual division of labour, and notions of 'the family' and family relations. I have highlighted the sociological factors that have led to the emergence and overlap of different social categories, such that kin themselves can be neighbours, colleagues, comrades and friends all at once.

The chapter has also located 'friendship' in a wider sphere of sociality and argued that what demarcates friendship from other relations are particular, 'idealized', perhaps even romanticized, notions of choice, voluntarism and freedom. Yet in reality, friendship, like other relations, is subject to rules and ethics of sociality informed by a local ideology – `ishra – about the bonds of living together. This argument reiterates the trend in recent scholarship that encourages us to focus on friendship within its social setting. In a context that values kinship highly because of its associated permanence, endurance and irreversibility, kinship then becomes an ideal, despite the diversity of practice. Through choice and enacting the expectations of `ishra, Arsalis use kinship as a model for other relationships and hence value friendships precisely because they become as close to kin as is possible.

Finally, documenting everyday friendships in a changing rural setting may contribute to the wider study of social relations across cultures. As is evident from this chapter, the language and idioms used to describe friendships are not different from those deployed in other societies. Therefore, while there might be 'little pragmatic sense in attempting to construct a rigid, globally applicable, definition of friendship' (Bell and Coleman 1999: 15), there definitely remains room for cross-cultural comparisons.

Notes

1. The term *qurba* literally means closeness. In Arsal it is used to denote kinship. Despite the usage of a common idiom, *qurba/ qarāba*, meanings differ from one Arab context to another (see Peters 1976; Mundy 1995).
2. Lineage theory has been misused to account for the 'backwardness' of Arabs – even by Arab scholars themselves (Mundy 1995) – and to 'facilitate their representation as especially divisive and violent'. For a critique, see Abu-Lughod (1989), Peters (1967), Eickelman (1981), Kuper (1988).

3. This was before Carsten revived the term more recently into a novel conceptual framework to be used 'in opposition to or alongside "kinship" in order to signal openness to indigenous idioms of being related rather than a reliance on pre-given definitions or previous versions' (2000: 4).
4. My familiarity with Arsal is based on a long-term and extensive knowledge of the area, built up during the course of ten years, and culminating in thirteen months' ethnographic research conducted between 2002 and 2003.
5. Local Municipality estimate for 2003.
6. According to the local Municipality, in 2003 herders made up only 10% of the population.
7. Each patronym in Arsal, as well as in other towns in Lebanon, is registered under a number in *sijill al-nufūs*, a registry originally instated by the Ottoman administration. Every time a child is born, he or she is added to the registry. Officially, therefore, an `ā'ila consists of the number of people sharing a registered patronym in one specific town.
8. Lebanon has a serious self-induced problem with statistics because no census has been conducted since 1923 when the population was divided equally between Christians and Muslims. Wishing to maintain a sectarian system based on this proportion, the government has avoided a new census, which might reveal that the ratio has altered and thus disrupt the political order. Arsal Municipality accordingly estimates the size of a lineage indirectly through a count of eligible voters in elections.
9. There are more than eight NGOs in Arsal, at least three of which are national and have branches outside the town.
10. There are eleven privately owned schools and one public secondary school in Arsal. Although there are small shops and quarries, there are no public offices, ministries or private companies.
11. Compare with Papataxiarchis (1991) who argues for a gender difference in the way friendship is conceived in Aegean Greece. While for women friendship is expressed in terms of domestic kinship, for men friendship is independent of kinship and the hierarchies it imposes.
12. In the past few years, people have been pressing the Municipality to build a park or space for families and children.
13. In the last few years, there has been a growing Islamic sentiment in the town. There are a variety of reasons behind this, including the introduction of satellite TV which exposes people to religious channels, the surge of piety teachers from the cities, and the increase in access to transport which has enhanced the self-consciousness of Sunni identity in a Shiite area.
14. 'Ba`īd `an al-`ayn, ba`īd `an al-qalb.'
15. There are other, though less important, events such as birth and religious festivals in which kin, neighbours and friends participate.
16. The television was powered by a car battery.
17. `Āshara is the verb from the noun `ishra.
18. Abu-Lughod argues that the Bedouins she studied tried to make 'quasi-kin' out of non-kin (1986: 63).

References

Abu-Lughod, L. 1986. *Veiled Sentiments. Honour and Poetry in a Bedouin Society*. Berkley, Los Angeles and London: University of California Press.

———. 1989. 'Zones of Theory in the Anthropology of the Arab World', *Annual Review of Anthropology* 18: 267–306.

Adams, R. and G. Allan (eds). 1998. *Placing Friendship in Context*. Cambridge: Cambridge University Press.

Allan, G. 1989. *Friendship: Developing a Sociological Perspective*. London: Harvester Wheatsheaf.

———. 1996. *Kinship and Friendship in Modern Britain*. Oxford: Oxford University Press.

Baalbaki, A. 1997. 'Transformations in the Pastoral Nomad System in the Village of Arsal', *Periodicals of the Institute of Social Sciences*, Lebanese University, Beirut (4): 67–84.

Bell, S. and S. Coleman. 1999. 'The Anthropology of Friendship: Enduring Themes and Future Possibilities', in Sandra Bell and Simon Coleman (eds), *The Anthropology of Friendship*. Oxford and New York: Berg.

Bloch, M. 1973. 'The Long and the Short term: the Economic and Political Significance of the Morality of Kinship', in Jack Goody (ed.), *The Character of Kinship*. London: Cambridge University Press.

Carsten, J. (ed.). 2000. *Cultures of Relatedness: New Approaches to the Study of Kinship*. Cambridge: Cambridge University Press.

Cohen, Y. A. 1961. 'Patterns of Friendship', in Yehudi A. Cohen (ed.), *Social Structure and Personality: A Casebook*. New York: Holt, Rinehart and Winston.

Eickelman, D. 1981. *The Middle East: An Anthropological Approach*. Englewood Cliffs, NJ: Prentice Hall Inc.

———. 2002. *The Middle East and Central Asia: An Anthropological Approach*. Upper Saddle River, NJ: Prentice Hall.

Geertz, H. 1979. 'The Meaning of Family Ties', in Clifford Geertz, Hildred Geertz and Lawrence Rosen (eds), *Meaning and Order in Moroccan Society*. Cambridge: Cambridge University Press.

Kuper, A. 1988. *The Invention of Primitive Society. Transformations of an Illusion*. London and New York: Routledge.

Mundy, M. 1995. *Domestic Government: Kinship, Community and Polity in North Yemen*. New York: I.B. Tauris.

Obeid, M. 1997. 'Pursuing Dreams … An Upstream Struggle', *Al-Raida* XV/79, Fall 1997.

———. 2006a. 'Uncertain Livelihoods: Challenges Facing Herding in a Lebanese Village', in Dawn Chatty (ed.), *Nomadic Societies in the Middle East and North Africa: Entering the 21st Century*. Leiden and Boston: Brill.

———. 2006b. *Close Bonds: Kinship, Politics and Livelihoods in a Lebanese*. Unpublished PhD Thesis, University of London.

Paine, R. 1969. 'In Search of Friendship: An Exploratory Analysis in "Middle-Class" Culture', *Man* 4(4): 505–24.

Papataxiarchis, E. 1991. 'Friends of the Heart: Male Commensal Solidarity, Gender, and Kinship in Aegean Greece', in Peter Loizos and Evthymios Papataxiarchis (eds), *Contested Identities. Gender and Kinship in Modern Greece.* Princeton, NJ: Princeton University Press.

Peletz, M. G. 1995. 'Kinship Studies in Late Twentieth-Century Anthropology', *Annual Review of Anthropology* 24: 343–72.

Peters, E. 1967. 'Some Aspects of the Feud Among the Camel Herding Bedouin of Cyrenaica', *Africa* 37: 261–81.

———. 1976. 'Aspects of Affinity in a Lebanese Maronite Village', in J. Peristiany (ed.), *Mediterranean Family Structures.* Cambridge: Cambridge University Press.

Pitt-Rivers, J. 1973. 'The Kith and the Kin', in Jack Goody (ed.), *The Character of Kinship.* Cambridge: Cambridge University Press.

Rosen, L. 1979. 'Social Identity and Points of Attachment: Approaches to Social Organisation', in Clifford Geertz, Hildred Geertz and Lawrence Rosen (eds), *Meaning and Order in Moroccan Society.* Cambridge: Cambridge University Press.

Uhl, S. 1991. 'Forbidden Friends: Cultural Veils of Female Friendships Andalusia', *American Ethnologist* 18(1): 90–105.

Chapter 5

A Matter of Affection: Ritual Friendship in Central India

Despite the general paucity of writing on the anthropology of friendship, one area in which the latter has received significant attention has been in the discussion of what are variously called fictive kinship, ritual kinship, ceremonial friendship or ritual friendship relations. That anthropologists have examined these kinds of relationships at the expense of less formal modes of association is entirely understandable: they have a ritual form that can be studied, and their sociology can be precisely plotted and compared in a way that may be more difficult with the nebulous and diffuse networks of 'ordinary' friendships. Alternatively, the focus on these ritualized forms may betray the biases of anthropological knowledge that valorized the 'jural' domains of life at the expense of the 'domestic', and which were heavily criticized by those who argued that this divided approach offered only a limited understanding of kinship, and by extension, gender and power. Either way, the study of ritual friendship has about it the air of mouldy pages in an old anthropology journal. Nevertheless, as I hope to show in the discussion that follows, there is still considerable analytical value in exploring ritual friendship, especially when, following our informants' lead, we place it in the context of other social relationships such as caste and brotherhood.

I look here at the structural role of ritual friendship among people in central India, and examine both how people talk about such a relationship and how they practice it. In particular, I raise questions about the way in which ritual friendship is opposed to ideologies both of caste and of brotherhood, and why the idea of love or affection (*prem*) occupies such a central place in its imagination. I suggest that the experience of disputes between brothers and the expectation that they will fall out with one another, coupled with a heightened fear of the power of witchcraft and sorcery, especially used within kin groups, leads people to see ritual friendship as a form of association which is safe from dispute. As such, in ideological terms it is constructed as founded purely on sentiment, unencumbered by material concerns and thus free from the sorts of entanglements that relationships with agnatic kin tend to suffer from. In a society characterized by a fear of malignant mystical attack, one creates a relationship of ritual friendship that is 'like brothers' but is ideally and ideologically disinterested. Whereas ritual friendship is always seen in terms of sentiment and affection (and, as a corollary, involving exchange which is not predicated upon calculation of a return), brotherhood is characterized precisely by the give-and-take of daily life: sentiment is present but it finds its basis in existing kinship relations. Where sentiment is bound up in other spheres of social life, such as in the relationship between brothers, there is the risk of dispute over land or other resources and jealousy has plenty of opportunities to rear its ugly head. And where jealousy walks, the fear of witchcraft and poisoning surely follows. The ideology of ritual friendship, on the other hand, is characterized by a lack of dispute or argument between friends. Through its emphasis on affection, ritual friendship becomes abstracted from a social life grounded in materiality, especially if, as people say, the best ritual friends are those who live far from one another.

In a manner not altogether dissimilar to the Chinese 'same-year siblings' described by Santos (this volume), the basis of ritual friendship in central India is sentiment: it is founded in the affection two people have for one another. It is not, however, restricted to these two people. Contrary to Pitt-Rivers' (1973) assertion that sentiment among friends is confined and therefore socially unimportant, in this case we can see that the ties of affection that bind people together are also conceptualized as bringing different families closer together. One could also argue that the sum of these individual ties of sentiment produces wider bonds between all people in a community such as a village beyond their own personal relations of kinship and friendship. For India in particular, others have looked at locality-based senses of belonging (e.g. Lambert 1996, 2000; Froerer, this volume) and have argued that the traditional emphasis on caste in India has relegated the importance of links between people who share a common residence (e.g. a village or a neighbourhood). Taking this line of reasoning further, I would argue that the existence of locality-based relationships enables people sharing the same physical space (a village) to think of one another as essentially the same, something that the ideology of caste works hard to negate. Sentiment is valued here between people who are friends, but one could argue that the consequences of sentiment have a wider effect on the imagination of a village community bound together by the ties of locality (as opposed to caste or kinship-based relationships). The importance of such an approach is that it recognizes that an ideology which ignores caste, as ritual friendship does, can exist alongside a contrary ideology that affirms caste. Ritual friendship, the sentiment it involves, and the ties of affection it builds beyond individuals, express the recognition of a fundamental affinity of people and the assertion of people as the same, an idea that caste denies. As such, looking at ritual friendship offers alternative bases for thinking about Indian society.

Ritual Friendship in Markakasa[1]

Forms of ritual friendship are common throughout central and eastern India (Orans 1965; Babb 1975; Jay 1973; Prakasam 1993; Skoda 2004). The generic Chhattisgarhi term used for ritual friendship in the village of Markakasa is *phul-phulwāri* of which there are several types.[2] The name given to the relationship depends in most cases on the substance exchanged at the ceremony creating the ritual friendship. One such substance is *prasād* (ritual gift of the deity) from the Jagannath Temple in Puri in Orissa, known as *mahāprasād*. This then comes to signify the name of the relationship and also the title by which one addresses the other. Taking one's ritual friend's name is not permitted, and a fine (a small amount of money or a coconut) is imposed for transgressions. Other common substances exchanged include *ganga jal* (holy water from the River Ganges) and *tulsi jal* (water sprinkled into the mouth using leaves of Indian basil, a holy plant). Both men and women can form these types of *phul-phulwāri*, but the friendships must be between members of the same sex. Of these three types of *phul-phulwāri*, *mahāprasād* is the most common in Markakasa.

People in Markakasa become ritual friends for different reasons and in different circumstances; in all cases, however, *prem* (love, affection) is described as the basis of the friendship.[3] For some, the friendship was already of long duration before the ceremony and they wanted to formalize and publicize their *prem*; for others, often those people who had struck up an acquaintance based on working together in another village or town, the ritual friendship marked the beginning of a more profound relationship. People who had performed the ceremony in their youth or childhood often mentioned that they became ritual friends because they used to walk to school together, play together or share food from one another's lunch boxes. For others it was because they had met working in the same gang on a government work project building a road or reservoir. One young Mahar (ex-Untouchable) man became *tulsi jal* with a man from a neighbouring village because they both liked racing bullock chariots and always ended up competing against each other. I formed a *mahāprasād* ritual friendship with a Markakasa man, Radhelal, the village shopkeeper. A fellow villager, Shamrao, had first suggested it to me, saying that we clearly had *prem* for each other, and went on to add that not only our *prem*, but the *prem* between our respective families, would increase. I was a regular visitor to Radhelal's house and knew his mother and brothers well, and he had attended my mother's brother's son's (MBS) wedding in Nagpur.[4] Now, if he ever went to Nagpur again, he, as my *mahāprasād*, could always call on my *māmā* (mother's brother) and so the *prem* would grow, Shamrao explained.

For a number of other people the *prem* also came after the ceremony: their fathers or grandfathers arranged their friendships in order to keep the families close and to enhance the connection between them ('*samanda vādna*'). In this situation the ritual friendship between individuals is a symbol of a wider union. Pardhu, a middle-aged Gond man with two *mahāprasād* relationships, told me that his first one was made when he was a child of about six or seven years old with a Rawat (cow-herder) boy from a neighbouring village. It was arranged by their parents to ensure that the relationship between the two families would endure. He met his second *mahāprasād* while they were both servants at the village headman's house and lived and worked there together. They became friends and decided to become *mahāprasād*. Interestingly, Pardhu's younger son has become ritual friends with the son of his father's second *mahāprasād*. Though the sentiment for the two ritual friends in cases of 'arranged friendships'[5] seems to be absent, what is in fact being affirmed and continued is the original sentiment that caused the old ritual friendship to be made. What is evident here is that *prem* does not map easily onto individual autonomous persons. Rather, sentiment is located among many different people and is thus more diffuse; but it is still constitutive of particular friendship relations between named and distinct individuals. Thus, we are dealing with a configuration of personhood and sentiment that looks very different to the one proposed by Carrier (1999), who claims that only a model of personhood that stresses individualism and autonomy (and one particular to a Western history) can produce the untrammelled sentiment necessary for the production of friendship (see also Killick and Desai's introduction to this volume).

That the children of ritual friends can themselves become ritual friends suggests a tension in the elaboration of the relationship as one of kinship. Brothers or other close relatives cannot become *mahāprasād* to one another, and since *mahāprasād* is conceptualized as being 'like brotherhood', it would follow that their respective children are also to be regarded as agnatic kin, and barred from forming ritual friendships with one another (cf. Prakasam 1993: 202–3). My data demonstrate that existing ritual friends do arrange the friendships of their children and in doing so they implicitly deny that they are 'real kin' or 'real brothers'. It suggests that in reality what is being created in ritual friendship is a relationship that looks very much like agnatic kinship or brotherhood but is in fact something rather different. Ritual friendship is not the same thing as 'fictive kinship'.

Whereas caste is relevant in much thinking in other spheres in village life, people are emphatic that it is not a consideration when choosing a ritual friend. Even to suggest it in connection with *phul-phulwāri* seemed distasteful to those I spoke to. Those who in other conversations and contexts were the most disparaging of the village Untouchables (Mahars and Chamars) were clear that *phul-phulwāri* was blind to caste. Most ritual friendships are formed out of caste, unlike marriage of course which is (almost) always, and ideally, contracted within caste. Of the forty-five relationships within the village, thirty-six were contracted with members of a different caste and nine were contracted within caste. Of the seventy relationships that Markakasa people contracted with people from other villages, thirty-eight were with different castes and seventeen within caste.[6] Ritual friendships also crossed the clean–Untouchable divide: of the thirty-six relationships contracted within the village but outside one's own caste, thirteen were between Untouchables and non-Untouchables.

Similarly there seems to be no concern to restrict the making of ritual friends to people of the same class: wealthier villagers made ritual friendships with poorer ones, poor with poor and wealthy with wealthy. All in all, the impression is of a rather chaotic 'system'. It was important that the two friends be at a similar stage in their lives: though I was closer friends with my landlord than with Radhelal, it was never suggested that I become ritual friends with the former, in large part because he was married and had children and I was not.

The ceremony is not complicated and takes about five minutes to complete. A ritual specialist is not always required. Most people made do with a member of the family or a friend, though some people did ask the village *baiga* (ritual specialist) or the barber (*nai*) to officiate. People often chose to perform the ceremony at the time of the annual village fair (*mandai*) or at weddings, in part because it is at these times that the largest number of witnesses will be gathered in one place, and partly because the feasting that goes on in any case at these times can be hijacked to celebrate the friendship ceremony too. Also, as mentioned above, the ideal, according to some people, is that the ritual friend live in another village, and it is at weddings and *mandai* that guests (*saga*) visit the village and old acquaintances from far away are given the opportunity to become something more intimate.

The two parties sit on wooden blocks (*pidi*) facing each other, and two mounds of clay or mud representing the goddess Gauri (Parvati) and her son, the god Ganesh, are placed on a plate. These are the divine witnesses to the ceremony. Each friend brings with him a plate containing a coconut, some money (five or ten rupees, but the same amount in each), a sprig of bound grass, red vermilion powder and a heap of husked rice grains (*chāwal*). The two friends anoint the gods with vermilion powder and then one another on the forehead. The sprig of grass is placed behind the other's left ear and then the plates are exchanged between the parties an odd number of times (five, seven, nine), so that they each end up with the other's plate. The friends feed each other the ritual substance (be it *mahāprasād, ganga jal* or *tulsi jal*) and then embrace. They then feed each other *pān* (a betel leaf concoction), and the coconuts are broken up and distributed among the assembly as *prasād* (the divine gift).[7]

Becoming a ritual friend is not necessarily an individual act. As mentioned above, it can involve a wider class of persons than the two friends. And the relationships that are created are not restricted to these two people. One's ritual friend's brothers and sisters become like one's own siblings; their parents are referred to, both when speaking to them and about them, as *phul bābu* ('flower father') and *phul dai* ('flower mother'). If the ritual friends marry then their respective wives also automatically become *mahāprasād* or *tulsi jal* to one another without a separate ceremony being required, and the same is often, though not always, true for husbands of ritual friends. Ritual friendship seems to borrow many of the attributes of 'real' kinship – kinship is after all an extremely powerful and accessible idiom – yet in ideological terms a different sort of relationship is imagined.

The Content of Ritual Friendship

The obligations that ritual friends have to one another are only loosely articulated. What is emphasized is not what ritual friends should and could do for one another, but simply that they have love (*prem*) for one another. Ritual friendship is of a different quality to other more casual forms of friendship. As one young man, Suresh, told me: 'Friendship (*dosti*) can break but *mahāprasād* is for life. It's a question of *vishwas* (trust or faith). The level of trust you have in a *mahāprasād* is different to that which you have in an ordinary friend'.

People generally say that if ritual friends live in different villages they ought to visit one another, which is a result of the *prem* that exists between the two. As mentioned above, life-cycle events such as weddings and death rituals are often occasions when those ritual friends who live a distance from one another may visit. The act of visiting friends and relatives in other villages is an important part of both men and women's lives. Through this act it is possible to create an imaginary landscape of relatedness, in which one comes to conceptualize other villages as linked with one through ties of sentiment. But this has implications between people living in the same village too: not only is the tie between the Markakasa person and his friends or relatives in the other village, but also with people in Markakasa who have friends or are related to residents of that other village. Thus, contrary to Pitt-Rivers' assertion, ritual friendship is capable of creating sentiment that extends beyond the two people who have directly formed the relationship. My landlord Dhansai's family's ties of friendship with a family in another village provide a good example.

About eighty years ago, a man of the Sidar[8] caste from a village called Patratola, fifteen kilometres to the east in what is now the state of Chhattisgarh, bought some land in Markakasa and became friends with Mayaram, the father of my landlord Dhansai. As he also had land in Patratola, he would only occasionally visit his holdings in Markakasa and when he did he would bring his son, Pyarilal, with him. Mayaram's eldest son, Kashiram, worked with Pyarilal and they helped each other out with their respective fields. In time they became good friends and decided to become *mahāprasād* to one another. Their fathers were happy too since it cemented the relationship between the two families. During Dhansai and his sister Didi's childhood, there was much coming and going between Markakasa and Patratola. They would often spend several days visiting each other's households and they considered Pyarilal their 'older brother'; his father was their *phul-bāba* ('flower father').[9] The links were strengthened by Pyarilal's sister marrying and settling uxorilocally on her father's land in Markakasa as a *lamsenin*.[10] Today the *lamsenin's* grandchildren are very close to Dhansai and Didi's family: they often work together, both in work gangs on government projects and as agricultural labour, and are among the most common visitors to the house. In addition, Pyarilal's father's brother's son (FBS), Samlal, who also inherited land in Markakasa, set up a house there and even now shuttles between the village and Patratola. His family is close to Dhansai's, too. Samlal's wife, for instance, cooks and cleans for Kashiram, Dhansai's brother, when his adopted son and daughter-in-law are away, and nursed his late wife before she passed away. Thus, though Kashiram's father's younger brother (FyB) lives in Markakasa, and they have cordial relations, it is to Samlal and his wife (his *mahāprasād's* FBS and a member of a different caste) whom he turns to in times of need. When Pyarilal's wife came to Markakasa to attend the wedding of one of the 'grandchildren' referred to above, she contrived to spend as many nights as possible with Didi's family, rather than sleep in the houses of her affines and caste-fellows. When I asked her why, she replied that there were tensions with both the other households relating to old disputes in

Patratola and so she felt more comfortable staying with Didi. This reveals another facet of the nature of ritual friendship that I highlighted at the beginning of the chapter: it is set up in contrast to the kinship relations one might have with one's real brothers (or one's husband's brothers, as in this woman's case).[11]

Along with visiting, also central is the idea that ritual friends should dine together whenever they can; it was said that one should always invite a *mahāprasād* to dine at one's house. Festivals such as Diwali were important occasions when dining between ritual friends living in the same village would take place. In cases where their ritual friends are members of an Untouchable caste, Markakasa villagers pursue different strategies. People often said that young, unmarried men and women could eat at the house of an Untouchable without censure or pollution regardless of whether they were ritual friends or not. When young people marry, however, they ought to stop. However, despite this general rule, all those who had conducted ritual friendships across the Untouchable/'clean' divide said they had no qualms about eating at Untouchable households and that they did not think about such things when it came to ritual friends. And, of course, Untouchables friends were invited to eat at clean caste households. Caste councils, though active in other areas of life such as marriage and divorce, did not police the 'breaking' of these dining rules.

Ritual friendships stand outside the key institutions and relationships of caste and kinship. In creating connections between people of different castes, whether they live in the same village or not, people express the idea that sentiment has a value that transcends that of caste. Put in other terms, the idea of difference that is promoted by an ideology of caste is countered by the idea of similarity involved in the ideology of ritual friendship. It is this similarity that permits and sustains *prem*. In the course of a telling off I received for having addressed my ritual friend in an inappropriate way,[12] a man explained to me that we were both the same and equal and should treat one another with respect: 'what is in you here', he said pointing at my chest (and heart), 'is in him there', pointing now at my *mahāprasād*'s chest. 'It is the same'.

As well as constituting this key ideological function, ritual friends can also offer more instrumental aid, particularly in times of need. The following story illustrates the way in which many people thought about the ideal friendship engendered by this type of relationship.

On more than one occasion (and indeed after my own *mahāprasād* ceremony was performed), I was told the story of Lord Krishna and Sudama. Krishna and Sudama were childhood friends (though not 'ritual friends') of different castes who had played and studied together. When Krishna defeated his evil uncle and took back his throne at Mathura, he told Sudama that if ever he wanted anything he need only ask. Sudama was a poor Brahmin and his ever-growing number of children compounded his poverty. His wife was something of a shrew by all accounts and pestered him to go and see his old friend Krishna, now a wealthy king, to ask for assistance. Sudama wanted to take a gift, as it had been so long since they had seen each other. All they had in the house however was *pohā* (flattened or beaten rice), hardly a suitable offering to a king; but Sudama grabbed a bagful and set off for Mathura. On his arrival, seeing the splendour of Krishna's court, Sudama grew ashamed of his meagre gift and decided not to give it to his old friend. Krishna greeted Sudama affectionately and washed the feet of his guest. But he had noticed the bag of *pohā* that Sudama was unsuccessfully trying to hide and snatched it from him. He opened the bag and began eating the *pohā* with such joy that his courtiers began whispering about this mysterious gift. 'It's the tastiest food I've ever had', announced Krishna. Sudama was happy but felt uneasy about asking Krishna for help. He left without mentioning the reason for his visit. When he got home, it was unrecognizable; where his hut had once stood there was now a beautiful palace. Krishna had known what his friend had wanted and provided it. This, I was told, was how ritual friends ought to behave with one another.

Ritual friends do help each other both financially and by providing their labour at life-cycle events. But this is not in itself unusual behaviour: 'ordinary' friends or neighbours often do the same. What is different is that the ritual friend can be relied upon to assist one because of the affection that exists between the parties, and because one trusts one's ritual friend to a greater degree than other people.

The Problem with Brothers

When I asked people in the village about the nature of the relationship between ritual friends, they would often reply that forming *mahāprasād* creates a bond like that of brothers, like the closest of brothers, and that it is even closer than brothers because there is no self-interest involved or reason to argue; there is '*sirf prem*' ('only love'). The proof that the relationship is only 'like brothers' is that the children of ritual friends can themselves become ritual friends, an act that would be prohibited if making of brotherhood was actually envisaged. Thus it is misleading at the level of analysis to lump together ritual friendship and kinship despite the apparent similarities in the content of the relationships between the two types of relatedness. I suggest that we can uncover the true meaning of ritual friendship if we instead oppose the categories of ritual friendship and brotherhood. Let us take a closer look at the relations between brothers.

Brothers are regarded as the closest of all kin relations but the relationship is also recognized as the most difficult to maintain successfully, especially after the brothers marry. Before marriage, brothers are seen as working happily together for the good of the common household; after marriage, however, with the arrival of wives, brothers become selfish and quarrelsome. This is, of course, as it is seen from the male point of view, but wives also share the view that the relationship between brothers is fraught with difficulty. The ideal household is one where all brothers, together with their wives, live together and work together without division or jealousy. But this is seen as too lofty an ideal to be realized and as a consequence people often said that having more than one brother was a recipe for trouble.[13] In fact, most households in the village have at one time or another been seriously divided because of disputes between brothers. Two of the castes in the village, the Mahars and the Desau Gonds, have each split into two factions as the result of fraternal quarrels. Brothers (and their wives) are seen as intensely envious of their siblings. The most common cause of disputes is over land and inheritance. At least until their father dies, brothers and their families farm the land together and hold the grain produced in common. Maintaining this arrangement can, however, be difficult and in several cases a division of property (*hissa*) has been made in the father's lifetime, so that brothers farm separately and hand over a portion of their grain to their parents. Moreover, accounts are certainly kept of how much labour one brother's household contributes to the other. The disappointing experience of brotherhood is for many in sharp contrast to the idealized vision of ritual friendship.

I returned to the village in April 2005 for a month of fieldwork, and a series of incidents involving my *mahāprasād*, Radhelal, highlighted the interested/disinterested dichotomy between brothers and ritual friends. Radhelal, as I mentioned before, is the village shopkeeper. In a tiny space of less than two metres by two metres, he stocks a rather wide range of household goods; he also buys and sells unhusked rice, *mahua* flowers (used to make alcohol), tamarind, and other farm and forest produce. The shop makes a handsome profit, and many people praise Radhelal not only for his fair rates and prices but also for his commercial skill. He is the youngest of four brothers and a recent event affected relations between them.

April is the time when the *mahua* flower, which is used to make alcohol, blooms and falls and is collected by villagers to sell. The sale of *mahua* flowers to private shops, however, is illegal; all *mahua* must be sold to the State's Tribal Development Council (*Adivasi Vikas Mahamandal*), which guarantees a 'fair rate'. For Radhelal, the buying and selling of *mahua* can be highly profitable but it is also dangerous. Forest officials regularly conduct raids, and the transportation of *mahua* between merchants – which often takes place at night – is risky and subject to interception. Tractors transporting *mahua* had been caught on two separate occasions in the area that month and had, together with the flowers, been confiscated by the Forest Department. According to Radhelal all the traders were nervous. But he could not sit on his *mahua* any longer; he was short of money and needed to sell it on. So one day before dawn he sent three bullock cartloads off to his buyer. Unfortunately, fifteen forest officials were waiting for them and impounded the carts and the produce. Radhelal rushed to the Forest Office as soon as he heard and managed, with the help of a local leader from a neighbouring village, to persuade the officials to release the carts and the *mahua* in exchange for a large sum of money. On his return, his brothers Naresh and Mer Singh berated him for his lack of judgement in selling the *mahua*. The income that he would have made was eaten up by the bribe he had handed over. His sister-in-law, Mer Singh's wife, also began to criticize him, suggesting that the shop had lost enough money, and that they ought to shut it and Radhelal should do something else. Naresh and Mer Singh agreed. This was a surprising statement since everyone knew how well the shop did and that it was as a result of the income from the shop that the household had grown so wealthy. Radhelal said as much to his brothers and sister-in-law. Angry and upset, he went to open his shop for business. Later that day, he came to my house and told me what had happened:

> I can't understand why they're behaving like this. I had to sell the *mahua*. And that's what business, running a shop, is like: you have to pay people off all the time. My brothers don't understand that because they don't run the shop. How can they say I should close it down? They don't like seeing me doing so well, that's what the problem is. They can see that I'm getting to know lots of important people, traders, and they can't bear it. They can't bear the fact that it's because of me that the household runs at all and if any of them want money it's me they come to.

That evening he stayed and ate with me and came again the following evening too. He said that he just did not feel like eating at home with his brothers. The atmosphere was bad and his mother was crying all the time. Though he has other friends in the village, it was striking that he chose to come to my house, the house of his *mahāprasād*, while he was fighting with his brothers. Compared to the intensely interested relationship he had with his brothers, our relationship was disinterested in that neither of us could constrain each other's action, nor were we involved in each other's household affairs. Significantly, whereas brothers are expected to fight and fall out, it is said that ritual friends never do.

This discussion of disputes and arguments among brothers (or agnatic kin more generally) is important because such conflicts, if not resolved satisfactorily, run the risk of involving magic, used to eliminate an enemy. Attacks of witchcraft and sorcery are fairly common, and most people have, during the course of their lives, been subject to unwelcome attention of this kind. Malignant spiritual attacks are of two broad types: those perpetrated by witches (*tonhi* or *saude*), who may or may not need a reason to attack, and those initiated by laymen with the help of a sorcerer/diviner (*baiga* or *pujāri*). The latter kind of spiritual attack is most commonly committed by close kin, in particular close agnatic kin, of which one's real brother is the ideal type. While a brother is often accused of attack, it is also common to suspect his wife, who also has an interest in harming her brother-in-law and his family. Consider the following example.

My landlord Dhansai had a longstanding dispute with his elder brother Kashiram that has only recently been resolved. The relationship between the two brothers has never been good, and was characterized by a dispute over inheritance and property. Kashiram, Dhansai's brother, has no children of his own, but he had adopted a boy around fifteen years ago when the child was eight. Adoption is common in cases of childlessness but the adopted child is usually someone from within the family, a brother's son or daughter for instance. The reasoning is simple: 'an outsider should not eat one's land'. In this case, Shanta, the adopted boy, although a relative, is not of their lineage. Dhansai felt great bitterness over this: Kashiram ought to have adopted one of Dhansai's children so that the land would remain in the family; Kashiram's four acres would instead go to this 'outsider'. In the midst of all these claims and accusations of betrayal, Kashiram's wife, according to Dhansai, went to see a *baiga* (sorcerer) to ask that he cast a spell (*mantra*) to kill him. Dhansai duly fell ill, with recurring headaches and unexplained weight loss, and was at death's door for the good part of a year.

One could argue that interested relationships, such as those involving brothers, are susceptible to the use of witchcraft and magic, especially as weapons in the course of a dispute. Ritual friendships are ideally disinterested relationships, and as a result could be interpreted as being free from the types of risks associated with interested ones. The terms interested and disinterested suggest that ideas and theories about gifts and exchange may prove useful in understanding ritual friendship.

In a recent chapter discussing ritual friendship in Orissa, eastern India, Pfeffer (2001, cited in Skoda 2004: 176) makes the intriguing observation that 'love, nothing but pure love is expected from and given to the [ritual friend]. They will never demand a buffalo but their alter egos will surely provide for them'. Though not expressed in quite the same terms, the ideology seems to be very similar to what I have described above. Firstly, that love, 'only love' (*sirf prem*), is the most important factor in a ritual friendship, and secondly, that gifts are given without any expectation of return. This is in sharp contrast with the type of exchange that takes place between brothers: although brothers and their families may appear to give to one another with no expectation of return in the short-term, accounts are certainly kept for the long-term. Over the course of one's life, generalized reciprocity eventually becomes balanced. Sahlins (1974) argues that generalized reciprocity, as a kind of open-ended responsibility, is the sort of arrangement that exists between close kin. The experience of agnatic kinship in Markakasa seems to suggest that over the course of time it has to become balanced, or at least have the semblance of balance, for any sort of relationship to endure. A permanent imbalance will lead to conflict and a rupturing of relationships.

Take the example of my landlord Dhansai again. His elder brother Kashiram and he have now reconciled and they live and work together. The adopted son Shanta and his wife were asked to go and live in her natal village and renounce their claim on inheriting his land. Kashiram is much older than Dhansai; he is in his late sixties and can only perform the least demanding of tasks, such as collecting tamarind or *mahua*. Dhansai supports his brother now; he pays for his medicine and the repairs to his cycle, and sweeps and cleans his elder brother's living quarters. But this is part of the deal. When the childless Kashiram dies, Dhansai will inherit his land. The acrimonious dispute of more than twenty years standing appears to have been forgotten.

No such accounts are kept with ritual friends: people are expected to give with no expectation of return. On my return that April, Radhelal would insist that I eat with him every evening; after the fifth dinner in as many days I remarked that I felt awkward that I could not reciprocate. (As I ate my meals with my landlord and his wife, I found it difficult to invite people to dinner.) 'But we're *mahāprasād*', he replied. 'That sort of thing doesn't matter, you should eat with me everyday'. The motivating force is sentiment and affection; there is no 'looking to the future'.

Seen in terms of reciprocity and the gift, the story about Krishna and Sudama, recounted earlier in the chapter and told to me almost every time I asked someone specifically about ritual friendships, can be considered in a new light. What is appealing about the story is not, as I had initially supposed, that it is a general statement about how friends should behave with one another. Rather, the essential point of the story might be that Sudama cannot ask his friend for anything but Krishna knows what he wants and gives it to him without Sudama's knowledge.[14] As Parry states: 'the genuine gift is never solicited and the gift should be made in secret' (1986: 461).[15] I am not suggesting that this holds true in reality for the types of exchanges that occur between ritual friends, merely that the ideology appears in contrast to the types of interested exchange that transpire between brothers. The gift between ritual friends does not need to be repaid.

Ritual friendship captures an 'image of eternity' (Graeber 2001: 218). Unlike the expectation of disputes with brothers (raised almost to the level of ideology), it is said that ritual friends never fall out. This can be seen in the exchanges that take place in the ritual which makes people into friends. As mentioned above, each party has a plate containing some money and rice which is passed back and forth between the parties five, seven, or nine times. The significance of odd numbers is not only that at the end of the process, each party holds the other's plate, but that as a result of this long back-and-forth, the parties become confused as to whose plate they are holding at any point during the exchange. This has two implications: firstly, it suggests that this type of exchange is represented in ritual as continuing indefinitely and as an 'image of eternity', explained by the prolonged series of exchanges; secondly, the fact of exchange becomes irrelevant because of the confusion caused by the passing back and forth – the knowledge that one has given to the other seems to be enough.

I should say here that I am not suggesting that the relationship between brothers is characterized by a complete lack of an 'image of eternity'. I am simply proposing that the type of reciprocity that goes on between brothers (or other agnatic kin) is subject to change from generalized to balanced (or in Graeber's terms, from 'open' to 'closed'; 2001: 220[16]), whereas the ideology of exchange which characterizes relations between ritual friends remains permanently 'open'.

This brings us neatly back to a discussion of equality and hierarchy, and the opposition of the ideology of ritual friendship to the ideology of kinship and caste. Taking my cue from Graeber, I contend that gifts do not need to be repaid between ritual friends because the relationship is not identified with inequality between the actors: 'Gifts have to be repaid when communistic relations are so identified with inequality [as in the case of brothers of the same household] that not doing so would place the recipient in the position of an inferior' (Graeber 2001: 221). The relations between ritual friends are not characterized by inequality but the relations between brothers (especially those who share a household) certainly are. By not repaying the gifts received from a brother, one places oneself in a position of inferiority in relation to that brother. Take the example of Dhansai and Kashiram once again. Dhansai provides for Kashiram and receives nothing in return for the moment. Kashiram, although older, is put in a position of inferiority as long as no return is made. This situation will change once Kashiram is dead and makes his return by giving his land to Dhansai. That ritual friends are regarded as equal is supported by the fact that, since sentiment is the basis of their relationship, they are not compelled to make a return: there is no question of an inferior or superior ritual friend.[17] Likewise, equality is a key element in the story of Krishna and Sudama: one man's commentary on it was that by giving Sudama a palace, Krishna was making Sudama the same as him, creating similarity out of the undesirable difference of inequality between friends.

And yet, are ritual friendships in reality, as they are experienced and not as they are idealized, ultimately about self-interest and is that why people make them? The idea held by some that ritual friends ought to be from different villages, ideally far away, seems to indicate that friendships are made to expand social networks beyond the confines of one's village and 'to get to know more people' – people one would not otherwise encounter. Interestingly, in answer to my questions about why people *married* less either within the village or to cousins than in the past, I was often told that to do so meant one did not get to know new people, and knowing new people was seen as valuable. By bringing the fear of witchcraft back into the discussion, however, one could alternatively suggest that the greater the distance between ritual friends, the smaller the chance the relationship could become interested and thus susceptible to the types of attack that occur among kin and neighbours. In contrast to Western notions of friendship, intimacy is actively discouraged between ritual friends. In stark contrast to 'ordinary' friendships, the ritual friendship is strictly non-joking and the injunction against referring to one's ritual friend by name is always enforced.[18] Distance and formality are necessary components of this type of relationship.

One could look at the benefits of ritual friendship in two ways: material and moral. Gana, a forty-five year old Teli man, has a *mahāprasād* relationship with a bullock-seller who visits the village once or sometimes twice a year. When I asked them and others why they had become ritual friends, they gave the stock answer: *prem* (love or affection). But it is also clear that for the bullock-seller, having a ritual friend in Markakasa means that on a cold winter's night he is fed and housed during his stay while the other members of his party shiver outside under the mango trees. He also has the moral benefit of being treated not as a complete outsider, as his fellow bullock-sellers are, but explicitly as a *saga* (guest) of the village because of his relationship with Gana. It is impossible to ascertain, however, whether this moral benefit would translate into material benefit, in the form of improved sales of bullocks for instance, but certainly in the eyes of Gana's fellow villagers there was a sense that they would get a fairer deal from a man connected with them in this way. Nevertheless, the cornerstone of the relationship is still idealized as being one of love and affection (*prem*), despite the actual experience of the ritual friendship once it is formed, which may involve material or moral benefit. The practice and reality of ritual friendship can be as disappointing as the relations with brothers: friendships made in youth can fall away in later life and, although I never heard of ritual friends arguing or fighting, simple avoidance can be the expression of a disagreement or of a sense of growing apart. After all, ending a marriage or building a separate house from one's brother signals the end or at least the suspension of those respective relationships. But how does one publicly end a friendship? In contrast, however, to the relations with brothers and wives, there is a strong presumption that ritual friends do not argue and that it is a lifelong association. Although the friendship is undoubtedly idealized, it is noteworthy that it is my informants who do the idealizing, and not the anthropologist who could quite naturally be accused of viewing their social world through rose-tinted glasses.

Conclusion

Friendship should indeed be seen as a process (Loizos and Papataxiarchis 1991), as a form of belonging that changes over the course of a lifetime: at different points in one's life certain relationships are privileged over others, and parents, peers, siblings, spouses, children, as well as friends, fade in and out. This process has important social significance. But as I have shown here, looking at friendship as structural (in both senses of the term), as well as functional, can also provide valuable insights into different forms of sociality.

By looking at the function of this particular form of friendship in the context of social life in Markakasa, it should be made clear that 'ritual friendship' is not at all the same thing as 'fictive kinship'. Despite the fact that ritual friendship is modelled on kinship to a certain degree (e.g. the use of kin terms), what is constructed in ideological terms is a type of association that is ultimately contrasted with kinship, not assimilated to it. The fear of witchcraft or magic, the expectation of disputes between brothers, and the accompanying disappointment one might feel about the fraternal relationship all contribute in large part, I suggest, to the construction of an ideology of ritual friendship that is typically disinterested and based purely on affection. Where there is no 'interest', at least in ideological terms, one can create a safe relationship which is not subject to spiritual attack or spectacular dispute. Ritual friendship also demonstrates that sentiment between people of different castes acts as a counter to the ideology of caste in certain spheres of social life, and also that this sentiment extends beyond the two individual parties to the friendship. In addition to affirming the social body of the village by connecting people across caste, kin and class lines and thereby emphasizing a fundamental affinity as members of a common humanity localized in a particular space, ritual friendship creates a landscape of relations with people outside one's locale, which has the effect of reinforcing ties with related people within one's village. Reorienting the focus so that ritual friendship is put at the centre of the analysis demonstrates how the classic tropes of Indian sociology – kinship and caste – can be seen in their proper context. It is precisely because caste and kinship are social arenas of such importance in people's lives that ritual friendship, with its emphasis on affection, takes the form that it does.

Notes

1. Markakasa is a pseudonym. It is a small multi-caste village located in a 'tribal' area at the eastern extremities of the state of Maharashtra, close to the border with the state of Chhattisgarh. Fieldwork was conducted for a total of twenty months (from 2002 to 2004, and again in 2005 and 2008). The research was supported by an Economic and Social Research Council Postgraduate Studentship (PTA-030-2002-00731), and Postdoctoral Fellowship (PTA-026-27-1681), an Emslie Horniman Award from the Royal Anthropological Institute, and an award from the Sutasoma Trust. I wish to thank Jonathan Parry, Veronique Benei, Evan Killick, and the participants at the 'Anthropology of Friendship' workshop and LSE South Asia Seminar for their comments on various versions of this chapter.
2. Jay (1973) refers to the word *mitān*, which he translates as 'friend', and which is used in the same way Markakasa people use *phul-phulwāri*; Jonathan Parry (personal communication) also reports the use of this word in and around the industrial city of Bhilai in Chhattisgarh. To my knowledge, Markakasa villagers never used *mitān* to refer to these specific ritual friendships, and indeed the title *mahāprasād* was sometimes used, incorrectly, as a generic term.
3. Okada also observes that mutual affection is the primary reason why people enter into similar sorts of ritual friendships in Nepal (1957: 214).
4. A large city 180 km to the west where my maternal uncle (MB) lives.
5. This is my category, not one that Markakasa people used.
6. In two cases, the Markakasa villagers did not know the caste of their ritual friend, which itself is striking in the Indian context. For the remaining thirteen relationships outside the village, I have no data as to the caste of the ritual friend.
7. It is important to note here that the ritual does not 'make' similarity out of difference. It simply affirms a pre-existing similarity that is enabling and constitutive of the *prem* between the parties.
8. A Scheduled Tribe under the Indian constitution and therefore 'Adivasi' but not Gond.

9. Although it was Kashiram who was Pyarilal's *mahāprasād*, the terminology used extended to his siblings.

10. *Lamsenin*: the wife of a *lamsena*, a man who lives uxorilocally and farms the land of his father-in-law.

11. Bloch's (1973) discussion of affinal and agnatic kinship may suggest a complementary interpretation. He argues, following Fortes, that affinal kinship relationships need to be constantly activated and 'used' in order to be maintained: thus they have force in the short-term. For the long-term, however, one knows that it is agnatic kinship relationships which endure and have the greatest moral force. This may be the case here, with 'affinal kinship' replaced with 'ritual friendship' in the analysis. There are a number of differences, however, not least that ritual friendship acts to make up for the failings of brotherhood and in the process is transformed into a different type of social relationship altogether. It is because one knows that the long-term experience of brotherhood may be ultimately disappointing that the ritual friendship based on sentiment has more moral force.

12. I was on my way to a musical performance in the village and said to my *mahaprasad*, 'Are you coming?' This offended a man who was standing nearby who proceeded to instruct me that my question lacked the requisite tenderness that one should display when speaking to a ritual friend. The correct formulation should have been 'Are you coming, *mahaprasad*?'

13. Thus, though strictly speaking the ideology of brotherhood involves harmony, the experience of failed fraternal relationships leads to the creation of an 'almost-ideology' of brotherhood as problematic.

14. That Krishna is a god is almost irrelevant in the telling of this story, and the contexts in which I was told it make this clear. It is not Krishna's divinity that is emphasized but his quality as a friend, and he realizes what Sudama wants because he has *prem* for him. It is not surprising that the story featured a god: throughout much of India stories of gods are told in exactly this fashion to signify exemplary behaviour to be aspired to by ordinary mortals.

15. Okada makes a similar observation regarding the practice of what he terms 'ritual brotherhood' in Nepal: 'A man has the right to ask his *mit* for help although the ideal situation is that both should be on the alert to assist each other without being asked' (1957: 217).

16. Whereas 'open reciprocity' means that which 'keeps no accounts because it implies a relation of permanent commitment' (Graeber 2001: 220), 'closed reciprocity' occurs when 'a balancing of accounts closes the relationship off, or at least maintains the constant possibility of doing so' (Graeber 2001: 220).

17. In fact, this is one of the few major criticisms of the *phul-phulwari* institution, voiced by a particular minority who dislike it because of its caste blindness, in particular the types of associations it creates between clean castes and Untouchables, and the emphasis placed on commensal dining in these sorts of relationships. In this the opponents seem to recognize the social value of these kinds of friendships, that the sentiment they create and express has implications beyond the individuals concerned and their households.

18. Ritual friends do drink alcohol with each other. However, among brothers, it is generally frowned upon for younger brothers to drink in the presence of older brothers: to do so would imply a lack of respect (*mariada*). This supports my contention that, in contrast to brotherhood, ritual friendship emphasizes the essential equality of the two parties.

References

Babb, L. 1975. *The Divine Hierarchy: Popular Hinduism in central India*. New York and London: Columbia University Press.

Bloch, M. 1973. 'The Long and the Short term: the Economic and Political Significance of the Morality of Kinship', in Jack Goody (ed.), *The Character of Kinship*. London: Cambridge University Press.

Carrier, J. 1999. 'People who can be friends: selves and social relationships', in Sandra Bell and Simon Coleman (eds), *The Anthropology of Friendship*. Oxford: Berg.

Graeber, D. 2001. *Toward an Anthropological Theory of Value: the False Coin of our Dreams*. New York: Palgrave.

Jay, E. J. 1973. 'Bridging the Gap Between Castes; Ceremonial Friendship in Chhattisgarh', *Contributions to Indian Sociology* 7: 144–58.

Lambert, H. 1996. 'Caste, Gender and Locality in rural Rajasthan', in C.J. Fuller (ed.), *Caste Today*. Delhi: Oxford University Press.

———. 2000. 'Sentiment and Substance in North Indian Forms of Relatedness', in Janet Carsten (ed.), *Cultures of Relatedness*. Cambridge: Cambridge University Press.

Loizos, P. and E. Papataxiarchis (eds). 1991. *Contested Identities: Gender and Kinship in Modern Greece*. Princeton, NJ: Princeton University Press.

Okada, F.E. 1957. 'Ritual Brotherhood: a Cohesive Factor in Nepalese Society', *Southwestern Journal of Anthropology* 13(3): 212–22.

Orans, M. 1965. *The Santal: a Tribe in Search of a Great Tradition*. Detroit: Wayne State University Press.

Parry, J. 1986. 'The Gift, the "Indian" Gift, and the "Indian Gift"', *Man* (n.s.) 21(3): 453–73.

Pfeffer, G. 2001. 'A Ritual of Revival among the Gadaba of Koraput', in H. Hulke and B. Schnepel (eds), *Jaganath Revisited: Studying Society, Religion and the State in Orissa*. New Delhi: Manohar.

Pitt-Rivers, J. 1973. 'The Kith and the Kin', in Jack Goody (ed.), *The Character of Kinship*. Cambridge: Cambridge University Press.

Prakasam, G. 1993. *Satnamis: the Changing Status of a Scheduled Caste in Chhattisgarh, Madhya Pradesh*. Unpublished doctoral thesis, University of Oxford.

Sahlins, M. 1974. *Stone Age Economics*. London: Tavistock.

Skoda, U. 2004. 'Ritual Friendship in a Converging Tribal and Caste Society', *Journal of Social Science* 8(2): 167–77.

Chapter 6

Close Friends: The Importance of Proximity in Children's Peer Relations in Chhattisgarh, Central India

PEGGY FROERER

It is widely taken for granted by laypersons and scholars alike that friendship is one of the fundamental ways in which people form connections and ties with each other. However, friendship as a specific subject of study has generally remained peripheral to the broader anthropological project, due largely to anthropology's traditional preoccupation with kinship. As noted in the introduction to this volume, this preoccupation, which can be traced back to the inception of the discipline, relates to the attempts of early ethnographers to 'establish ethnology as a science as exact as physics or chemistry' (Bouquet 1993: 114). As an institutionalized system that was underpinned by ascribed social ties, kinship became the subject within anthropology that was potentially rendered 'scientific' by the genealogical method (cf. Holy 1996: 144–55).

In contrast to kinship, friendship in many societies is one of the least institutionalized of all social relationships. Viewed at its simplest as being a companionable relationship that exists between two individuals, friendship is commonly construed by scholars as a relationship that is 'achieved' rather than ascribed and is 'voluntary' rather than constrained (Paine 1969; Cohen 1961). Anthropologists' attempts to systematically engage with the subject have been sporadic at best (Pitt-Rivers 1973; Jay 1973; Wolf 1966), although there has been a recent resurgence in interest (Bell and Coleman 1999, Santos-Granero 2007).

Emphasizing the importance of friendship is particularly valuable in forcing anthropologists to consider how a specific kind of (non-kin) relationship figures into our understanding of social life, and how, in turn, existing social structures impact upon this relationship. In spite of the ethnographic attention that this subject has recently received, it is a social relationship that continues to be viewed more as a way of elucidating a greater anthropological understanding of kinship, than as an independent subject of analysis. Even Bell and Coleman, in the introduction to their volume, acknowledge that a consideration of the role of friendship in social life serves 'not least as a means of producing an anthropology that understands kinship more explicitly in the context of other forms of social ties' (1999: 2).

In central India, where the research for this chapter is based, this 'friendship-kinship binary' (Reed-Dahany 1999: 144) is complicated by the existence of caste, which remains the principal category around which any discussion of social identity traditionally takes place. As Lambert (2000: 73) points out, the endogamous character of caste is implicitly accompanied by 'a putative hereditary principle [that is] coterminous with the outermost limits of [biological] kinship'. Consequently, the consideration that kinship has received has generally been subsumed within broader ideas of caste relatedness (cf. Mandelbaum 1970: 33; Mayer 1960). The privileged position that caste has in the anthropology of India, and the subordinated relationship that kinship has to caste, means that any consideration of ordinary, non-kin relationships like friendship that may occur beyond (or in spite of) the domain of caste has been largely neglected.[1]

Anthropologists of India might protest that the existing studies on 'ritual' or 'ceremonial' friendship (commonly called '*mitān*' in Chhattisgarh) are surely an exception to this charge. A more institutionalized kind of social relationship, ritual friendship is a formal arrangement made between two individuals who are usually the same sex and age and who are often, but not always, from different castes and villages (see Dube 1949; Jay 1973; Skoda 2004; Desai this volume). Individuals who enter into such an arrangement typically observe an 'affinal-type dyadic relationship' (Jay 1973: 155) and participate in life-long ritual obligations that are normally reserved for kin. It is perhaps because it is a more institutionalized social relationship,characterized by scholars as a form of 'fictive kinship', that the subject of ritual friendship has been given greater attention in the ethnographic literature.

Rather than ritual friendship, this chapter is concerned with what has been termed 'ordinary friendship': those 'unofficial bonds constructed between persons' (Bell and Coleman 1999: 4) that involve mutual acknowledgement and a shared understanding, and that are not based on ties of blood or heredity (cf. Parekh 1994: 95–6). In line with other contributions to this volume, the objective of this chapter is to consider the ways in which such friendships, which are referred to locally as *jod* (friend) or *saheli* (girlfriend), are formed in the course of everyday activities and through shared experience.

As noted above, one of the characteristics regularly attributed to notions of friendship is voluntarism, or the assumption that friends are freely chosen by the parties involved. Writers like Allan (1979), Cohen (1961) and Fehr (1996) have challenged this assumption by examining the social conditions that affect the formation of friendship. For example, the manner by which friends meet, the frequency with which they are able to interact, and the activities in which they engage are all subject to a range of complex conditions and social constraints over which individuals may have little control. Particular constraints might include age and gender, as well as (within India) caste or ethnicity. In this chapter, however, I wish to examine how another such constraint – proximity – impinges upon the formation of ordinary friendship.

As Erwin (1993: 181) observes, contact is a fairly obvious prerequisite in the construction of relationships; in turn, the idea that individuals who inhabit the same physical environment are more likely to become close friends than those who do not seems equally self-evident. However, the specific ways in which proximity facilitates social interactions and the formation of friendship have received very little direct attention within the anthropological literature.[2] In India, the issue of proximity is related to the idea of 'residential locality', which traditionally constituted a 'third dimension' (Lambert 1996: 93) – after caste and kinship – that was used by anthropologists to characterize social identity. With the demise of 'village studies', attention to locality as a component of social identity also declined, becoming subordinated to analyses of caste (Lambert 1996: 101; cf. Dumont 1964).

It would of course be naïve to suggest that caste (and, by extension, kinship) is not important to understanding the particular nature of social relations in India. However, in an attempt to consider an alternative discourse, and in order to highlight an issue that has been passed over within the ethnographic literature, this chapter focuses specifically on how proximity – not caste or kinship – serves as the pivotal factor around which ordinary friendship is both constructed and constrained. Particular attention is given to children and young people's interactions because, as my informants maintain, it is through 'doing things together' during childhood that close friendships are most commonly formed.[3] In the final part of the chapter, I will briefly consider how proximity remains an important feature for adult friendships. I will also return to the issue of how these ties cut across caste and kinship obligations and how they have the potential to impact upon communal relations. In this way the chapter fits with the broader thesis of this volume in showing how friendship, as a distinct social relationship, is of central importance to everyday lives.

The Village and the *Para*

This chapter is based on research that was carried out between 2002 and 2003 in a predominantly *ādivāsi* (tribal) village that I will call 'Mohanpur', located in a densely forested region of Chhattisgarh, central India.[4] Like many tribal communities in this part of India, the village is geographically cut off from the urban mainstream due to thick jungle and inaccessible roads. Most people earn their livelihoods locally, through a combination of rice cultivation and the collection and sale of non-timber forest products. In spite of recent road construction that has cut the five-hour commute to the town to just under two hours, most villagers have never made the forty-kilometre journey. Due to the lack of electricity, there is also little access to 'popular' Indian or Hindu culture via television and other media. This relative geographical and cultural distance from the Hindu and Indian 'mainstream' contributes to the general 'backwardness' with which this and other villages in the surrounding area are associated.[5]

The village population of nearly 900 is divided into eight *jātis* (castes) and is spread across 165 households. The politically and socially dominant Hindu community, which makes up three-quarters of the population, is comprised of three high-caste *ādivāsi* groups (Ratiya Kanwar, Majhuar and Dudh Kanwar) and four non-*ādivāsi* groups (Yadav, Panika, Chohan and Chowk/Lohar). The Oraon *ādivāsis*, all Catholics, make up the remaining quarter of the village. All castes are endogamous.

The local caste hierarchy follows the same order listed above and is most visibly expressed in terms of rules of commensality.[6] For example, the four high caste groups (Ratiya Kanwar, Majhuar and Dudh Kanwar, together with the Yadav) indulge in the symmetrical exchange of food and drink (see Parry 1979: 97). None of these castes takes food from any village 'low castes' (Panika, Chohan, Chowk/Lohar), although all low castes can take food from high castes. Moreover, no Hindu castes will take food from the Christian Oraons. With respect to the public expression of relations between specific caste communities, such prescriptions are 'founded on an ideology of pollution' (Parry 1979: 101) and are strictly enforced and respected by the caste communities as a whole. Amongst individuals, however, such rules are liberally but quietly broken, with high-caste individuals frequently sharing meals and drink with their low-caste friends.

The village is geographically small, with an area of roughly 1.5 square kilometres that is divided into thirteen wards or '*paras*' (cf. Mayer 1960; see map). Households within the same *para* are often built around a communal courtyard or linked together by a shared wall or footpath. The number of households that form a *para* range from as few as seven to as many as eighteen, and *paras* are usually divided from each other by a road or fenced boundary and gate.

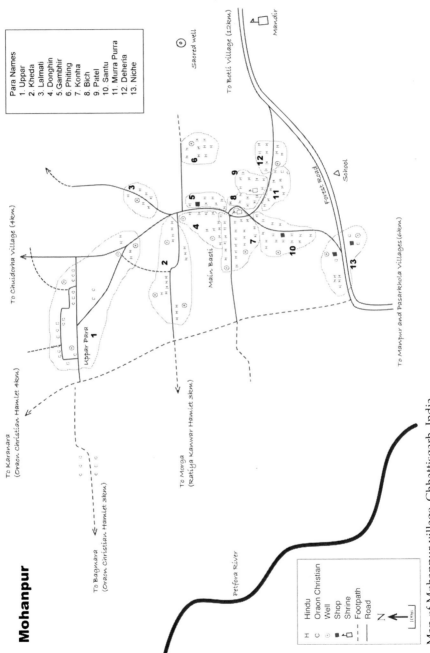

Map of Mohanpur village, Chhattisgarh, India

Each *para* has a specific name that reflects its geographical location, its individual founder or its current residents. For example, the neighbourhood where the majority of the Oraons reside is known as 'Uppar *para*', or the 'upper neighbourhood' located a half-kilometre beyond the main part of the village; 'Patel *para*' is where the current village headman (the Patel) resides; and 'Lalmati *para*' is distinguished by the red-coloured earth (*lāl māti*) that is common in this part of the village.

In the early 1960s, and up until very recently in many villages in rural India, *para* divisions often reflected caste (and, by extension, kinship) divisions: high- and low-caste groups and families typically lived in separate clusters (cf. Mayer 1960: 132–6; Fuller 1992: 12–5). Nowadays, however, all *paras* in the village are comprised of households belonging to at least two different castes. For example, high-caste Ratiya Kanwar households share Patel *para* with Majhuar and Chohan households; the low-caste Oraons share the Uppar *para* with Dudh Kanwar and Ratiya Kanwar households; and Majhuar, Ratiya Kanwar and Panika castes live together in Konha *para*. Equally, the practice of a kind of kinship-based 'residential locality' (Lambert 1996: 93), where members of the same kin group traditionally lived within close proximity of each other, and where there was no distinction between 'friends' and 'family' within the same *para*, has also declined in favour of a more contemporary practice that sees members of the same Ratiya Kanwar, Majhuar and Oraon families spread across different *paras*. While this practice, which has occurred only in the past couple of decades, is related to population growth and other practical matters like the availability of land on which to build or extend a household, what I am interested in here are the implications of this spatial rupture, and the increasing importance that social (and political) obligations to proximity-based friends have assumed over more traditional obligations based on caste and kinship.

What is important about the nature of *para* divisions is that, while local rules of untouchability tend to define the official, 'public' relations between different caste groups, the informal, everyday contacts enjoyed by those who live in the same *para* tend to produce social connections between individuals that override existing caste rules (cf. Mayer 1960: 132). This affinity is promoted by the shared activities (agricultural, recreational, ritual) in which *para* members regularly participate together. It is also reinforced by the fact that these same individuals – particularly women – may not have close contact with those who live in different *paras*. For example, in the absence of 'official' business (i.e. selling mats, buying alcohol) or a special ritual occasion, people rarely make casual visits to their acquaintances and fellow caste members outside of their own *para*. People are also less likely to attend the ritual events sponsored by members of their own caste and even kin who live in a different *para* than they are to attend those events sponsored by members of different castes from within their own *para*. For most individuals, in other words, there is a sense of loyalty to 'my people in my *para*' (*ham log, hamāre para*). As we shall see in the ethnography below, this is often accompanied by suspicion or distrust for 'those people' who live in a different *para* (*un log, dusre para log*).

At this stage, it is important to bear in mind that 'my people' (*ham log*) can and does include individuals from different castes, whereas 'those people' (*un log*) includes members of the same caste. Even in this very small village, then, we find the application of systematic distinctions between 'us' and 'them'. While the present chapter is restricted to an ethnographic examination of the way in which the issue of proximity impinges on the formation of friendship (and, by extension, the creation of non-friends) and cuts across traditional caste and kinship ties, this kind of analysis has broader appeal, particularly in the way in which proximity, as a factor in the creation of ideas about 'us' and 'them', can provide greater understanding of the construction of communal identity and conflict (see Froerer 2007). I will return to this issue briefly at the end of the chapter.

The Exclusivity of the *Para*

In part because I lived in the Uppar *para*, which was mainly inhabited by Oraon Christians and located nearly half a kilometre from the rest of the village, and in part because of my broader research interests in ethnic group relations (see Froerer 2006, 2007), my awareness and understanding of the kinds of constraints that impinged upon the formation of ordinary friendship were, unsurprisingly, hampered by my assumption that caste and, by extension, religion, were the chief determinants in the creation of individual social relationships. I thus initially ignored what would later become increasingly apparent: that the formation of friendship is underpinned not by caste or kinship, but by close proximity, or the experience of living in the same locality.

I first began to think about the salience of proximity to the formation of friendship when, early on in my fieldwork, I was invited for a picnic by the children and youth from Kheda *para* (comprised of Ratiya Kanwar, Dudh Kanwar and Majhuar families). Locally, a picnic is a special event that is often, if not always, organized and attended exclusively by young people on the occasion of a holiday or festival. On the agreed date, children will be dispatched to all households within their *para* to ask for donations of rice and lentils, along with pots and other items necessary for the preparation of a large meal. In very rare cases, a generous individual will donate a small chicken, making the occasion particularly special.

Once all the items are collected, the children and youth will trek toward the designated picnic site, which is usually located several kilometres away along the banks of a local river. Upon arrival, the smallest children are usually ordered to scavenge around for firewood while older ones carry water from the river or dig a fire pit. After the cooking is underway, the children will play with their closest friends and age-mates before bathing and preening themselves in preparation for the meal.

What is striking about the picnic is that it is an event in which participation is invariably limited to those children and youths belonging to the same *para*: children from different *paras* are always excluded, and *paras* do not organize picnics together. Smaller *paras* where fewer children reside will neither organize a picnic nor be invited to join an outing that has been organized by a different *para*. Indeed, some effort goes into making the event an exclusive, *para*-led affair. When I questioned the Kheda *para* children about why they did not extend the picnic invitation to their friends who lived outside of the *para*, I was informed that this would be out of the question. 'We never invite children from a different *para* to accompany us', I was told adamantly by one adolescent girl, 'Picnics are only for children from our *para*'.

Competition with other *paras* to organize the best picnic contributes to the exclusivity of the event. On the day of the Kheda *para* outing, young people from the Patel *para* had also organized a picnic. Having decided upon a picturesque location in the surrounding jungle, two of the older Kheda *para* youth set off very early to stake out their site before children from the Patel *para* could do so. As it happened, the latter had chosen what they considered to be a more beautiful site along a different river. Both groups returned from their respective picnic outings boasting that their experience had been far superior to that of the other *para*.

While not particularly unusual in itself, this pattern of *para* exclusivity is extended to other activities. These include fishing or hunting parties, which will be organized by individuals from one *para* at the exclusion of individuals from other *paras*. Sometimes, participants will run into members from another *para* who are engaging in the same activity, at which point they may assist each other or participate together in the activity. More frequently, however, they will compare results – who has caught the most fish or killed the biggest bird – before carrying on the activity with members of their own *para*. This pattern is also reproduced in the context of village-wide ritual or social events, such as weddings, funeral rituals or festivals. At such occasions, children, youths and adults tend to congregate with members of their own *para*. While a child might indulge the occasional request by a school friend from another *para* to join him at the event, this request is equally likely to be turned down with the excuse that 'I think I'll stay with my people from my *para*'.

In short, I found that the sort of exclusivity that underpins the *para* picnic and other events was part of a wider pattern of social interaction, which sees children, youths and even adults from the same *para* participating in activities together. Significantly, the exclusivity of such events is not related to caste or kin but to locality. As mentioned above, no *para* is comprised exclusively of single-caste households, and the respective picnics were attended by children from all castes in each *para*. What is interesting for the purpose of this chapter, and the subject matter of this volume as a whole, is how this pattern of exclusivity, which is based largely on physical proximity, affects the formation of friendship and the creation of non-friends amongst children.

The *Para* and the Formation of Friendship

At its most basic level, the formation of everyday friendship relations, particularly among children, can be seen as limited to those with whom an individual comes into regular contact (cf. Erwin 1993: 183). In Mohanpur, it is the *para* that serves as the primary context that facilitates this kind of contact. From before a child is weaned (which normally happens from around the age of three), he or she can be found in the company of an age-mate or slightly older or younger child from his *para*, engaging in different kinds of 'pretend play' together. Such activities often mimic adult work and might include weaving 'mats' with strands of grass or pulling 'water' out of an imaginary well to take a pretend bath. Young children also play 'house' or 'farmer' together, or imitate and incorporate aspects of different ritual activities (weddings, healing rituals, possession) that they have recently witnessed into their play. Older children's play begins to assume more locally gendered forms: girls will paint fake tattoos on each other's hands and feet, or make necklaces or rings out of strands of grass; boys will practice hunting with their home-made slingshots. All children will invariably be found engaged together in the favourite local game of '*bati*' (marbles).

In addition to playing, children from the same *para* will carry out household chores together. Small children, for example, are often charged with carrying out minor tasks, like protecting freshly parboiled rice from chickens or collecting fallen fruit from a nearby tree. From around the age of four or so, children are able to bathe themselves and wash their own clothing, and two or three young children from the same *para* are invariably sent off together to the nearest well to carry out these tasks. Slightly older children (aged five or six) will be allowed outside of the confines of the *para*, charged with greater responsibilities like running errands to the village shop, which they will often do hand-in-hand with a friend from the *para*. Such responsibilities are also typically manifested along gendered lines. For boys, tasks might include the collection of small sticks for firewood or jungle grasses for fodder, and for girls, washing the previous meal's dishes or collecting the cow dung from the household courtyard. All children from around aged twelve onward participate in seasonal farming activities, such as sowing, weeding and harvesting. For the ostensible purpose of sharing the workload, and so that they will not get 'fed up' (*kiskat lagthe*), children will carry out such tasks in the company of their *para* friends. While more could be said about the specific kinds of activities in which children participate, the important point here is that children in the same *para* invariably engage in such activities together (*sange-sange*).

Research in sociology has, unsurprisingly, shown that friendships tend to develop when individuals are placed in a context where they regularly participate in joint activities. In what sociologist Scott Feld (1981: 1025) has called the 'focus of activity' theory, the more activities that individuals share with each other, and the more constraining the 'focus' or context in which such activities are shared, the more likely it is that they will become 'interpersonally tied' through friendship (cf. Feld and Carter 1998).

Locally, the *para* serves as this kind of context in which the everyday activities that children engage – doing chores, playing, eating – are combined with special events like picnics and hunting and fishing outings that are organized exclusively by and for members of the *para*. It is because shared activities tend to be organized by children living in the same proximity that the *para* serves as a particularly powerful facilitator in the formation of friendship. As one 12-year old girl from Gambhir *para* told me, children become friends because they 'live together and do things together: they play and work, they sleep together, they study together; they go everywhere together (*sange sange*)'.

While most friendships are created between those of the same age and gender living in close proximity, not all children have the privilege of living in a *para* with similar gender or age-mates. At the time of my fieldwork, the number of children in each *para* varied between six (Lalmati *para*) and twenty-four (Konha *para*). In *paras* with fewer children, proximity can even supersede age and gender in the formation of friendship. Take the case of Ravi, an eight-year-old boy, and Lalita, a fourteen-year old girl who lived in Uppar *para* who, for different reasons, were left behind on a daily basis as their age-mates attended school. As there were no other children their age in their particular *para* throughout the day, Ravi and Lalita struck up a close friendship. In tandem with same-age friendships, theirs was cultivated through the engagement of shared activities that included grazing cattle and buffalo, running errands to the village shop, and generally joking around and teasing each other throughout the day. When asked about their relationship, they admitted that each was the other's preferred '*jod*' because they 'did things together everyday'.

While this example is slightly unusual, the significance of shared activities – 'doing things together' – is clearly crucial to the formation of friendship. It is also through participation in the same activities that, notwithstanding caste identity, the association between children's friends and their loyalties to their *para* is specifically manifested. This can be illustrated with the friendship shared by four Ratiya Kanwar children (two girls and two boys aged seven and eight) from Deheria *para*. The two girls, Champi and Sankumer, were a year apart in age and school class and were each other's 'best friend'. The two boys, Jaggu and Gajanand, shared a class with Sankumer and were also 'best friends'. Being from the same *para*, the four could regularly be found together, helping each other complete their chores, picking fruit from the jungle and playing intense games of *bati*.

One afternoon, I found the group preparing to visit the village shop to buy sweets. Sankumer suggested that they avoid the shortcut through Murra Purra *para*, which lay adjacent to Deheria *para*, and instead go the long way, via the main village road. Murra Purra *para* (which consisted of Ratiya Kanwar, Oraon and Majhuar households), I was informed, was not a very nice *para*, as its occupants included three girls (two Ratiya Kanwars and one Oraon) who allegedly 'bullied' Sankumer. Champi, the eldest in the group, ruled out taking the main village road, and the four proceeded through Murra Purra *para*, where they found the three girls playing *bati* in the centre of the path. Champi ordered them to move so that the group of four could walk past. One of the Ratiya Kanwar girls protested that 'this is our *para*', in response to which Champi gave her a shove and told her that she smelled of urine. The other two girls scooted away as the group proceeded on its way. After visiting the shop, Sankumer insisted that the group return by road, thereby avoiding Murra Purra *para* and the three girls altogether.

Through this example we see how the *para* not only serves as the central 'focus' or context around which children engage in shared activities, but becomes the primary focus around which children's friendships and loyalties are formed. It is also important to note that, while friendships are manifested in terms of shared *para* proximity, they are not explicitly based on shared caste identity: in the example above, the Deheria *para* children happened to be from the same caste; the Murra Purra *para* children, like those from most local *paras*, were from different castes. Non-friends, in turn, are constructed in spite of shared caste identity: as we saw above, both *para* groups were comprised of Ratiya Kanwar children. Shared caste identity, in other words, is not the most important factor in facilitating the formation of friendship between children who live in different *paras*.

Instead, it is shared time and experience that serves to build up a degree of intimacy and allegiance between individuals that goes beyond the social connections and ideologies of sameness associated with caste. 'People prefer those from their own *para* because they know them best', I was told by an adult male informant from Konha *para*: 'They are like family. You can sit comfortably with them, you can tell them anything. It does not make any difference if they are from a different caste or family.' The preference for friends from the same *para* is also related to reciprocity and trust. 'People from your own *para* share their time and assist each other during *bara kam* [weddings, funerals, rice harvest], when there is a lot of work to be done', this same informant explained. Whereas you can trust people from your own *para*, 'you do not know if you can trust people from different *paras*. When you do not see them every day, you will not know how they will act at certain times, or if you can rely on them when you need them'.

Children express similar sentiments. After the Kheda *para* picnic, I started asking different children about their friends, and about the friendship-*para* pattern that was becoming increasingly visible to me. The main reason that children gave for why they preferred spending time with friends from their own *para* was because the latter 'shared things' like slingshots, marbles or sweets from the local shop. Children from the same *para* also 'play nicely with you and help you out with your chores'. Moreover, children from the same *para* look out for each other while they are at school and when they are involved in activities together outside of the *para*. People from different *paras* live 'outside' (*bahar*) and separate (*alag*), and are thus regarded with more reservation. 'They might be ok', I was told by another child; 'they might help you or play nicely with you, but you cannot be sure because they are from a different *para*'.

Like adults, then, children seem to recognize the importance of familiarity, trust and reciprocity that is generated in the context of shared proximity and the kinds of activities and interactions that this shared proximity facilitates. For this reason, they prefer to spend time and are more likely to become friends with those people who, regardless of caste, reside in the same *para*.

School, Age and Gender

While proximity seems to supersede caste in terms of affecting the formation of friendship, the *para* is not the only local context where it serves as an important feature in the formation of friendship; the other obvious context is the local school, the main venue where children from different *paras* have the opportunity to meet and engage in school-based activities together. After the school day ends, however, the children invariably bid farewell to their school friends and go off to their respective *paras*, where they will become absorbed in chores and other activities with their *para*-based friends (for specific discussions on the importance of schooling in the creation and cultivation of friendship, see papers by Santos, Rodgers and Evans, this volume). Therefore friendships that revolve specifically around school-based activities have little chance to flourish outside of the school setting. Such friendships are also weakened by the fact that most children leave school after Class 5, if not before, after which they may no longer come into regular contact. In short, once schooling ends, the increased level of contact and associated activities promoted by the proximity that children shared within the school setting also cease, diluting and bringing to an end the friendships that were formed there.

Lack of contact and lack of participation in shared activities not only results in the weakening of friendship ties; it also leads to the creation of a sense of distrust and even fear. After completion of their primary school studies, children sometimes begin to express a strong dislike for their peers from other *paras*. For example, Gurmati, a twelve- year-old Ratiya Kanwar girl from Kheda *para*, insists that she 'does not like' (*acchā nahi lagthe*) her age-mates who live in Patel *para* and Konha *para*. These are the same girls (all Ratiya Kanwar) with whom she was studying and whom she counted as her 'best' friends until she completed Class 5 one year previously. Nowadays she finds them to be quite bullying and even threatening, and claims to get on only with those from her own *para*. She especially dislikes the Ratiya Kanwar girls who live in Konha *para* and Patel *para* because they 'create a lot of tension'. She feels scared when she sees them nowadays, as they call her names: 'If I see them on the way to the shop, I will walk the other way'.

What is interesting is that Gurmati does not have any age-mates in her own *para*. Having rejected the girls from other *paras*, her friendship circle is limited to the four Majhuar and Dudh Kanwar girls who are four and five years her junior who live in Kheda *para*. Like Gurmati, the girls from the other *paras* also claim that they dislike their ex-classmates who live in different *paras*. Indeed, I rarely saw children and young people, especially girls, in the company of those outside of their own *para* after the completion of their studies. Only one girl from Konha *para* admitted that she thought she could become friends again with some of the girls from a different *para*, but only if she had the opportunity to meet and 'do things together' with them more often.

In addition to age, another important feature that affects the formation of friendship is gender. As discussed earlier in this chapter, boys and girls within the same *para* can and do become good friends. However, from around the age of six or seven – an age which, incidentally, coincides with the beginning of school – and with few exceptions (of the sort mentioned above) children typically begin to demonstrate a preference for same-sex friendships. This preference is reinforced by restricted movement (for girls) and increased freedom (for boys). For example, girls are normally expected to return home directly after school, whereas boys have more freedom to roam about. With the exception of communal labour activities like weeding or harvesting rice, or participating in public road works, girls from different *paras* rarely get the opportunity to meet up with one another – even those from the same caste – and are instead confined to their own *para*. Restricted movement means that girls are unable to regularly associate with those beyond the proximity of their immediate surroundings. Consequently, they come to rely almost entirely on their *para*-based friendships, irrespective of both age and caste identity.

While girls' friendship loyalties and expressions of dislike could be attributed to the fact that their movements are more restricted to their *para*, such sentiments are similar amongst adolescent boys. As mentioned above, boys have more freedom to spend beyond the confines of the *para*, and can often be found hanging out in more neutral or public spaces, like the village square or on the terrace of the local council building. Contexts such as these are preferred over the homes of boys from different *paras* because, as a young man from Kheda *para* named Shantilal told me, people feel uncomfortable visiting different *paras* unless it is for a specific purpose. Importantly, even in these public spaces, boys tend to prefer to hang out with those from their own *para*. *Para*-based loyalties thus extend beyond the immediate proximity that constitutes their formation. Once again, this is related to trust and familiarity. 'People do not trust those from different *paras*', explained Shantilal: 'Sometimes, if you walk into the *para* of your school friend, his *para*-people might be sitting there talking about something. Then they will immediately stop talking when they see you. It is like they were talking about you, or talking about something that they did not want you to hear. This causes tensions and makes you feel very badly.' The potential for this kind of tension not only dissuades older boys from forming friendships with those from different *paras*, but also reinforces the preferences and loyalties that people feel for the friendships that they have with those from within their own *para*.

Friendship and Proximity in Adulthood

Thus far, I have shown how the formation of friendship is influenced more by proximity than by other social categories. For children, these relationships revolve predominantly around the shared experiences that such proximity facilitates: picnics, play, chores. But the importance of the *para* for the facilitation of friendship is not restricted to childhood; it also continues into adulthood. In the final part of this chapter I will briefly examine this process, before considering the impact that *para*-based friendships have on wider social relations.

After childhood, which ends at the time of marriage (between the age of fourteen and sixteen for girls and boys), both men and women continue to demonstrate a preference for those in their *para*, thereby underlining the continued importance of proximity for the maintenance of friendship. While friendships amongst adult men are usually extensions of those that they cultivated during the course of their childhood, friendships amongst women tend to be different from those they enjoyed as children. This is because women's childhood friendships are invariably severed at the time of marriage. Following patrilocal traditions, the new bride will leave her natal village and go and live in her husband's village, where her in-laws will place increased demands on her time and labour, and where her movements will invariably become even more restricted. Consequently, she has limited opportunity to return to her natal village and meet her childhood girlfriends who, due to their own marriages, are in any case unlikely to be still resident there. While these new brides express a sense of loss and nostalgia for their childhood *para*-friendships, they invariably form new ones through activities and experiences that they share with the girls and women from their husband's *para*. The issue of proximity, in other words, remains fundamental to the kind of friendships that women will form in the course of adulthood.

As in childhood, friendships within adulthood continue to revolve around 'doing things together', such as labouring in the fields, fishing, hunting, carrying water, collecting firewood – all activities that are normally carried out in the company of one's *para* friends. Such friendships, which, as we have seen above, are often formed because of shared proximity and in spite of caste and kin-based relationships, also carry with them more serious communal and political implications. For example, *para*-mates, regardless of their caste, tend to support each other against their non-*para* caste-mates when faced with village-wide decisions over issues such as grazing or water rights, and sometimes even in disputes over land and electoral politics. This can be illustrated with an incident that occurred in 2004, when the Oraons from Uppar *para* sided with their Ratiya Kanwar *para*-mates in a disagreement over land that the latter had with two Oraon families in Niche *para*. In the past, the Niche *para* Oraons would have expected to receive full support from the Uppar *para* Oraons, with whom they shared both caste and kin relations. When the dispute was ultimately decided in favour of the Ratiya Kanwar families, it caused a serious rift within the Oraon community. The Niche *para* Oraons accused the Uppar *para* Oraons of breaking their communal obligations, and refused to have anything to do with them; the Uppar *para* Oraons, while regretting the ensuing rift, insisted that they had an obligation to back their *para*-mates, with whom they had been friends since childhood and with whom they shared communal living space. This rift spilled over into the rest of the Oraon community and continues to plague intra-Oraon caste and kin relations to the present day. More recently, Niche *para* Oraons refused to vote for an Uppar *para* Oraon candidate during a local council election that occurred nearly three years after the initial land-based rift, in spite of the fact that the candidate happened to be a member of their own caste and kin group. Instead, they gave their support to the local Ratiya Kanwar candidate from their own *para*, claiming that not only did they owe electoral loyalty to their friends with whom they shared residential proximity, but that they could no longer trust their caste and kin to extend reciprocal support.

While caste and kinship remain salient categories around which social and ritual activities and ideologies revolve, what is interesting here is how proximity-based friendship can supersede caste and kinship ties, not only in the course of everyday relations, but also in terms of local disputes and politics. Perhaps more interesting is the way in which ties that revolve around proximity-based friendship can have an effect on broader 'us' / 'them' communal and relations. Locally, as elsewhere in India, communal ties based on caste, kinship and religion serve as a notoriously powerful vehicle through which individuals and groups can promote their own group over others in order to effect a particular kind of social and political agenda. The fact that the Oraons and Ratiya Kanwars were Christian and Hindu, respectively, was incidental in the examples narrated above. That religious affiliation was superseded by friendship and proximity in the examples cited above is itself very interesting, because it goes against recent patterns throughout India that have seen allegiances based specifically on religious affiliation becoming the most prominent social category in the context of communal tensions and violence (see Froerer 2006, 2007). Indeed, the particular incidents outlined above occurred in the wake of a period of Hindu/Christian communal tension that had troubled the village for several years. Against this backdrop, what was perhaps most striking about the first example was the way in which the Uppar *para* Oraons compromised their relationship with their own caste and kin-mates ('my people') in their desire to avoid tensions with their Ratiya Kanwar neighbours ('those people'), from whom they would expect to receive reciprocal support in future. The consequences of such a move, which resulted in the more recent example of the Niche *para* Oraons withholding political support from their Uppar *para* caste and kin-mate, went beyond the creation of a rift within the local Oraon community. This example has demonstrated how friendships formed and facilitated through proximity and shared experiences in childhood have the potential to cut across traditional caste and kin-based relationships and, potentially, to permanently alter social and political allegiances in adulthood.

Conclusions

It is not particularly surprising that proximity serves as the principal facilitator for social interaction, given that individuals who have close physical contact are more likely to form close personal relations than those who do not (cf. Erwin 1993). Locally, the importance of proximity is underscored by the way in which the very act of living in the same locality promotes engagement in shared activities. As we saw in the ethnography above, it is specifically through 'doing things together' that friendships are most commonly formed. More importantly, participation in joint activities such as those that revolve around work and play serves to foster familiarity, trust and reciprocity, all of which are deemed by both children and adults to be important values that underlie the formation of friendship and that spill beyond the *para* confines.

What is interesting and unusual in this case is that these kinds of activities revolve predominantly around a specific locality, the *para*, which serves as an especially constraining 'focus' or context in which such activities are shared (cf. Feld 1981). While the school experience also provides an important context wherein proximity and shared activities can aid the formation of friendship, such friendships have little chance of flourishing outside of the school setting. As we saw above, children and youth – and even adults – tend to prefer those who live in the same *para*, with whom they have had the opportunity to develop close relations. Children who do not share the same proximity, or whose physical contact with friends has been disrupted (for example, by the completion of the school experience), tend to become non-friends and are even regarded with distrust.

One reason for focusing on the specific way in which proximity impinges upon and facilitates the formation of ordinary friendship in this part of India has been to draw attention to an alternative discourse to that of caste (and kinship) in understanding and characterizing social relations. As mentioned earlier, the idea of 'residential locality' has been used in the past as an analytical tool in anthropologists' attempts to understand the particular nature of social relations in India (cf. Lambert 2000). However, kinship and caste remain powerful idioms within which social relations like friendship are invariably subsumed.

My ethnography has shown, in contrast, that 'residential locality' or proximity can serve as the primary local constraint that shapes the formation of friendship. The affinities and loyalties that children and adults show toward those in their own *para* not only impact upon the formation of friendship, but can also supersede caste and kinship ties and obligations. Such affinities can, in turn, be contrasted with the distrust that people express for those from other *paras*, including members of their own caste and kin group. It is the *para* that forms the centre of social and, as we have seen, political engagement for those who may or may not be from different castes, and who reside within its boundaries. The proximity that helps to generate friendship between *para* members is compounded by the exclusive nature of the activities that are organized around *para* members. Together, these factors facilitate interaction and help to create bonds and intimacies between people who are otherwise unrelated.

This chapter represents an attempt to render explicit some of the ways in which proximity constructs and constrains the formation of friendship. While this examination has been restricted to an ethnographic account of friendship between individuals, this kind of analysis has wider implications. In particular, as we saw with the example of adult-based friendship, recognizing that proximity is a pivotal factor that underpins how people choose their friends and non-friends potentially provides greater insight into understanding phenomena that figure into the creation of 'us' and 'them', allies and 'others' or the construction of communal identity and conflict.

Acknowledgments

The fieldwork for this paper took place over a ten-month period between September 2002 and September 2003. I am grateful to the Economic and Social Research Council (grant number 1 SAN S281) for funding this research. Special thanks are due to my friends in Chhattisgarh. I am also grateful for the feedback that I received from Caroline Osella and Simon Coleman, together with others who attended the original workshop at which this paper was first presented. I would especially like to thank the editors of this volume for their useful suggestions.

Notes

1. Caroline and Filippo Osella's (1998) article on friendship in Kerala, south India, which shows how friendship relations, particularly among young men, serve to contest and even 'subvert' caste and other forms of hierarchy (1998: 190), is a rare exception to this. Lambert (2000) has also tried to move beyond

traditional caste-specific discussions of kinship that rest on an assumption of shared biology by examining a form of relatedness that is based on locality and created between members of differentiated groups. This kind of relatedness, however, is commonly described as 'fictive kinship', not 'friendship'.

2. Limited sociological research has been conducted (see Fehr 1996; Festinger, Schachter & Back 1950). Within anthropology, more general issues related to proximity, including the broader conceptual and material dimensions of 'space', 'place' or 'landscape' and their role in the production of social life (see Hirsch and O'Hanlon 1995), have received greater attention.

3. Locally, the notion of 'childhood' typically depicts a status category that continues until marriage, which normally occurs between the ages of fourteen and sixteen for both girls and boys.

4. Although I prefer the term '*ādivāsi*' (original inhabitant), which is used by local people themselves, my alternating usage of this term with 'tribe' and 'caste' throughout this chapter reflects the impossibility of a clear distinction between these terms (see Bailey 1960; Dumont 1961; Sundar 1997: 156–90).

5. Popular stereotypes about *adivasis* that contribute to the 'backward' label and persist within mainstream Indian society include living within forested environments, speaking a tribal dialect, holding animistic beliefs, hunting and gathering, and drinking and dancing (see Pathy *et al.* 1976).

6. The ranking of local groups does not follow the mainstream caste hierarchies found in other parts of India (cf. Singh 1993). Like Mayer's study of caste hierarchy in the central Indian village of Ramkheri (1996: 34–5), this ranking represents the broad consensus of villagers and is based on local norms of pollution and untouchability, which revolve most visibly around rules of commensality.

References

Allan, G. A. 1979. *A Sociology of Friendship and Kinship*. London: George Allen & Unwin.

Bailey, F. G. 1960. 'Tribe' and 'Caste' in India. In *Contributions to Indian Society* IV: 7–19.

Bell, S. and S. Coleman. 1999. 'The Anthropology of Friendship: Enduring Themes and Future Possibilities', in S. Bell and S. Coleman (eds), *The Anthropology of Friendship*. Oxford: Berg.

Bouquet, M. 1993. *Reclaiming English Kinship: Portuguese Refractions on British Kinship Theory*. Manchester: Manchester University Press.

Cohen, Y. A. 1961. 'Patterns of Friendship', in Yehudi A. Cohen (ed.), *Social Structure and Personality: A Casebook*. New York: Holt, Rinehart and Winston.

Dube, S.C. 1949. 'Ritual Friendship in Chhattisgarh', *Man in India* 29(2): 98–102.

Dumont, Louis. 1961. 'Tribe and 'Caste' in India. In *Contributions to Indian Society*: 6.

———. 1964. 'A Note on Locality in Relation to Descent', *Contributions to Indian Sociology* 7: 71–6.

Erwin, P. 1993. *Friendship and Peer Relations in Children*. Chichester: John Wiley and Sons.

Fehr, B. 1996. *Friendship Processes*. London: Sage Publications.

Feld, S. L. 1981. 'The Focused Organization of Social Ties', *American Journal of Sociology* 86(5): 1015–35.

———. and W. C. Carter. 1998. 'Foci of Activity as Changing Contexts of Friendship', in Rebecca G. Adams and Graham Allan (eds), *Placing Friendship in Context*. Cambridge: CUP.

Festinger, L., S. Schachter and K.W. Back. 1950. *Social Pressures in Informal Groups*. London: Tavistock.

Froerer, P. 2006. 'Emphasising Others: the Emergence of Hindu Nationalism in a Central Indian Tribal Community', *The Journal of the Royal Anthropological Institute* 12: 39–59.

———. 2007. *Religious Division and Social Conflict: The Emergence of Hindu Nationalism in a Central Indian Tribal Community*. New Delhi: Social Science Press; London: Berghahn Books.

Fuller, C. 1992. *The Camphor Flame: Popular Hinduism and Society in India*. Princeton: Princeton University Press.

Hirsch, E. and M. O'Hanlon, 1995. *The Anthropology of Landscape: Perspectives of Place and Space*. Oxford: Oxford University Press.

Holy, L. 1996. *Anthropological Perspectives on Kinship*. London: Pluto Press.

Jay, E. J. 1973. 'Bridging the Gap Between Castes; Ceremonial Friendship in Chhattisgarh', *Contributions to Indian Sociology* 7: 144–58.

Lambert, H. 1996. 'Caste, Gender and Locality in Rural Rajasthan', in Chris Fuller (ed.), *Caste Today*. Delhi: Oxford University Press.

———. 2000. 'Sentiment and Substance in North Indian Forms of Relatedness', in Janet Carsten (ed.), *Cultures of Relatedness*. Cambridge: Cambridge University Press.

Mandelbaum, D. G. 1970. *Society in India*. Berkeley: University of California Press.

Mayer, A. 1996. 'Caste in an Indian Village: Change and Continuity 1954–1992. In C. Fuller (ed.), *Caste Today*. Delhi: Oxford University Press.

———. 1960. *Caste and Kinship in Central India*. London: Routledge.

Osella, C. and F. Osella. 1998. 'Friendship and Flirting: Micro-Politics in Kerala, South India', *The Journal of the Royal Anthropological Institute* 4(2): 189–206.

Paine, R. 1969. 'In Search of Friendship: an Exploratory Analysis in "Middle-Class" Culture', *Man* 4(4): 505–24.

Parekh, B. 1994. 'An Indian View of Friendship', in Leroy S. Rouner (ed.), *The Changing Face of Friendship*. Notre Dame, Indiana: University of Notre Dame Press.

Parry, J. 1979. *Caste and Kinship in Kangra*. London: Routledge.

Pathy, J. *et al.* 1976. 'Tribal Studies in India: an Appraisal', *The Eastern Anthropologist* 29(1): 399–417.

Pitt-Rivers, J. 1973. 'The Kith and the Kin', in Jack Goody (ed.), *The Character of Kinship*. Cambridge: Cambridge University Press.

Reed-Danahay, D. 1999. 'Friendship, Kinship and the Life Course in Rural Avergne', in Sandra Bell and Simon Coleman (eds), *The Anthropology of Friendship*. Oxford: Berg.

Santos-Granero, F. 2007. 'Of Fear and Friendship. Amazonian Sociality beyond Kinship and Affinity', *The Journal of the Royal Anthropological Institute* (N.S.) 13(1): 1–18.

Singh, K.S. 1993. *The Scheduled Castes*. Delhi: Oxford University Press.

Skoda, U. 2004. 'Ritual Friendship in a Converging Tribal and Caste Society', *Journal of Social Science* 8(2): 166–77.

Sundar, N. 1997. *Subalterns and Sovereigns: An Anthropological History of Bastar 1854–1996*. Oxford: OUP.

Wolf, E.R. 1966. 'Kinship, Friendship and Patron-Client Relations in Complex Societies', in M. Banton (ed.), *The Social Anthropology of Complex Societies*. London: Tavistock Publications.

Chapter 7

Making Friends, Making Oneself: Friendship and the Mapuche Person

MAGNUS COURSE

In this chapter I seek to describe how the Mapuche concept of friendship, which in many ways resembles the stereotypical Western model of friendship, emerges from a definitively non-Western conceptualization of the person. I hope to show that Mapuche friendship can accurately be described as being based upon individual autonomy, voluntarism, affection, and a rejection of the constraining aspects of kinship. In other words, it can be described by the same terms which writers such as Allan (1996), Carrier (1999) and Paine (1969) have used to characterize Western middle-class friendships (see also Killick and Desai, this volume). Like these writers, I accept the idea that notions of autonomy and voluntarism underlying the local concept of friendship imply a particular understanding of the person as a locus of autonomous intentionality, in other words, as an 'individual'. However, I disagree with their implication that this notion of the person as individual is the unique product of Enlightenment thought, a point made explicit in the writings of Mauss (1985 [1938]) and Dumont (1985). Put bluntly, this chapter constitutes part of a wider rejection of Mauss's famous claim that the notion of the person as individual was 'formulated only for us, among us' (1985 [1938]: 22).[1] The point is not to deny that the Western version of the person as individual has followed a particular historical trajectory, but rather to deny that such a conceptualization is necessarily unique to the West. Such a position necessarily requires an exploration of the entire realm of social relations of which the person is a part and which constitute part of the person; a process which will lead us to review the mutually exclusive yet mutually constitutive realms of Mapuche kinship and friendship.

The Mapuche, whose name means literally 'the people of the land', are one of the largest indigenous groups in the Americas. Around one million Mapuche people live in Chile, while a further 40,000 live across the

Cordillera in Argentina. Yet despite this numerical strength, they have received relatively little attention from anthropologists, perhaps because they fit into neither the 'Andean' nor 'Amazonian' culture areas into which most studies of Amerindians have been divided. The Mapuche are perhaps best known for their successful 350-year military resistance to Spanish conquest. However, they eventually succumbed to defeat at the hands of the Chilean army in 1883, and over the next forty years were subject to a process of 'reduction' – a confinement on limited and impoverished reservations. Population growth and increasing usurpation of land by forestry companies and ranchers have led to an increasingly vocal Mapuche political movement demanding the return of lost lands and greater autonomy. Mapuche society covers a wide spectrum, from monolingual Spanish-speaking bureaucrats in Santiago and Temuco, to monolingual Mapudungun-speaking subsistence farmers in the Mapuche southern heartland of Chile's Eighth, Nine and Tenth Regions. The research upon which this chapter is based was carried out in the neighbouring communities of Piedra Alta and Isla Huapi, located between Lago Budi and the Pacific Ocean in the Ninth Region. All of the people with whom I worked were subsistence farmers, living on small isolated homesteads. The vast majority of the population was bilingual in Spanish and the Mapuche language, Mapudungun.

I start this chapter with a brief sketch of the general features of the Mapuche conceptualization of the person before moving on to demonstrate its relevance to Mapuche friendship. The model I put forward is not one formulated explicitly by Mapuche people, but rather one which I have deduced from various statements about what does and does not constitute acting as *che*, as a 'true person'. In addition to such statements, I have also deduced features of the model from the implicit theories of personhood informing ritual practice. This analysis leads me to suggest that the Mapuche conceptualization of the person is best characterized as 'centrifugal' – an open-ended movement outwards from 'given' kin relations to 'chosen' friendship relations. It is the singularity of volition in making friends which, I suggest, leads to a singular or individual notion of the person as the key locus of value. Having described the various forms of social relations involved in the conceptualization of the person, I go on to focus on one of these forms: friendship among adult men, the paradigmatic form of which is the exchange of wine. 'Exchange' for the Mapuche, as for the Ashéninka described by Killick in this volume, cannot be wholly reduced to individual acts of giving but is ultimately an ongoing social relationship maintained through delayed reciprocity. Having explored the role of friendship in the conceptualization of the living person, I go on to look at the relevance of friendship relations to the person upon death, in particular to the role played by friends in the *amulpüllün* funeral discourses. I end the chapter with some reflections on the relationship between kinship and friendship, consanguinity and affinity, and the status of the Mapuche person as 'individual'.

The Centrifugal Person

The argument I advance in this chapter is based upon the role of friendship in the Mapuche representation of the person, referred to as *che* in Mapudungun. As many other writers have demonstrated, the status of true personhood is rarely a self-evident category in Amerindian societies (Taylor 1996, Viveiros de Castro 1998). Rather it is something which must be constructed, demonstrated, and ultimately attributed. The Mapuche are no different in this regard; *chengen*, 'to be a true person', is a demonstrable quality rather than a permanent state. One must demonstrate the conjunction of proper human physicality with the capacity for proper human sociality in order to be considered *che*. Thus a variety of spiritual beings which engage in human social practices of reciprocal exchange are not considered *che* because they lack human bodies. Likewise, beings which possess human bodies yet fail to demonstrate proper human sociality, such as infants and drunk people, are also not considered to be *che* (Course 2009). My focus in this chapter is not on the physical aspect of the Mapuche conceptualization of the person, but rather on the nature of proper human sociality. What are the forms of social relations which serve to define true persons?

Central to any understanding of the Mapuche person is the concept known in Mapudungun as *küpal*, a concept translated by Mapuche people into Spanish as *descendencia*, 'descent.' Each person is the product of the combination of their mother's menstrual blood and their father's semen. Both of these substances transmit both maternal and paternal *küpal*; semen thus links a child to both paternal grandfather and grandmother, while menstrual blood creates a link to both maternal grandmother and grandfather. Mapuche people thus place great importance on their *meli folil* or 'four roots' – a metaphorical allusion to one's four grandparents. *Küpal* is understood to be a 'given' component of the person: fixed, immutable and permanent from the moment of conception. Its influence is visible in each person's physical characteristics, in their relations with spirits, in their capacity to fulfil certain social roles, and in their moral behaviour.

As well as being an essential aspect of the person, *küpal* can also be understood as the basis of a relationship between persons. Thus someone can be said to 'share' *küpal* with all of their consanguineal kin. The totality of those with whom one shares *küpal* is referred to as *reñma*, a term equivalent to 'kinship' in a generic sense. Yet although at one level *küpal* suggests a theory of cognatic descent, in terms of sharing *küpal*, the term also takes on a distinct patrilineal bias. A virilocal tendency means that men spend most of their lives with those whom they share *küpal* with, whereas married women tend to be separated, both socially and spatially, from such people. Thus the cognatic concept of *küpal* becomes a patrilineal concept when its meaning is extended from a component of personhood to the level of the inter-personal relations. This co-residence of men, un-married women and children who share *küpal* leads to the idea of being of *kiñe küpal*, of 'one descent'. Relations between those patrilineally-related co-residents who share *küpal* are predicated on a notion of similarity and identity which leads to an ethic of obligatory mutual assistance and solidarity. Yet such relations are also often fraught with problems, particularly as they often hinge around attempts to assert authority between and within different generations, attempts which challenge what I seek to illustrate is the fundamental autonomy of the Mapuche person.

Matrilateral relations are referred to as *küpal ñuke püle*, literally 'descent by the mother'. These relations are characterized by perceived difference and supposed equality of status. People enter into exchange relationships with their matrilateral kin, whereas they very rarely exchange with their patrilineal kin. Relationships created through marriage often closely resemble those with matrilateral kin. Indeed, matrilateral cross-cousin marriage (*ñukentun*) was previously an idealized and preferred form of marriage.[2] The concept of *küpal* therefore refers to many things – to both an essential aspect of the person and to the form of certain relations, to both patrilineal relations and cognatic relations. It is perhaps the polysemic quality of this central aspect of the Mapuche person which has led to confusion amongst ethnographers who have sought to understand the person through the social aggregates of which they are members. Relations of identity between people of *kiñe küpal* are a key factor in the composition of 'groups' such as *comunidades* and *lof*. In the Mapuche context, the Spanish term *comunidad* refers to a legally-constituted group of people resident on one reservation; the Mapuche term *lof* refers to a localized group which may span one or more reservations. Although in some cases *kiñe küpal*, *lof* and *comunidad* are synonymous, in others they are not. We can generalize by saying that *comunidad* is primarily a jural concept, *lof* a territorial concept, and *kiñe küpal* a kinship concept.

Yet this discussion of the Mapuche person omits one crucial fact: to be a true person, to be *che*, one must go beyond relations with one's kin, whether these be maternally or paternally related. While such kinship relations are chronologically precedent, it is those relations which a person creates through their own volition during the course of their life which constitute them as *che*. It is here that the central importance of friendship in the constitution of the Mapuche person becomes apparent. Indeed, as I argue below, relations with non-kin in the form of friends constitute both the realization and demonstration of the autonomous volition which lies at the heart of the Mapuche notion of *che*.

These relations which go beyond those of 'kinship' fall under the rubric of what I call the 'sociality of exchange', the paradigmatic form which is the relation between friends (*weniiy*), and it is these relations and their relevance to the Mapuche representation of the person that are my focus in this chapter. Ideally this exchange is reciprocal and occurs at games of *palin* (a highly ritualized sport resembling field hockey), at *ngillatun* fertility rituals, at funerals, and in everyday interactions. As I shall seek to demonstrate in the text which follows, it is impossible to overestimate the importance of friends as it is through the activation of the capacity to form relationships with un-related others that one becomes a true person. Such a conceptualization of personhood is clearly open-ended and externally oriented towards others. Indeed, Mapuche sociality could accurately be described as centrifugal, a constant movement outward, both in metaphorical terms of social proximity and the literal meaning of geographical space.

The Wine-Drinking Friend

In this section I wish to describe more fully the capacity for the sociality of exchange which I suggested above was one of the criteria upon which attributions of personhood were based. In particular, I elaborate upon one of the most immediately obvious and ideologically elaborated forms of such sociality: the exchange of wine between adult male friends. Whereas kinship relationships are characterized, at least from ego's point of view, as being 'given', in that they preceded his or her existence and came into being without his or her intentionality, friendship is very much predicated on personal autonomy and intentionality. It is this exercise of autonomy and intentionality which serves to distinguish the Mapuche person as an individual, to differentiate one from a generic background of kinship identity in which one can only ever stand as part of a wider aggregate; I suggest that it is this form of sociality which corresponds to the attribution of full personhood.

Fundamental to my argument is the point that all Mapuche people participate in what I term the sociality of exchange as it is this which defines them as persons. For children it is constituted primarily through the exchange of speech acts, for women it is constituted through the gifts of bread, sugar, eggs, chickens and *mate* tea which they make when visiting other women. However, my focus in this chapter is on adult men. For men, the sociality of exchange occasionally takes more elaborate forms, including the three institutions of formalized friendship: *trafkintun*, *konchotun* and *compadrazgo*. *Trafkintun*, or sometimes simply *trafkin*, refers to the exchange of pretty much anything. When a man swaps a sack of oats for a sack of wheat, he is engaging in *trafkintun*. However, the word is usually only used when the exchange is considered to be of some import, not necessarily in the object exchanged but in the relationship created. Men who have engaged in *trafkin* call their exchange partners *trauki*, an abbreviated form of *trafkin*. This relation is said to imply not only the exchange of goods, but also the exchange of affection and respect. The Capuchin lexicographer Augusta defines *trafkin* as 'a friend with whom one has exchanged gifts of whatever kind' (1991 [1916]: 221). The purported equality of the participants is demonstrated by the fact that this term is often used to replace the reciprocal term *chedkiiy* meaning 'father-in-law' and 'son-in-law', a term sometimes perceived as suggesting an intrinsic inequality. As my friend Justo, a man in his early sixties, explained to me, 'I call my son-in-law *trauki* so as not to offend him as we are friends.'

The practice of *konchotun* is these days rarely referred to by this name in the area around Lago Budi. Previously, *konchotun* would occur at games of *palin* or *ngillatun* rituals when one man would slaughter a lamb in honour of a particular friend. The relationship would be sealed when the act was reciprocated in the territory of the initial recipient. The two men would then refer to each other by the term *koncho*, a term defined by Augusta as 'a title of friendship between two men who have given each other lambs in the respective ceremony' (1991 [1916]: 93). I suspect that the term *kon*, now used to refer to 'invited guests' for whom an animal has been slaughtered, is in some way derived from the term *koncho*, although some informants stated that the two were distinct.

Compadrazgo is the institution introduced to Mapuche people by the Catholic Church in which a person acts as *padrino*, 'godfather', or *madrina*, 'godmother', at a child's baptism or confirmation.[3] The most important component of the *compadrazgo* relationship is the relationship between the parents of the child and its godparents who refer to each other as *compadres*. However, unlike in other parts of South America, *compadrazgo* is not used by Mapuche people to create relations with people of greater wealth or influence. Rather, Mapuche people seek out those they perceive as being of a similar social standing to themselves (see also Killick this volume for a similar case in which an indigenous group display a dislike of hierarchical differentiation in such relationships). It is perhaps because of its significant overlap with the pre-existing forms of institutionalized friendship mentioned above that *compadrazgo* seems to be less important among the Mapuche than amongst certain other Amerindian peoples

(Gudeman 1972). It is important to mention that these formalized friendships are not inherited, or at least not perceived to be inherited, as they are in other parts of the Americas. Although one is expected to be respectful and caring towards the formal friends of one's parents, there is no expectation that the formal relation be carried over.

The vast majority of friendships, however, fall outside all of these formalized institutions, and are referred to simply as *weniiywen*, 'friendships'.[4] It is the exchange of wine between male friends which is in many ways the paradigmatic activity of both friendship and of the sociality of exchange. Almost every social event involves the exchange and sharing of wine. Chief among the larger of such gatherings are football tournaments, funerals, the sport of *palin*, the gambling game of *rayhuela*, and *pago*, the monthly social security payment. But many drinking groups form for no particular reason outside the houses of clandestine wine-sellers. In short, whenever two or more men are gathered together there is a good chance that they will set to drinking wine.

A drinking group will almost always form a circle, although how well defined this circle is depends to a large extent on how much has already been drunk. The donor of the wine will quietly present the unopened carton he has recently bought to a person of his choosing, who, upon its reception, will appear simultaneously shocked and delighted. Ideally the receiver will open the carton, pour wine into the single glass available, and drink about half the glass before refilling it and handing it with his right hand back to the initial donor. The donor will then likewise drink from the glass and hand it back to the receiver. The fact that the receiver drinks first is a demonstration that he trusts the donor and does not fear being passed poison (*fiñapue*). However, receivers frequently first pass the glass to the donor before themselves drinking, particularly in situations where the donor is not well known. Such precautions are regarded as nothing more than common sense due to the perceived relation of wine to poison and witchcraft which will be discussed further below. After this initial exchange, the receiver proceeds anti-clockwise around the circle of drinkers, serving each person in turn in exactly the same manner. Everyone present in the circle will be served regardless of age or gender. A refusal to drink is utterly unacceptable and is usually interpreted as being tantamount to an accusation of witchcraft.

Once the circle has been completed, the initial receiver will himself drink (or if he served himself first, drink again) and then set the glass and carton down. When he feels that a sufficient interlude has passed, he will take up the glass and carton and once again proceed to serve anti-clockwise around the circle. However, this time he will not make any particular effort to serve first the donor of the carton but will start serving with whoever happens to be the first person to his right. This process is repeated until the carton is empty at which point the receiver hands the empty carton and glass back to the donor and thanks him. More than one carton may simultaneously be passing around the circle and the servers have to concentrate to make sure that they do not miss out any of the drinkers. If a drinker is accidentally skipped over he or another drinker will immediately point this out and the server will apologize and rectify the error. The denial of wine to someone is to deny the fact that they are *che*, a person. The etiquette of serving wine is informal, but inflexible. From an early age children are explicitly taught that drinks are always served with the right hand, that the order of serving is always anti-clockwise, and that all present must be served.

It seems to me that there are two different things going on in this process. The first is the exchange of wine between two friends and the second is the communal sharing of this same wine between all present. Such sharing serves to delineate one's status as *che* and thereby create the prerequisite for exchange between persons. Thus what interests me here is the fact that the communal sharing is ideologically suppressed and viewed simply as an indirect consequence of the initial exchange between two friends. I believe that this way of thinking about exchange and of elaborating exchange is common to many aspects of Mapuche society: that complex social processes and institutions involving many people are nearly always ideologically transformed into a direct exchange between just two persons.[5]

Let us look at the ethnographic data once more to see how such an ideological transformation of exchange is achieved. The fact that the 'owner' of the wine always gives it to someone else, rather than sharing it out among all present, immediately creates a situation in which the number of actors has been reduced from many to just two, and, furthermore, a situation in which something has been 'given' and not simply 'shared.' This linguistic differentiation exists in Mapudungun as the verb roots *elu*- 'to give' and *inakon*- 'to share'. It is worth pointing out here that the serving of wine is never understood as, or confused with, the giving of wine. This point is made clear by the fact that only the receiver of the wine ever thanks (*mañumun*) the donor. People have to concentrate to remember exactly which person gave them the carton of wine so as to thank them and only them. Upon the act of presentation the donor makes it clear exactly to whom the carton is to be given, usually specifying some reason or other. These speech acts of thanking and presenting serve to define clearly the two participants in the exchange. The exchange, which in purely material terms is between one person and the group, is presented as an exchange between two individuals. Mapuche men always remember who has given them wine and to whom they themselves have given wine. Such memories create almost tangible bonds with which people map the history of their social relationships.

It is perhaps worth noting here that the exchange of wine is not understood by Mapuche people as being necessarily reciprocal. People always say that they give through affection, never through any obligation to reciprocate. In many situations people deliberately avoid direct reciprocation. If a group of three men are drinking, each person will always give a carton to the person who had not previously given to them. Indeed, when someone does reciprocate directly, the receiver (who was initially the donor) frequently admonishes them saying that they gave through *cariño*, the Spanish term for 'affection', and not because of any expectation of a return. The emphasis is thus placed on individual volition in choosing to whom wine will be given and a relation of friendship is thereby acknowledged. Nevertheless, behind these assertions to the contrary there does seem to exist the notion that receiving implies giving and vice versa. The giving of wine both implies and creates a relationship which is by definition a two-way relationship. Whilst the wine itself may not be reciprocated, it is assumed that the *cariño* which the giving of wine implies will be reciprocated. The acceptance of the carton demonstrates the acceptance of this relationship.

I suggest that the giving of wine is used in two ways: firstly, to express and affirm existing relationships; and, secondly, to open the possibility for creating new ones. Wine is generally not given between close patrilineal relatives such as brothers, fathers and sons, paternal uncles and nephews, i.e. between those of *kiñe küpal*. It is, however, exchanged between affines, maternal uncles and nephews, *compadres* and neighbours, all of whom are considered primarily as 'friends'. I would suggest that this is because the exchange of wine between patrilineal relatives would, in a sense, be both redundant and superfluous as there is something in the relationships between such people which is inevitable and intrinsic. As I have explained above, the giving of wine is a symbol of affection and its acceptance a symbol of trust. Wine is also the vehicle for the creation of new relationships. Upon my arrival in Piedra Alta I was constantly presented with carton after carton of wine. This was not due to my novelty value as a foreigner, but to the fact that Mapuche men frequently seek to give wine to anyone unknown to them, whether Mapuche, Chilean or English.

I have spoken above of wine as a 'value' as in a sense it serves as currency in a moral economy. Mapuche men also frequently drink other alcoholic beverages such as apple cider (Map. *manshana pülko*, Sp. *chicha*) and corn beer (*mudai*). Yet the giving and sharing of these drinks is not elaborated to the degree which the giving of wine is. I would suggest that this is because whereas *chicha* and *mudai* are produced domestically, wine must be purchased with cash. This externality to the domestic economy gives it the sense of being an object of pure value.[6] Just as money is used in the material economy, wine serves as the chief currency of the moral economy. This becomes clearer when we see that these two currencies operate in rigidly segregated spheres of exchange which in turn correspond to distinct genders. Wine is never sold by men, only ever given. It is women who are wholly responsible for the large-scale clandestine sale of wine. The husbands of the many women who sell wine go to great lengths to avoid being associated in any way with the actual financial exchange. They will always look away when money is handed over and walk off immediately if any dispute over a payment breaks out.

If I am right in seeing the exchange of wine as one of the primary vehicles for constituting friendship relationships between Mapuche men, we should not be surprised to discover that it is also the primary vehicle for denying and destroying such relationships. Indeed, it is largely through the poisoning of wine that witches, *kalku*, seek to tear the world apart. The Mapuche world is full of evil, of creatures, beings and spirits all intent on destroying the lives of true persons, of *che*. Perhaps the most feared component of the forces of evil are not the headless riders, the flying skulls, or the living hides, but the witches resident among one's very own consanguines, affines and neighbours. It is these witches, the human anti-humans, who are the most prevalent and most present evil in the world. It was previously believed that all deaths were caused by witches; however, these days people also acknowledge the reality of *winka kutran*, 'Chilean diseases'. Nevertheless, the majority of illnesses and deaths are still understood as being caused directly by witches.[7]

Through this description of the exchange of wine I have sought to demonstrate two things: firstly, that the giving and sharing of wine can be understood as a fundamental form of sociality among Mapuche men, a form I refer to as the sociality of exchange; and secondly, that such a mode is a clear example of the Mapuche practice of ideologically transforming complex social exchanges involving multiple actors into simple dualistic exchanges between two individuals. This second point is key as it reveals a representation of friendship which proposes the person as the locus of individual volition rather than as part of a supra-individual aggregate. I further argue that wine serves as a medium for both the expression and affirmation of existing relationships as well as a means for creating the possibility of new relationships. The refusal to participate in the exchange of wine is perceived as a refusal to participate in society. This refusal is taken a step further by witches, *kalku*, who through their reversed participation in the exchange of wine seek to negate the social value which wine implies.

The Dead Friend

The open-ended notion of the person expanding centrifugally through friendship relationships means that death poses a very particular ontological problem for Mapuche people, namely that the webs of reciprocity through which persons have constituted themselves remain unfinished; there are outstanding debts which must be cleared. This notion of 'debt' is not confined to material objects, but to the notion that sociality is itself a process of generalized exchange. In other words, death leaves such relations in limbo, and by removing the person from the realm of sociality leaves them in a diffuse and 'unfinished' state. The project of self-creation is brought to an abrupt halt, but still short of its final destination. The responsibility of 'finishing' the deceased necessarily falls to those still alive.

Upon reaching old age, both men and women voice their fears about leaving things 'unfinished' (Map. *dewmalay*, Sp. *sin terminar*) and 'abandoned' (Map. *trangey*, Sp. *abandonado*). Women tend to focus especially on the question of who will care for their garden and who will finish their weaving. Men, on the other hand, tend to worry about who will pay off the debts of hospitality they have accrued as guests of friends at funerals, games of *palin*, and *ngillatun* fertility rituals. We have seen that this sociality of exchange is based upon a notion of reciprocity – indeed, it is this mutually obligating reciprocity which keeps friendship relationships, *weniiywen*, perpetuated through time. Death inevitably cuts such reciprocity short, and proves an insurmountable obstacle to the repayment of the inevitable debts every adult has accrued.[8] Many older men attempt to resolve this dilemma by staying at home and withdrawing from the webs of sociality before death catches up with them. This change in social status is described simply as 'He no longer goes out' (Map. *tripawelay*, Sp. *ya no sale*). Nevertheless, such attempts can do nothing more than diminish the problem. This is because the extent to which the person is predicated on relations with others far surpasses the remembrance of material exchanges of wine and meat. In other words, the problem is not so much one of resolving a financial transaction, but rather of severing the cumulation of a lifetime's relationships conceptualized as a series of exchanges between individuals.

This problem is dealt with by a form of funerary discourse known in Mapudungun as *amulpüllün*, literally 'the making go of the spirit'. The explicit purpose of this form of discourse is to 'finish' or 'complete' (*dewman*) the deceased (Course 2007). And just as it is to friends to whom one must turn to create oneself in life, so it is to friends that the responsibility of completion in death falls. Just as in life the autonomy of the Mapuche person is premised on their relations with others, so too in death it is the task of others to secure this autonomy through the termination of the networks of sociality through which the deceased constituted themselves. *Amulpülliin*, then, is the final word in the dialogue of the person's life.

The *amulpülliin* always consists of three stages: the *pentukun*, the greeting between the speakers; the *nutramtun*, the biography of the deceased; and the *mariepull*, the toasting of the deceased. I will return to the *amulpülliin* in more detail in the analysis which follows, but first I provide a simple overview of the events. The headman of the host *lof*, or in some cases the deceased's closest male relative, asks two people to come and give the formalized funerary discourse, which is sometimes known by the general term for 'oratory', *wewpin*, and sometimes by the term *nutramtun*, translatable as 'history' or 'biography'. The two speakers, referred to as *wewpife*, 'orators', face each other across the coffin. The speaker who represents the host *lof* starts the usual sequence of *pentukun* which involves a lengthy description of his own family history and achievements, interspersed with questions to his counterpart. The counterpart responds with his own description. Once the *pentukun* is over, the *nutramtun*, the biography of the deceased begins. The *nutramtun* is over when each speaker picks a bottle from those lined up on top of the coffin, takes a long swig, and then hands it across the coffin to his counterpart. These bottles lined up along the coffin are known as the *mariepull*.[9] Once the two *wewpife* have exchanged bottles, people from the surrounding crowd come forward to grab bottles, take a few swigs, and pass the bottle to anyone who happens to be standing close by. The drinking of the *mariepull* marks the end of the *amulpülliin*.

Let us begin our analysis of the *amulpülliin* by focusing on the identities of the two primary orators, the *wewpife* or *wewpin*. Ideally, at the funeral of a man, one of the speakers is a close patrilineal relative of the deceased, someone with whom they shared *kiñe küpal*. The other speaker should belong to the *kiñe küpal* of his mother, his matrilateral kin. In other words, one speaker represents 'consanguines' and the other 'affines'. These days, however, there are many instances when there is no one from one or both of the relevant *kiñe küpal* who is sufficiently skilled to give such an elaborate discourse. In this case a speaker is selected from the *lof* of which the relevant *kiñe küpal* is part. Failing that, the relevance of kinship ties is subsumed by that of geographical ties as it is stipulated that in the absence of speakers from the relevant *lof*, the two speakers must come from *lof* located either side of the deceased's *lof*.

The host *wewpife*, that of the *lof* hosting the funeral, starts the discourse with the *pentukun*, an elaborate mixture of greeting and autobiography. In the *pentukun* the speakers outline their own relation to their *meli folil*, the 'four roots' of their *küpal*, but particular emphasis is given to patrilineal descent and the *kiñe küpal* to which it gives rise. The discourses take the form of a dialogue, the first speaker outlining an aspect of his descent and then inquiring of his counterpart the same aspect of his descent. The speakers then go on to comment at length on their own achievements: the places they have been, the places they have worked, the events which they have organized and any Chilean dignitaries they may have met.

Once the *pentukun* greeting has come to an end, the host *wewpife* commences the *nutramtun*, the biography of the deceased.[10] He outlines the aspect of the deceased's *küpal* which relates to his own position as representative of the deceased's patri-relatives. The speaker representing the deceased's matrilateral kin confines himself to outlining the deceased's matrilateral genealogy. Both speakers take great care in not missing out any relatives they deem to be of significance. In effect, this genealogical aspect of the *nutramtun* serves to unravel the paternally-derived and maternally-derived elements of the deceased's person by making them explicit. Such elements can be seen as corresponding to consanguineal and affinal elements of the person and are, in a sense, abstracted and generalized to a level beyond that of the person. What is stressed is the place of the deceased in a chain of relations stretching back through time, and therefore in what could be seen as an enduring 'group'. At first glance, then, the *nutramtun* would seem to echo the funeral rites described for Melanesia and elsewhere which 'disintegrate' the person into the patri- and matri-groups from which they were composed. This disintegration is simply a shift in scale between the congruous units of the 'dividual' and the 'group' (Strathern 1988). However, as we shall see, there is far more to the *nutramtun* than the citing of genealogy, and there is far more to the Mapuche person than the sum of their paternal and maternal parts.

Once the recounting of the genealogy of the deceased is over, the host *wewpife* starts to recount in great detail the events of the deceased's life. Every place they visited, every *palin* and *ngillatun* in which they participated, every anecdote they told, and most importantly, every friend they made – all must be recounted and made explicit. Once the first *wewpife* has recounted what he knows of the deceased, the second *wewpife* starts to add details of which the first speaker may have been unaware. This in turn prompts the initial speaker to respond with yet more details of the deceased's life. The alternating dialogue has a competitive edge, and it is this competitive element to the *nutramtun* which ensures that no stone remains unturned in the biography of the deceased. My informants always impressed upon me the necessity of recounting the negative aspects of the deceased's life with just as much care and veracity as the positive. 'Just as the person was in life, so we must describe them in death', proclaimed Roberto, one of the most experienced *wewpife* in the area: 'If they were a great footballer, we tell of their goals and put their shirt on top of the coffin. If they were a great *palife* [*palin* player] we tell of their great games and clash *wiño* [*palin* sticks] over the coffin. That's how it must be if the person is to be completed.' Once the two *wewpife* have exhausted their reminiscences of the deceased, the headman of the host *lof*, or in some cases the deceased's closest male relative, ask the gathered crowd of the deceased's friends if anybody else wishes to add anything. For as the person creates themselves in life through friendship relationships, it falls to friends to bring this process of self-creation to its culmination. These friends, both men and women, must come forward and state anything which they feel the *wewpife* may have overlooked.[11] The combined effect of the *nutramtun* is said to be that it 'finishes' or 'completes' (*dewman*) the person.

To explain how the *amulpülliin* achieves this 'finishing' of the person, I wish to utilize the concepts of transgredience and consummation as described by Mikhail Bakhtin in his early essays '*Author and Hero in Aesthetic Activity*' (1990 [1923]) and '*Art and Answerability*' (1990 [1923]). For Bakhtin, the self is necessarily constituted through its relation with an other. Both self and other only have meaning in relation to each other. Hence, Bakhtin's concept of being is essentially triadic: the self, the other and the relation between the two. These two poles of self and other are ultimately two different ways of perceiving time and space, the former marked by its openness, the latter by its closedness. The Bakhtin scholar Holquist notes: 'For the perceivers, their time is forever open and unfinished; their own space is always the center of perception, the point around which things arrange themselves as a horizon whose meaning is determined by wherever they have their place in it. By contrast, the time in which we model others is perceived as closed and finished' (2002: 22). The implication of this is that it is only from the time/space of the 'outside' that the person can come to be seen as a unique, consummated whole. The achieving of this consummation by the other is predicated on what Bakhtin calls 'transgredience': the ability to fully know the person as object and to thereby fix them in a particular time and space.[12]

In other work (Course 2007), I have argued that the Mapuche people conceptualize the person in a similar way, as inevitably constituted through its relations with 'others', whether these be chronologically prior 'others' of paternal and maternal kin, or chronologically subsequent 'others' approached through the sociality of exchange. The value of the Bakhtinian approach in revealing the function of the consummation of the Mapuche person realized in *amulpülliin* is made evident when we review a famous passage considering the 'hero' as deceased and the 'author' as *wewpife*:

> And this being outside in relation to the hero enables the author to collect and concentrate all of the hero, who, from within himself, is diffused and dispersed [...]; to collect the hero and his life and to complete him to the point where he forms a whole by supplying all those moments which are inaccessible to the hero himself from within himself; [...] and to justify and to consummate the hero independently of the meaning, the achievements, the outcome and success of the hero's own forward directed life. (1990: 14).

The *amulpüllün*, then, creates a meaningful whole out of a life constituted through relations with others. It creates a 'whole' through condensing what is diffuse. This essence corresponds to the uniqueness of an individual life. It is only this 'whole', cut free of the relations from which it was constituted, that can move on into an unknown and unspecified realm. It is only others who, from the necessary perspective of 'outsidedness', are capable of achieving the transgredience necessary to consummate the person. Thus, as Bakhtin notes, 'Biography is bestowed as a gift' (1990: 166). However, this 'gift' is of a different nature to that envisaged by Mauss (1990 [1925]), as the very nature of the 'gift' of *amulpüllün* is to remove the recipient from the realm of sociality and thus remove the possibility of reciprocation.

The fact that the deceased is now cut free of the relations of reciprocity through which they constituted themselves is made clear in the *mariepüll*, the ritual toasting at the end of the *amulpüllün*. In stark contrast to the careful and meticulous exchange of wine described above, the drinkers in the *mariepüll* seize bottles and gulp down wine themselves before passing them on to anybody else. There is no concern with maintaining the anti-clockwise direction of the bottle, with ensuring that all are served, nor with thanking anybody: the bottles are dumped unceremoniously on the ground when empty. I suggest that just as the 'gift' of biography, the *nutramtun*, is by its very nature impossible to reciprocate, so too the *mariepüll*, which stands as the 'gift' of wine from the deceased, is also destined to never be returned. The whole point of the *mariepüll* is that it marks the end of reciprocation, and therefore the end of sociality.

We have seen that death is the cessation of sociality, but paradoxically it is a cessation which must be achieved by others. This is true in both the morally negative causation of death by witchcraft, and in the morally positive consummation of the deceased by the *wewpife* and friends. The fact that all deaths are caused by the ill-will of others, namely *kalku* witches, becomes especially salient in funerals as it is the paradigmatic positive other, in the form of the friend, who enables death to be a consummation of the singular person and thereby secure autonomy. It is to this uniqueness of the individual person that I now turn to in my concluding remarks.

Conclusions

In this chapter I have sought to show how, firstly, friendship relations are central to the Mapuche conceptualization of the person, and secondly, that such relations are premised on an idea of an autonomous and intentional individual. The attribution of personhood is dependent upon going beyond the initial given relations of kinship characterized by the concept of *küpal*, and going on to create friendship relationships with unrelated others through one's own volition. Indeed, it is the very act of choosing – of demonstrating volition – which defines one's friends as friends and oneself as *che*. The mechanics of the exchange of wine, the paradigmatic form of the sociality of exchange, serve to emphasize a particular dyadic relationship between two autonomous individuals, momentarily severed from the other social relations around them. I hope to have shown that the sociality of exchange forms the basis of a life-long project of self-creation: a constant actualization of the capacity for personhood through engagement with others. It is this 'open-endedness' of the Mapuche person which endows it with a certain centrifugality, a desire to expand relationships with others ever outward. This same 'open-endedness' also creates the necessity of 'finishing' the person in the *amulpüllün* described above. It is for this reason that the sum of the Mapuche person is always more than its constituent parts. One must take into account that the person is also constituted as a residue of the various relationships into which it has entered during life. The implication of this is that the person is unique and irreducible to any other level. The open-endedness of the person makes it fundamentally incongruous with social aggregates to which it might belong. It is, then, hard to envisage the Mapuche person as a 'dividual' in the sense utilized by Marriot and Inden (1977) for India and Strathern (1988) for Melanesia; but does this allow us to speak of an 'individual'?

Up until now I have been somewhat hesitant in using the term 'individual' in reference to the Mapuche person. As Louis Dumont (1970, 1985) has pointed out, the concept of the 'individual' as an autonomous unit has a particular history specific to the Western context in which it arose. Likewise, Mauss pointed out that the concept of the 'person' has also travelled its own political and historical trajectory (1985 [1938]). I do not wish to detract from either of these approaches, which rightly warn us of the danger of unquestioningly imposing upon other peoples units of analysis particular to Western thought. Yet this should not blind us to the fact that certain non-Western societies may well have developed independently their own concepts which resemble in many ways those of the 'individual' and the 'person'. As I stated in the introduction, I am not convinced by Mauss's claim that the notion of the person as individual is 'formulated only for us, among us' (1985 [1938]: 22). There is a tendency in some anthropological writing to suggest, in a pseudo-evolutionary way, that the notion of autonomous individuals is the unique invention of the Enlightenment and that other peoples have yet to surpass the fact of being simply 'parts' of 'wholes'. Yet it seems to me that, for the Mapuche at least, the model of the person as an autonomous individual who enters social relations through his or her own volition is just as applicable (or perhaps one could argue, inapplicable) as it is anywhere in the Western world. As I have attempted to make clear above, Mapuche persons are engaged in a process through which they create themselves through the friendship relationships which they enter into during their lifetimes. The unique persons to whom such a process gives rise cannot be reduced to 'parts' of any 'whole'. I would suggest that this is not the result of contact with colonialism, Christianity or capitalism, but rather a genuinely indigenous aspect of the Mapuche concept of the person. Whereas the Western 'person' is created through the extra-familial institutions of the state or church (Strathern 1992), the Mapuche person must create themselves through a constant process of engaging with others, a process which ends only at death.

Yet the Mapuche individual which emerges through friendship is clearly a relational individual. Any opposition of 'individual' and 'relational' persons seems to me to be highly problematic, or at the very least misplaced, in terms of the Mapuche case. Personal autonomy is a pre-requisite in creating relations with non-kin, yet it is through these relations that the autonomous person emerges.[13] This is not as tautological as it might at first seem, once we appreciate that the emergence of self and other occurs as a dialectical process over time.[14] I would further suggest that for Mapuche people 'kinship' and 'friendship' are in a similar dialectical relationship – mutually exclusive yet mutually constitutive. It is through relations of kinship which the initial aspects of the person, both physical and social, emerge. Yet true personhood, which is necessary to reproduce relations of kinship, only emerges through relations which are by definition outside the realm of kinship – those of friendship.

Acknowledgments

This paper is based upon twenty-six months of research carried out in 2001–2003, 2006 and 2007 in Piedra Alta and Isla Huapi between Lago Budi and the Pacific Ocean in Chile's Ninth Region. The research was supported by an Economic and Social Research Council studentship and a British Academy Post Doctoral Fellowship. I thank both of these institutions for their support. I am also grateful to the participants and organizers of the workshop at which the original version of this paper was presented. Further thanks go to Evan Killick and Amit Desai for their insightful editorial comments and suggestions.

Notes

1. Admittedly, Mauss starts his famous paper with several caveats to the end that his argument is confined to the representation of the person in law. Yet, as several commentators have noted, by the end of the paper he seems to be making a much larger claim (Carrithers, Collins and Lukes 1986).
2. This partial equivalence of matrilateral kin with affines is echoed in Mapuche kinship terminology, which has both 'Iroquois' and 'Omaha' features (see Course 2005).
3. Couples who marry in church also choose what are known as *padrinos de casamiento*, 'marital godparents'.
4. The suffix *-wen* refers to a mutualistic dyadic relation.
5. This imposition of duality upon essentially non-binary phenomenon is a key theme in Mapuche thinking, not just in the context of social relationships, but the world in general.
6. The opposite is apparently the case in many other parts of South America where it is its location within the domestic economy which endows alcoholic beverages with their value (see for example Descola 1996; Gow 1989).
7. See Bacigalupo (2007) for more information on Mapuche understandings of illness and curing.
8. I should point out that death not only leaves 'unfinished' those relationships predicated on the sociality of friendship, but also those relationships given at birth: the relations with those whom one shared *kiñe küpal*, and the relations with one's matrilateral kin, not to mention the extension of these modes of sociality through having one's own children.
9. The term *mariepull* would seem to be derived from the numeral *mari epu* meaning 'twelve'. However, the actual number of bottles lined up usually exceeds twelve, as every *lof* member and relative participating in the funeral as a host must provide a full bottle of wine, or more usually, *chicha*.
10. Due to the prohibition on photographic or audio recording of ceremonial discourses I am unable to provide word-for-word transcriptions of *nutramtun*. My analysis is based upon my memory of the discourses, and upon discussions with the orators themselves held at a later date.
11. It is not just the words and conscious actions of those present which must mirror the life of the deceased, but even the elements themselves: it is said to always rain during the funeral of a stingy person, while sunshine accompanies the departure of the generous. Those who lived violent lives are sure to see their funerals marred by brawling and arguing.
12. The perspectival cosmology outlined by Viveiros de Castro (1998) can be viewed as just such a struggle for transgredience. But whereas the

consummation of the dead Mapuche person ensures its autonomy; for the living, transgredience would be a reduction to the status of victim, a point to which I return in the conclusion to this thesis.
13. Although autonomy and volition are necessary in keeping kinship relations alive, they play no role in their creation.
14. This is the one of the chief contributions of 'post-structuralist' thinkers to twentieth-century thought – yet it is an idea which may well have been at the heart of Amerindian philosophies for far longer.

References

Allan, G. 1996. *Kinship and Friendship in Modern Britain*. Oxford: Oxford University Press.
Augusta, F. 1991 [1916]. *Diccionario Araucano*. Temuco: Editorial Kushe.
Bacigalupo, A.M. 2007. *Shamans of the Foye Tree: gender, power, and healing among the Chilean Mapuche*. Austin: University of Texas Press.
Bakhtin, M. 1990 [1923]. *Art and Answerability: Early Philosophical Essays* (translated by V. Liapunov). Austin: University of Texas Press.
Carrier, J. 1999. 'People who can be Friends: Selves and Social Relationships', in Sandra Bell and Simon Coleman (eds), *The Anthropology of Friendship*. Oxford: Berg.
Carrithers, M., S. Collins and S. Lukes (eds). 1986. *The Category of the Person*. Cambridge: Cambridge University Press.
Course, M. 2005. 'Borges, the Mapuche, and the Mother's Brother's Son', *Cambridge Anthropology* 25(1): 11–30.
———. 2007. 'Death, Biography, and the Mapuche Person', *Ethnos* 72(1): 77–101.
Descola, P. 1996. *The Spears of Twilight: Life and Death in the Amazon Jungle*. London: Flamingo.
Dumont, L. 1970. *Homo Hierarchicus: the Caste System and its Implications* (translated by M. Sainsbury). London: Weidenfeld and Nicholson.
———. 1985. 'A Modified View of our Origins: The Christian Beginnings of Modern Individualism', in M. Carrithers, S. Collins and S. Lukes (eds), *The Category of the Person*. Cambridge: Cambridge University Press.
Gow, P. 1989. 'The Perverse Child: Desire in a Native Amazonian Subsistence Economy', *Man* 24: 567–82.
Gudeman, S. 1972. 'The Compadrazgo as a Reflection of the Natural and Spiritual Person', *Proceedings of the Royal Anthropological Institute of Great Britain and Ireland for* 1971: 45–71.
Holquist, M. 2002. *Dialogism: Bakhtin and His World*. London: Routledge.
Marriot, M. and R. Inden. 1977. 'Towards an Ethnosociology of South Asian Caste Systems', in K. David (ed.), *The New Wind: Changing Identities in South Asia*. The Hague: Mouton.
Mauss, M. 1985 [1938]. 'A Category of the Human Mind: the Notion of Person; the Notion of Self' (translated by W.D. Hall), in Michael Carrithers, Steven Collins

and Steven Lukes (eds), *The Category of the Person*. Cambridge: Cambridge University Press.

———. 1990 [1925]. *The Gift: the Form and Reason for Exchange in Archaic Societies.* London: Routledge.

Paine, R. 1969. 'In Search of Friendship: an Exploratory Analysis in "Middle-class" Culture', *Man* 4(4): 505–24.

Strathern, M. 1988. *The Gender of the Gift: Problems with Women and Problems with Society in Melanesia.* Berkeley: University of California Press.

———. 1992. 'Parts and Wholes: Refiguring Relationships in a Postplural World', in Adam Kuper (ed.), *Conceptualising Society*. London: Routledge.

Taylor, A.-C. 1996. 'The Soul's Body and Its States: An Amazonian Perspective on the Nature of Being Human', *Journal of the Royal Anthropological Institute* 2(2): 201–15.

Viveiros de Castro, E. 1998. 'Cosmological Deixis and Amerindian Perspectivism', *Journal of the Royal Anthropological Institute* 4(3): 469–88.

Chapter 8

The Value of Friendship: Subject/Object Transformations in the Economy of Becoming a Person (Bermondsey, Southeast London)

GILLIAN EVANS

The thing about you, Obi, yeah, is you're tough, but you ain't really got any
friends.

Gary, age 11, Tenter Ground Primary School.

In this chapter I consider some key questions in the study of friendship, including what it means to make friends, how similar different forms of friendship are, and what the study of friendship can teach us about human relations more generally. The friendships I focus on here are those between groups of boys aged ten and eleven in a primary school classroom at Tenter Ground, a school in Bermondsey, a predominantly working-class area of central southeast London. I also draw on my own experiences, as an ethnographer making friends in the context of fieldwork, to examine what defines friendship as distinct from other kinds of relations.

Bermondsey, in comparison to the multicultural areas of southeast London surrounding it, is distinctive because it remains a predominantly white working-class area.[1] Although multiculturalism is a feature of the school and also of the many social-housing estates where Bermondsey's children live, it is not typical of Bermondsey as a whole, where a large part of the white working-class population continues to imagine the community in terms of closely defined kinship and residence or 'born and bred' criteria of belonging. Focusing on social class differences and how they intersect with other kinds of differentiations in Britain such as gender, race, ethnicity and cultural background, my wider research investigates how such distinctions come to be hierarchically valued, locally defined and embodied in practice. In particular I am interested in how it is that for certain kinds of young working-class men, the development of what is considered to be an appropriate disposition – a specific ethical stance towards the world and others in it – usually leads to failure at school. Indeed, it became clear to me during my research that educational failure was something of a prerequisite for becoming valued as a certain kind of working-class man; in this case a Bermondsey *bod* – a young man with a tough street reputation to maintain and a potential future in the economy of crime which flourishes in Bermondsey.

In order to find out more about how this particular way of becoming valued as a man arises as an oppositional stance to more dominant values which are substantiated in British institutions, such as schools, I conducted fieldwork in Bermondsey between 1999 and 2000. My main fieldwork site was a primary school but I also conducted ethnographic research in homes, on the street, in youth clubs and other relevant places in Bermondsey where I sought to discover how nascent Bermondsey *bods* make sense of all the various expectations – from parents, teachers, peers at school and young men on the street – about who they are expected to become in order to be valued by others.

Key to this research is the focus on processes of learning. Following Lave and Wenger's theory of situated learning (1991) and Toren's broadly phenomenological and anthropological model of learning (1990, 1999), I am concerned in my work with the question of how humans come to be the specific kinds of people that they are: collectively distinctive and uniquely particular (Evans 2006a). In this chapter I focus on the part that friendship plays in the process of becoming a particular kind of person and, among working class boys in Bermondsey, I consider what weighting is given to friendship relative to other kinds of relationships, such as kin relations and relations with teachers in the institutional setting of the school.

Disruptive Boys

Whilst educational statistics generalize about them, it soon became clear to me that certain kinds of working-class boys fail at school more than others. These most 'disruptive' of boys jeopardize not only their own chances of success at school but also that of other kinds of working class boys and girls who are more willing to learn. A downward spiral of failure is thus created in schools, like Tenter Ground, where this kind of subversion goes unchecked because the authority of adults is undermined from the lowest to the highest levels of the school hierarchy.

Most disruptive among these 'failing boys' tend to be those boys who are allowed, at home, to seek the freedom to play out on the street where, at a young age, they quickly learn, in relation to gangs of older boys who rule the street, how to withstand intimidation and actual physical violence.[2] In time these young boys learn how to become intimidating themselves and even, I argue (2006b), to enjoy violence which eventually becomes to them a kind of social good, one which subverts every value that education establishes for children. In the safety of the school, protected from the bullying of older boys on the street, these boys become a force to be reckoned with and the school becomes an arena where pecking orders are constituted on an hourly basis. Gary – nascent Bermondsey bod, charismatic leader among his friends, dominant in the class and school, bully to less daring and weaker boys as well as staff members for whom he has no respect – is labelled as one of the most disruptive boys at Tenter Ground (a failing primary school) but he is, nevertheless, one of the most academically able boys in his class: it takes more than brute force, as Obi – the new boy – must learn, to become peer group leader at Tenter Ground.

Gary

Gary is not an easy boy to get to know. Like many of the older boys, he is sulky, reticent and reluctant to be in the classroom where application to schoolwork is expected. Particularly surly, Gary resists any attempts on my part to get to know him: I smile at him, he ignores me; I greet him, he ignores me; I am insignificant to him and he is intimidating to me. For at least the first three months of my fieldwork this impasse between me and the disruptive boys continues until one day I realize, quite by chance, how it is possible for me to make friends with them. Before I describe this day, however, I first want to skip ahead a few months to describe what kind of influence Gary wields at school. In so doing I show how the disruptive boys' peer group is constituted on an on-going basis in relation to their subversive antics at school and, on the basis of this description, I introduce two main arguments pertaining to wider debates in the anthropology of friendship.

February 10 2000: supply teacher

When I enter the playground one cold February morning, there is a rabble of Year Five/Six (age ten to eleven) boys outside the steps leading inside the school; some of them, including Gary, are wrestling on the ground. I presume that the rest of the class must have gone inside because it is already after nine o'clock (when school proper is supposed to begin) and the playground is otherwise deserted. I approach the boys and ask, 'What's up?' They explain that Christine, their teacher, is away again. I ask them what is going to happen and Nathaniel,[3] one of Gary's best friends, responds: moaning and groaning, he tells me that the class will probably be split up as usual and divided between other teachers' classes. I manage to persuade the boys to come upstairs with me and on our way up we meet Baqir, who is crying, and being comforted by his best friend Basim.[4] These two boys have much in common with the disruptive boys because of their passion for football and computer games, but just like the more imaginative and artistic boys, such as Kevin and Anthony,[5] they are rarely involved in instigating any of the violent skirmishes which preoccupy the disruptive boys. Even though they are valued by the disruptive boys for their goal-keeping skills on the football pitch, Baqir and Basim are, nevertheless, quite often on the receiving end of their team mates' violence. I stop on the stairs to ask Baqir what happened and he tells me that Victor[6] kicked him in his bad leg. I take Baqir by the arm and lead him up the stairs, distracting him from his tears by talking about his number one passion, which is Manchester United football club.

We reach and enter the classroom where Mara, the head teacher, has just finished taking the register. She is explaining to the children that they are going to have a supply teacher for the day and while they wait for the teacher to arrive she begins the numeracy hour with some mental maths challenges. Mara fires times tables questions at individual children whom she calls by name. As soon as she does so, levels of movement and noise amongst the children begin to increase and the boys start to taunt each other when they get their maths questions wrong. Mara stops the questions to manage the boys' behaviour and when they take no notice of her she responds, shouting loudly, 'Shut up!' All the children find Mara's rudeness hysterical and some of the boys cover their mouths, feigning shock. Mara then gives up on mental maths and tells the children to go to their numeracy tables where the numeracy task for the morning is written on sheets.

For the duration of the numeracy task I join a table where Nathaniel, Gary, Daniel,[7] Kevin and Anthony are sitting. Daniel, like Nathaniel, skirts around the edges of disruption and sometimes finds himself at the centre of trouble as he tries to impress Gary. Making good the opportunity that Christine's absence presents, Gary is intent from the very beginning of the day on having a laugh.[8] He tries to distract Nathaniel who has started working on the numeracy sheet: in a tone indicative of their friendship, he repeatedly calls his name to try and get his attention, 'Nat, Nat,' and Gary begins to jibe Nathaniel, attempting to stop him from working, 'Don't start Nat, you're just copyin' that lot.'

Then, without warning, the supply teacher walks in. He is a small and slight man, about thirty years old, dressed formally in suit trousers with shirt and tie. Every teacher knows that the impression they create on children is formed within the first few minutes, if not seconds, of their entering a classroom and this teacher looks scared. Mara introduces him to the class. His name is Chris; he is Australian. Gary immediately takes up the bait and begins to entertain the boys at his table, 'Kray, did he say Kray? Yeah look at '[h]im. He looks like one of the Kray twins, don't he?[9] Is it Ronnie? Is it Reggie?' Chris ignores Gary and reinforces the numeracy task that has been set while Nathaniel makes a vain attempt to manage Gary's behaviour; showing his irritation he mutters, 'Just get on with your work man.'

Soon after Chris arrives, Mara leaves the room and immediately the levels of noise and movement begin to rise. Ade[10] gets out of his seat and comes over to Gary's table. Gary says to him, 'Chris is coming; you scared in'it?' Mark,[11] Ade's friend, then joins them and begins to jibe Nathaniel, 'Nat, you better give me the rubber, man.' When they manage to get the rubber away from Gary, Ade and Mark go back to their table. Gary gets up and follows them, saying to Ade, 'Give me the rubber you fat head.' Ade playfully refuses. Gary goes on taunting Ade in a teasing tone, 'Just give me the rubber before I bang your face in.' Changing tack, Gary adopts the Jamaican accent that he has been trying to perfect, 'Hey! Rasta!' Mark calls across the class to Nathaniel, taunting him, adopting a mock fighting posture, 'Nat, Nat, just watch out right!' Kevin responds sarcastically, doubting Mark's credibility, 'Oh right Mark!' and Daniel joins in the teasing, 'Nat, he's gonna stab ya.' Daniel then turns on Kevin – one of the imaginative boys – who has taken the risk of making his presence felt and asks him accusingly, 'Do you believe in Santa Claus?' Kevin ignores him. Daniel then attempts to get Gary's attention out of having teased Kevin, 'Gary, I just asked Kevin if he believes in Santa Claus and he just stared back at me.' Gary responds, 'Yeah course he does, that's why he puts his milk out and prays, "Please Santa."'

Gary continues to taunt Ade, posturing and making mock fight challenges. Then he turns to Kevin and says disdainfully, 'Get a life.' Kevin retaliates quietly, under his breath, 'I've got a life' but he continues to focus on his work, keeping his head down. Ade approaches Gary's table again, 'Give me the rubber!' Gary replies, teasing Ade still, 'Go away dog! Don't start boy!' Ade walks away, swearing under his breath. Gary flicks the numeracy task paper and declares, 'I'm not doing it anymore.' Daniel leans back on his chair and Gary turns on Anthony, 'You're a baby man, you even cuss babyish.' He then turns to Nathaniel, trying to provoke him, and says, 'Anthony said you know a slut and it's your mum.' But at that moment Gary and Daniel are suddenly distracted by Martin – an overweight boy who is most often the victim of all the disruptive boys' assaults – who is making loud sheep noises on the other side of the classroom. Astounded, Gary joins in even more loudly and he and Daniel collapse into giggles. Nathaniel, meanwhile, is still trying to concentrate on his work. Gary picks up some pencils and starts to throw them across the room at other boys. Kevin, sensing the ensuing chaos, says calmly, 'Where's that man, Chris?'Gary states matter of factly, 'Ronnie Kray? He's a legend,' and then resumes throwing pencils across the classroom, which finally descends into chaos: Victor, who is good at gymnastics, is doing a handstand in the book corner. Anthony and Kevin get up and leave the table; trying to avoid the trouble, they attempt to join a different table, but Rochelle, the classroom assistant sends them back.

Suddenly, Obi, who is the latest contender in the disruptive boys' peer group and most recent addition to the class from Nigeria, is up out of his seat and fighting with Victor. Obi looks more like a boy of thirteen or fourteen years old rather than ten or nearly eleven and he is physically intimidating; violently he pushes, shoves and attempts to punch Victor and as they tussle, they bump into other children, tables and chairs, causing mayhem around them as they fall fighting to the floor. Astonishingly, Nathaniel is still trying to complete the numeracy task.

After play time, during literacy hour, a similar chaos ensues: Gary gets up, and, without permission, leaves the classroom. He climbs up on the gym equipment which is stacked outside the classroom and he bangs on the windows at the top so that everyone can see him through the glass. Ade and some other boys immediately run out to join him. Chris sends someone to get Mara, the head teacher. Gary and the other boys run off to hide somewhere in the school and Mara comes back into the classroom. She reprimands the children about their behaviour and threatens to tell their parents; she then tells the boys that football club has been cancelled because of their misbehaviour. Mara explains to the other children that Gary is going to be sent home and she leaves the class again.

No wonder, then, that when the boys discuss amongst themselves who is the ruler of the school, Obi dismisses Mara outright. I listen to them arguing about which of them rules the school and Gary tries to dismiss Obi's desire to be a contender for leadership by saying, 'The thing about you, Obi, yeah, is you're tough, but you ain't really got any friends.' Being the ruler at Tenter Ground, then, is not just about being the toughest boy; it is about using toughness as one means to integrate a group of boys within a hierarchy of fraternity. That is why so much good-humoured teasing precedes the fighting and why the fighting is often, but not always, more about a display of bravado than it is about actual bodily harm. The boys make trouble and, in so doing, they fight their friendship into existence; for them it can become fun, whilst for others the disruptive boys' enjoyment may become a continuous source of stress to be endured. When I ask Obi why he keeps picking on other boys in the classroom, he turns to me and smiles; in his thick Nigerian accent he explains, 'It's sweet for me – like honey.'

Commonality and Conflict

Whilst Gary emphasizes toughness, adult computer game competence and knowledge of other, specifically adult-like and male concerns in his peer group, he excludes babyish, child-like, weak, soft, girl-like, cartoon and dinosaur-loving boys like Anthony. As for Anthony, he has no desire to be like Gary, or to be part of his group, and he is able, therefore, to effectively tolerate and ignore Gary's continuous and aggressive character assassination. He is physically submissive in the face of Gary's antagonizing antics, but his persistent affirmation of the kind of things that he is preoccupied with and the world which he enjoys, is an effective form of resistance. Not seeking to be a contender in Gary's pecking order of toughness, Anthony rarely comes to physical blows with Gary; each is the antithesis to the other of what it means to be a ten-year-old boy.[12]

Observing the way that boys' peer groups are formed at school, I begin to appreciate how, within any friendship group, the structure of social relations emerges with respect to twin processes of participation: both commonality and conflict are implied. Gary's friends have things in common but they are also competing, within this concern that they share, for toughness in fights or skill in football, to be the toughest and the best. They compete against each other, but only within the parameters of their shared preoccupation. Because a balance is constantly being struck, in any peer group, between these processes of commonality and conflict, there is inevitably a degree of tension. The boys' ability to manage this tension determines the extent to which they can remain friends, continue competing for equality against each other and not fall out irrevocably, for example over fights that have gone too far.

At the same time, depending on the specific form of participation that is required within each group, boundaries are continuously negotiated on the basis of who can and who cannot be included. There is, therefore, conflict arising within the group, over the competition for equal competence in relation to the specific form of participation required and, from the inside out, there is also conflict with those who are excluded from belonging to the group. This conflict with outsiders then becomes another thing that group members have in common. These boundaries, formed against those who cannot belong, can be quite fluid and open, or otherwise they can be ruthlessly defended and breached only by physical assertion, such as when a new boy at school, like Obi, proves himself to be a good fighter and therefore to be a potential contender for leadership among the disruptive boys.

Situated-ness

So what does this detailed case study help us to understand? Friendship, in this case, seems to be based on spontaneous relations of admiration rather than affection as some writers, such as Carrier (1999), have suggested. Admiration derives from the discovery of a mutual, but potentially fiercely rivalrous interest in and/or ability with respect to specific bodily and object-centred competencies, such as football, fighting and disrupting the authority of the teachers in classroom and school. This leads me to suggest that friendship here is founded on relations of competitive equality in which each competing party (not necessarily in a dyadic relation) of two or more people struggles to be equally as good at, if not better than, his rivals in a particular activity which often requires highly specific skills. Whether this potential for friendship becomes consolidated depends, however, not only on each party's ability to manage the emotional complication created by the on-going, creative tension between hierarchy and equality, friendship and rivalry, but also on an intersection of admiration across several spheres of competence. Inseparable from this competence is the capacity to thoroughly enjoy the intensity of such relations so that, in the end, it is clear to all that making friends in this way can, for the select few, be fun. Therein lays the particular attraction of friendship for these kinds of boys.

Spontaneous admiration may, in time, lead to relations of mutual support and trust but I hesitate to confirm that affection lies at the heart of friendship because the relations between Gary and his cohorts is often so fiercely rivalrous that it has a self-destructive quality; this is true of many of the 'gangs' of boys who play out on Bermondsey's streets. There appears, therefore, to be an additional tension in friendship relations – and I cannot say whether this is peculiar to boys' friendships or not – between balancing forces of creativity and destruction. Paradoxically, competition between friends can take a potlatch-like form in which boys and young men who are friends can be seen to compete against each other to destroy themselves and each other. In the game of 'Roast Chicken', for example, a group of friends as young as eight years old gets inside an abandoned car, sets it on fire and sees who dares to be the last to get out. This kind of phenomenon, where the meaning of friendship is made through violence and a flirtation with self-destruction, raises important questions about how far an anthropology of friendship can move, beyond assumptions of amity and intimacy, towards a more rigorous methodology with respect to the study of affect which is at the heart of the matter.

The second point I want to make about friendship based on Gary's case study is that Gary – just like Anthony, but with an entirely different definition of what counts as competence – brings himself into being, on a continuous basis, in relation to the question of who he can become relative to his friends. In other words Gary is always, and I would say inevitably, as Anthony is too, constituting his idea of himself in social relations (see Course's contribution to this volume for a similar discussion of how for the Mapuche, male personhood is achieved in the sociality of exchange between friends as drinking partners). As Gary continues to fight his friendships with Ade, Nathaniel, Daniel and other tough boys, like Victor, into existence on a daily, indeed hourly basis, he ruthlessly excludes those other boys who try to contend for a position in the group or those boys who are exactly the kind of boys he despises – weak and submissive, childish and uninteresting boys, like Anthony, whom Gary likens to girls. As Gary constitutes his developing sense of his own masculinity – his idea of who he can be in relation to others – he is, therefore, simultaneously defining who he is not and has no intention of becoming. For Anthony and other boys like him, their consolation for having to constantly withstand Gary's dominance is that they are reasonably certain that his antics will lead him to nothing but trouble in future. There is a reason, then, not to follow him and to feel glad not to be part of his troublesome group of friends.

At the same time as all of these complicated processes are going on within and between the various peer groups at school in which the differences between kinds of boys and between boys and girls are constituted, Gary is also able to defy teachers' expectations about whom it is good for a boy to become and he is defiant in this respect. In this light friendship can be seen to be a force of resistance in which those competing for equality within specific domains create a sense of self-value that might be entirely at odds with the hierarchical constraint of other kinds of expectations. Insofar as Gary continues to rule the school he is successful in his guerrilla warfare and it continues to be a battle for boys, like Nathaniel, to negotiate what it means to become a working-class boy and do well at school.

The point I want to emphasize in all this is that Gary is, with respect to his friendships at school, completely 'embedded'. He is working out his social position vis-à-vis others and he is 'situated' in those relations. It makes little sense, therefore, to describe him as an individual, as, in any simple way, the author of his own existence. Gary cannot know who he is without this process of making sense of other people's ideas of who he can be, and the same is true for all the children, all the time. Friendship is, therefore, a learning phenomenon and it is never accomplished; it is an on-going process. In relation to the structural dynamics of his friendships with other boys and his defiance of the figures of authority in school, Gary brings himself into being, as a particular kind of working-class boy, via an alternative economy of becoming. In so doing, he prepares himself for a specific kind of manhood in which failing at school is a prerequisite for developing a tough reputation on the street.

This continuous social process of making sense, from one situation to another, either acquiescing to or resisting the constraints on whom it is possible for any person to be, is what being situated is all about and it is, I suggest, what all humans everywhere are going through all the time. In other words situated-ness is a primary condition of human being. This means that contrary to conventional ideas about the so-called autonomy of the modern Western person, all persons, whether they are Melanesian, Western European or otherwise are subject to similar processes of inter-subjective learning/development in child and adulthood (Toren 1999). What we require, then, to understand how persons like Bermondsey *bods* come to be both collectively distinctive and uniquely particular is a theory of the situation and this, I suggest, requires a rigorous theory of learning and a model of ethnographic fieldwork in which comparison across situation – in this case home, neighbourhood and school – becomes possible.[13]

So rather than thinking about human relations in terms of a dichotomy between those societies characterized by situated persons engaged in personalized relations of exchange and those typified by autonomous individuals participating in the impersonalized relations of the market (Carrier 1999), we might more usefully think of a continuum of situated-ness. Course (this volume) contests the idea that the notion of the person as an individual is a singularly Western phenomenon. His notion of the 'relational individual' and mine about a 'continuum of situated-ness' force us to clarify exactly what is meant by individuality. Course's focus on the construction of personal biography and on self-narrative is productive, directing attention ethnographically to the mechanisms through which the inevitability of thorough going sociality is backgrounded in favour of a foregrounding of self-production. In the Western case, this would be a fascinating line of enquiry. Along this continuum it becomes clear that, due to particular historical circumstances, some people have more choice than others, both within any one society and when comparing one society with another, about whom they are able to bring themselves into being in relation to.

The more choice any person has about who to fraternize with, the more likely they are, as Carrier points out, to talk of the importance of friendship. What becomes clear, when there is a high degree of choice,[14] is that of all the people one encounters, at school for example, only a select few will become one's friends. It is this unpredictability, evident throughout other papers in this volume as well, that, in part, makes friendship a most interesting phenomenon. It is a mistake, however, to imagine that friendship can be defined as always being a spontaneous and unconstrained dyadic relation of affection (separated from other ties in the world) which is characterized by exchange without obligation between persons equally free to choose whom they associate with. In the next part of the chapter I go beyond the focus on what is specific about inter-subjective relations among boys in the classroom at Tenter Ground School and examine the critical significance of objects in the formation of the boys' friendships.

16 December 1999: Pikachu

The disruptive boys' reluctance to be 'good' at school raises the problem of my own participation. I am careful not to involve myself in the classroom in a way that renders me like a teacher or her assistant and yet I am obviously not a child either. For the first three months I am largely an adult person who observes and makes notes. I do not challenge bad behaviour or tell on children to the teacher and it is easy, therefore, for the children to ignore me if they choose to do so. In particular I struggle to find a legitimate periphery from which to get to know the disruptive boys better. For obvious reasons I cannot participate in the pecking order of disruption, which dominates social relations in the classroom, and I cannot fight or play football, which are the boys' main preoccupations in the playground. I am, therefore, a marginal and largely irrelevant person to them. All of this changes, however, on a single day in December. Just before the children break up from school for the Christmas holidays, my status in the classroom transforms dramatically.

The children have endured a week of inspections in which they have been expected to be on their best behaviour. Christine is proud of them because they have tried really hard and she takes this effort as a sign of their regard for her; the children knew that it was important to Christine that they behave well and work hard during the inspection. She laments the fact that the inspector did not get to see any personality in the children, but at least disruption was minimized, so Christine is pleased. The good news is that the school has not been demoted from 'serious weaknesses' to 'special measures', but it remains a school with serious problems and the stress that an inspection creates has taken its toll. As a reward for good behaviour Christine suspends formal learning for the whole day and declares that the children are first going to do fun tasks followed by free time in which they can choose what they want to do. The children are excited and in jubilant mood.

In the morning the children begin by helping to make the backdrop for the infant classes' Christmas nativity; they work at their numeracy tables in small groups. I join the table where Gary, Anthony, Kevin, Nathaniel and Daniel are sitting. The task is to draw stars on card and to cut out the best one to make a stencil. This stencil is then to be used to make lots of stars from silver paper. The boys are dissatisfied with the wonky stars they have drawn and I show them how to make more uniform ones using two regular triangles. Anthony, who is the most competent artist at the table, is not interested in my assistance since he is taking great pleasure in making his stars as irregular as possible; their lack of uniformity delights him. Gary, seeing the stars that Daniel and Nathaniel have managed to make with the stencil I made for them, reluctantly accepts a stencil from me for himself and we all begin to make silver stars together.

Every now and again I write a couple of notes down on my pad. Suddenly Gary turns to me and, engaging me for the first time, asks inquisitively, 'D'you 'ave to write everythin' that we do down?' and I respond, 'No, I just try to write down as much as possible that I think is interesting about the way that children learn.' Later, Gary points to my notes and says to Nathaniel, as if he is feeling left out, 'She never writes anythin' 'bout me in that book.' I turn the book towards him and show him where his name is: 'Look, your name is written down there more than anyone.' Seeing that it is true, Gary asks, 'Why?' and I tease him saying, 'Because you do the most talking, that's why.' Gary smirks and concentrates on his stars again, happily singing the lyrics to the latest chart-topping songs as he works.

Anthony works quietly on his own, every now and again directing conversation towards his friend Kevin. During the star-making activity, as with any task in the classroom, there is constant comparison between the boys of how each of them is coping with the task and a running commentary on the various conversational exchanges that take place between them. Nathaniel, who is pleased with the stars he is making, addresses me for the first time in three months by my first name. I am surprised to hear my name after having been ignored by the boys for so long and I am pleased that the relaxation of formal learning has allowed the terms of engagement between myself and the boys to shift, if only slightly. Gary, noticing these signs of developing familiarity, looks up from the star he is making and scrutinizes me, staring closely. I ignore him, continue making stars and wonder whether he is feeling encouraged or threatened by these signs of budding intimacy between himself, other children and me.

As we work, Kevin and Anthony begin talking about Pokemon. Kevin brings out of his pocket a small poster with about thirty cartoon characters that I have never seen before, drawn on one side. On the other side a single character – Pikachu – takes up the whole page.

I ask the boys who these characters are and they introduce me to Pokemon. These are creatures they have become familiar with through watching television cartoon programmes on Friday afternoons and Saturday mornings.[15] Abruptly Gary interrupts, changing the subject and attempting to engage me again on his terms; he asks, ''ave you got a car?' I let him know that I have and he asks me what kind. 'A Mercedes',[16] I tell him and he's impressed, 'Rah [wow],' he says, and this sparks off a conversation amongst the boys about what cars they like and what cars their dads have got. Anthony, bringing the conversation back to himself again, then tells Kevin about his birthday, which was the day before and he lists some of the things he received as gifts. He speaks proudly about the ten-pound note he was given and tells Kevin that he's going to buy two Pokemon toys with it. He lifts up his school shirt to show Kevin his Darth Maul[17] Star Wars T-shirt that he is wearing underneath his uniform. Kevin admires it and Anthony goes on to talk about the Action Man[18] things he received. Daniel intervenes then, saying disparagingly, 'Hello, which planet d' you come from if you still like Action Man?' Gary joins in and starts teasing Anthony about how childish he is because he is also still 'into dinosaurs'.

Noticing this differentiation, that Gary and Daniel emphasize, between the kind of things Anthony is passionate about and the things they like to discuss, such as cars, I come to Anthony's aid. Distancing myself from Gary's disparaging remarks, I ask Anthony if he has been watching the 'Walking with Dinosaurs' series on television and he has, so we talk about the awesome sea dinosaur that it features. Losing interest and probably disgruntled because I resisted the humiliation of Anthony that he and Daniel were trying to effect, Gary gets up and leaves the table. He joins some other boys who are now playing board games in the book corner.

Having engaged the boys for the first time about things that have nothing to do with schoolwork, I realize that the problem I face in the classroom is one of how to interact with Gary, as one among the more dominant boys in the class, without having to participate in what he does to gain influence which, in part, involves intimidating and antagonizing other, apparently weaker boys, like Anthony. Some boys, like Daniel for example, face the same difficulty and, in trying to impress Gary, they often participate in intimidating and antagonizing behaviour which then gets them into a lot of trouble. Witnessing the constant challenges Gary makes to boys whom he perceives to be either a threat to his dominance or to be weaker and more childish than he is, I resist the temptation to protect the weak child and to antagonize the bully. This is the route that many members of staff have taken with Gary but I am not here in the school to discipline children, but rather to understand how social relations between them are formed in the classroom and school. Of course I am continuously pushed against my own ideas of what constitutes acceptable behaviour in children and it is difficult to observe disruptive boys without becoming infuriated. I note the ways in which Gary attempts, on a daily basis, to wield his influence in the classroom and also how other children, like Anthony for example, skilfully resist this influence. What emerges is a constant state of flux: the various peer groups are seen to be in a constant process of formation and transformation, from moment to moment and over time. The problem for me is how to participate in these complex relations in a way that takes me beyond the more passive observations of the past three months.

As Christine approaches our table Daniel tries to tell on Gary because he abandoned the task and went to play games. Daniel does not dare, as Gary does, to do as he pleases in class, so he is disgruntled. Coming to Gary's defence, Christine tells Daniel that Gary probably got bored with making stars. She instructs them all to finish the star they're making and then to choose what they want to do. Daniel quickly finishes his star and then goes to join Gary and the other boys in the book corner. Kevin and Anthony ask Christine if they can stay at the table to do some drawing and when she agrees, I stay with them. Martin joins us and sits next to Kevin. I decide to do some drawing too. I ask Kevin if I can borrow his Pokemon poster. He agrees happily and, using a black felt tip pen on A4 white paper, I start to copy Pikachu. After a few seconds I realize that Anthony is staring at me. Focusing intently and with complete surprise on my drawing, which is an almost exact replica of Pikachu, Anthony pulls Kevin by the arm and tells him to look at what I am doing. Within seconds all the boys have been alerted to my achievement. Suddenly the table is crowded with boys who are praising my drawing, 'That's bad man [excellent],' 'Rah man, that's bad,' 'She's a good drawer man,' 'Can you do one for me?' 'Can you do one for me?'

Realizing, with amazement, what a stir I have caused with my Pikachu drawing I stay calm, as if it is nothing, and say, 'This one is for Kevin, but I could photocopy it for other people.' Suddenly and without warning the Pikachu drawing is hot property, everyone wants a copy, and for the first time this means that I am the focus of the boys' attention. When Anthony sees the reaction from all the boys he teases Daniel, 'I thought you said Pokemon was borin'' and now you're carryin' on like they're bad.' Unwittingly, and to Anthony's surprise, I have created something that is of specific significance to all the boys, not just to Kevin and Anthony's imaginative and creative friends; I am as surprised as Anthony is by the immediacy of the social effect my creation has.

Subjects and Objects: Popularity and Friendship

What is astounding about this moment during my fieldwork is how much it reveals theoretically: objects are obviously crucial to the way that social relations among children (and, indeed, adults) are both formed and transformed. Because of what I demonstrated that I could do and am able to produce: something that matters to the boys – this object, a drawing of Pikachu, and a specific form of physical competence, being good at drawing – I become for them, in a single transforming instant, a person of significance. This is not a note in my fieldwork diary, about which they could not care less; this is a drawing of Pikachu about which they care a great deal.

I understand, then, how the objects which children attend to (as well as the physical competency that relating to the object requires) become the bridges over and through which they encounter and make sense of each other in particular ways. This means that if we are to understand children's social relations we have to find out, in any situation, which specific objects and practices mediate peer group formation. It is an understanding of the specificity of those objects and practices that gives us the key to discovering not only the significance of peer group relations to children but also how they are transformed over time. What is particularly interesting about this observation is that it enables an analysis of how, in the process of learning how to participate appropriately, children are coming to appreciate how the value of subjects and objects becomes mutually specified, created and transformed in social practice over time. For example, I found, quite by accident, a way to participate that makes a difference to the boys and which makes me, therefore, instantaneously a person of value and, thereby, a person worthy of incorporation into the various friendship groups.[19]

The Pikachu moment is therefore significant in that it marks the point at which the bind of formal learning is removed in order to allow the terms of participation, for me and the boys, to change dramatically. In this case, quite by accident, the freedom of choice allows for the potential of friendship to spontaneously emerge. Suddenly the boys are all calling my name, asking each other if I am an artist, and dominant boys, who up until now have been physically removed and reluctant to engage me, push closer. They shove other boys out of the way so they can sit next to me at the table and watch me draw. Even Mark, Ade's sidekick, who never speaks to me and is often silent and withdrawn in the classroom, asks me quietly and politely if I will make a copy of the drawing for him. I experience directly what I have already begun to appreciate from observation alone: popularity and indeed friendship among children is predicated on a shared and finely differentiated physical mastery towards objects of specific significance. It is children's bodily competence in relation to specific objects in certain environments that marks the difference between them. For me, it was not because I could draw really well that I became popular, but because I could produce something of value to all the boys – Pokemon drawings. It is the specificity of the object and the competence associated with its production that counts.

This is what situated-ness is all about: in each situation, which has its own structural, spatial and temporal constraints, an economy of value is being constituted through particular kinds of exchange and physical competencies in relation to which each person must make sense of their position vis-à-vis others. What makes this even more complicated is the fact that what is expected of any person in one situation may vary considerably in another.[20] This does not necessarily mean, as has been suggested (Carrier 1999), that no stable or unified self endures from situation to situation; to assert this, I suggest, is to undermine the phenomenal plasticity of human learning in which, from birth, what one learns in one situation is inevitably accommodated to what one has learnt in another. Out of these continuous accommodations, a position of relative equilibrium is reached over time (Piaget 1971).

The Emotional Significance of Social Transformation

By focusing on processes of learning, I have been able to make an in-depth analysis of how boys like Gary come to develop an appropriately masculine and oppositional bodily disposition, one that adequately prepares them for the rigours of a particular kind of working-class, or indeed 'under-class', life on the street. I understand this social process of development to be an on-going evaluation, which is worked out in practice and which depends on emotional reasoning about the value – the goodness or rightness – of what participation and increasing incorporation into a group of friends feels like and is worth. It is important to remember that every specifically structured form of participation, such as fighting, implies an ethic, which is a continuously emerging understanding about what it is good, and by implication bad, for people to do and through doing, to become. In this on-going appraisal, which I describe as the constant feeling of what it is like either to desire to do or not to do what others consider appropriate in order to belong, knowledge and emotion are inseparably related through complex processes of learning (Furth 1987; Damasio 1995).

> Startled by the dramatic change in my popularity, I promise the boys that I will try to photocopy the drawing at lunchtime. I make my way to Eileen's office to ask for permission to use the photocopier, but I am wary because I worry that she might refuse my request since it has nothing to do with schoolwork. Keenly aware that the seal, which formal learning places on children's interests outside school, is now punctured, I worry that it will be me now who is perceived by the teachers as being disruptive. Outside the office I find a gaggle of boys waiting for me. Persistent and not to be put off, they ask if I have copied the picture yet. I tell them that I haven't and I knock on Eileen's door. As I go in, Ade, as if he has picked up on my reticence, follows to check and make sure that I won't let him down. I explain to Eileen that we have done some Pokemon drawings and ask her if she would mind if we photocopied them. She notices the boys crowding eagerly round the open door, smiles and gladly agrees. At her favourable

response, the boys rush into the office and crowd around the photocopier. I make twenty-four copies, one for each child in the class and I thank Eileen.

Filled with excitement now, the boys and I rush back to the classroom together and I feel, for the first time, the thrill of the camaraderie that competitive access to a difficult peer group grants me. I understand then that this is part of what friendship is all about: the reward of the social process of learning how to participate effectively, in any situation, is the change in one's feelings as one's sense of value in relation to others transforms. Reaching the classroom and having to settle down again for the register, I begin to appreciate how irksome is the restraint that classroom participation places on other kinds of interaction between children. Exchanging excited glances and gestures, the boys are eager to get their photocopies and find it difficult to concentrate on afternoon registration. Having taken the register and sensing the excitement, Christine allows us to go on drawing in the classroom. Boys rush to sit next to me at the table and I give out photocopies to the sea of hands; the girls, seeing that something is being given out, become interested for the first time and take their copies gladly.

Immediately the boys differentiate between the value of the original drawing and the photocopies. The original becomes the hottest property and I give it to Kevin because he let me copy his poster. Christine asks us if we would mind moving to the library (adjacent to the classroom) because she needs to get some children that she can trust to continue to work quietly, in the classroom, on the large backdrops for the nativity. She leaves Rochelle in charge and joins me to supervise the disruptive boys in the library. She is amazed, however, to see how focused the boys are on colouring in the Pikachu drawing and quietly she asks if I would mind her leaving me to get on with it while she goes back to the classroom. Astonished myself by the change in the boys' behaviour, I agree to be responsible for them for the first time.

The competition amongst the boys to achieve something and to complete a task happily, rather than trying to disrupt it or to endeavour sulkily not to have to engage with it, makes a welcome change. The boys' smiling happy faces make all the difference. What is significant about this moment is the realization in me that these boys are indeed capable of cheerful, still and quiet concentration on a task but for it to be enjoyable it has to be a task that is meaningful to them.

As we colour in, concentrating happily, I begin to realize what Christine already knows, which is that to judge the boys on the basis of their brooding, sulky dispositions in the classroom would be to misrepresent them. Their personalities, suppressed during formal learning and in order to meet the requirements of classroom participation, emerge all of a sudden, not gradually but in a single transforming moment of significance. What is most important about the change in the boys is the difference in their emotional state and therefore their bodily disposition:

the surliness is gone. The subject is not numeracy or literacy which appear to be abstract and therefore tiresome skills for the boys to have to learn. Pokemon means something to them and they are happy to learn from me how to draw, colour in and bring to life characters from the world with which they are passionately engaged outside school. More than anything, the freedom of friendship presents particular possibilities for the creation and transformation of value – of subject, of objects and of feelings about what being human is like. We should not be surprised, then, to read Rapport's (1999) description of his informant Arthur's joy at playing dominoes with his friends and to see this described by Arthur as some of the best moments of his life.

Participation as Exchange

Focusing on the specific kind of competencies that I must acquire in order to continue to be a person of particular significance – a friend – for the boys has made me consider the exact process of how these relationships are built. Whether on the football pitch, or in a fight, drawing, or when talking about experiences with objects that they possess, such as computer games or Pokemon toys, learning how to participate effectively in the peer group always means working out what among them constitutes an appropriate relation of exchange. Exchanges can be verbal, physical, or, in terms of actual objects, such as photocopies of Pokemon drawings, they can involve a trade; it is because an on-going process of exchange is involved that the social dynamic of peer group formation is always observed, in practice, as a spatio-temporal flux. This is because the formation of friendships, as much as the making of enemies, is never achieved. It is a continuously emerging social process in a specific material environment and it depends on children's evolving understanding about how best to participate in these exchanges, which in the special case of friendship takes the form of a competition for equality.

This means, to a certain extent, that the social structure of the disruptive boys' peer group, and within it any boy's social position vis-à-vis the others, is always defined by the question of who has enough influence to define what constitutes an appropriate exchange for the group and, by implication, who is able to place a limit on the question of whom will be allowed to make those kinds of exchanges. Friendship cannot therefore be isolated from politics: friendship can easily become the grounds for a resistance movement. At school the battle between teachers and disruptive boys is all about who has the authority to decide for children what constitutes appropriate exchange relations at particular times in specific spaces. The problem is that there is a huge discrepancy between adult ideas about what constitutes a legitimate exchange for a child to be making and the kinds of exchanges which certain kinds of boys are working out amongst themselves, at school, at home and on the street. The theoretical and, indeed, methodological point to emphasize is that without exchange relations there can be no social participation, and without exchange relations humans cannot learn whom it is possible for them to become. Learning is therefore an exchange phenomenon, and a study of friendship must focus on what is characteristic about the particular kinds of exchanges that make the relative freedom of friendship so thrilling.

Notes

1. Bermondsey was once known as the larder of London because of an industry focused on foodstuffs imported via the docks from countries all over the world. A closely knit and fiercely protective community grew up around this industry and despite the closure of the docks and associated industries in the 1970s, Bermondsey people continue to feel fiercely proud about and defensive of their locality.
2. See Froerer (this volume) who explores how gender differences affect boys' increased capacity to enjoy the freedom to explore the territories they inhabit and, thereby, to extend the range of their relations and influence.
3. Nathaniel is the son of first-generation Ghanaian immigrants.
4. Both of these boys are the sons of first-generation Bangladeshi Muslim families.
5. Kevin and Anthony are both boys from families with roots in the local area: Anthony is from Bermondsey but Kevin travels to school from an estate in Walworth. Compared to Gary though, these white boys are relatively weak, more interested in drawing and imaginative play than fighting and submissive in the face of Gary's bullying antics.
6. Victor is another boy of West African origin who is a serious contender for leadership among the disruptive boys.
7. Daniel, like Gary, is a Bermondsey boy; he lives with his single father who is devoted to and protective of him.
8. This kind of self-differentiation on the basis of belonging to types of boys' peer groups at school – those who want to 'have a laff' and those, the ear 'oles', who are more determined to listen to the teacher – was described in Paul Willis' classic 1970s ethnography of working-class schooling, *Learning to Labour*. At Tenter Ground, the distinction between subversive and well-behaved boys is not clear-cut. Any number of boys might be involved in 'low-level' disruption such as chatting and 'messing about' whilst only a few will be involved in the kind of full-scale disruption caused by, for example, fighting in class.

9. The Kray twins – Ronnie and Reggie – were infamous gangsters from the East End of London who built up a criminal empire. They were probably London's most notorious gangsters during the 1960s.
10. Ade is the son of first-generation Nigerian immigrants; he has only recently joined the school and still has a thick Nigerian accent.
11. Mark is the son of second-generation Nigerian parents; like the other boys in the class of second-generation African descent, his accent is slight.
12. Schools in Britain are structured socially on the basis of age-set organization into classes. What interests me here is how boys of the same age differentiate amongst themselves into opposing friendship groups. Santos (this volume) also explains how schools bring together children from different agnatic and village groups, thereby extending the range of possible ways of building relationships. In Bermondsey the mixed age groups of friends that occupy the territory of any one local estate often come into conflict with mixed age groups from other estates. These tensions are dissipated at school where age-set organization mitigates against territorial affiliations.
13. From this point of view it becomes possible to understand that what the minority of highly disruptive boys have in common is that they are all having to make sense of a complex set of situations that could be called a particular kind of working-class background. In practice, this means that they may be likely to have home lives that are disrupted for various reasons, attend failing schools and be working out how to survive on 'mean' streets. This kind of background differentiates a boy, like Gary, who is said to have a chaotic home life, an older brother with a tough street reputation and relatively unlimited spending power, from a boy like Anthony, who is growing up in a working-class family, but a different kind, where he is not allowed to play out, is protected from the street by his 'aspirational' mother and her capacity to care for him is not disrupted by the struggles of working-class life.
14. The more choices any person has about who they can become, the more likely they are to be engaged in explicitly representing those choices and their outcomes to themselves and others in discourses of 'identity-formation'. In this way a person becomes valued in relation to the continuous assessment of choices made, which foregrounds and makes of choice a fetish – a thing that somehow conceals the relations of its own production – relative to what is forced into the background, which is the taken-for-granted worth of constrained embedded-ness (in kin relations, for example) in which there is far less choice about how to be and become one's self. It is important to understand, however, that by choice I do not mean to imply a complete freedom – in any situation – for any person to do as they please, but rather a complex process through which a person – in any situation – makes sense of who she or he can be in relation to both the social constraints of the present moment and the embodied history of whom she or he has been in the past.
15. Pokemon was originally an electronic computer game on the Nintendo Game Boy hand-held computer games console developed in Japan, but most of the boys at Tenter Ground heard of it through watching television. Part of the extraordinary success of Pokemon is due to the exploitation of multi-media

international marketing opportunities; most of the children's parents subscribe either to satellite or cable as well as terrestrial television systems.

16. Laughing to myself, I do not mention the fact that my Mercedes is twenty years old and cannot go faster than twenty miles per hour uphill.

17. Darth Maul is a (Jedi) knight; he fights on behalf of the dark side (evil) in the Star Wars movie called Phantom Menace.

18. Action Man is an action figure designed for boys' play; it is the equivalent in boys' affections to what Barbie is for girls.

19. After having got used to being ignored by Gary for months on end I am unnerved when, in time, he begins to hail me out as his 'spee'. On the first occasion, not having heard the term before and later learning that it is a Jamaican patois term, I ask Gary what it means and he tells me: 'best friend'. Although hard-won, my friendship with Gary did not survive the school trip at the end of term, a week away on a residential course, where I was forced, because of a staff shortage, to adopt more of a teacher-like role towards the boys. The kind of detailed data I was able to collect about children's social relations was the outcome of a very clear negotiation with school staff at the beginning of the fieldwork in which I was able to argue how important it was that I was there to observe and to participate in children's relations and not to be presented as a teacher, classroom assistant or teacher's helper.

20. Although it may seem as if the regime of value created in friendships – at school, for example – is somehow bounded and separate from other ways of creating value, such as through kin relations and the economy of the household, it is equally true to say that when making exchanges in the present, children always assess the likely impact of each others' lives outside school. It is the past history of specific kinds of participation and the influence this history has on the form that exchange relations take in the present that informs what sense we make of who we are, in relation to the idea that others have of who we can be. We are all constantly trying to make sense of our own and each other's history and we do this, moment to moment, as an evaluation of our own and one another's capacity to enter into meaningful relations of exchange.

References

Carrier, G.C. 1999. 'People Who Can Be Friends: Selves and Social Relationships', in S. Bell and S. Coleman (eds), *The Anthropology of Friendship*. Oxford: Berg.

Damasio, A. 1995. *Descartes' Error: Emotion, Reason and the Human Brain*. New York: Quill.

Evans, G. 2006a. *Educational Failure and Working Class White Children in Britain*. New York, Hampshire: Palgrave Macmillan.

———. 2006b. 'Learning, Violence and the Social Structure of Value', *Social Anthropology* 14(2): 247–59.

Furth, H.G. 1987. *Knowledge as Desire: an Essay on Freud and Piaget*. New York: Columbia University Press.

Lave, J. and E. Wenger. 1991. *Situated Learning: Legitimate Peripheral Participation.* Cambridge: Cambridge University Press.

Piaget, J. 1971. *Structuralism.* London: Routledge & Kegan Paul.

Rapport, N. 1999. 'The "Bones" of Friendship: Playing Dominoes with Arthur of an Evening in the Eagle Pub', in S. Bell and S. Coleman (eds), *The Anthropology of Friendship.* Oxford: Berg.

Toren, C. 1990. *Making Sense of Hierarchy: Cognition as Social Process in Fiji.* London: Athlone.

———. 1999. *Mind, Materiality and History: Essays in Fijian Ethnography.* New York: Routledge.

Willis, P. 1977. *Learning to Labour. Farnborough: Saxon House.*

Afterword

Making Friendship Impure: Some Reflections on a (Still) Neglected Topic

Simon Coleman

When Sandra Bell and I decided to put together an edited volume on friendship (Bell and Coleman 1999), we realized early on that the subject had a long but curiously patchy academic past. Writers in history, philosophy and the social sciences had a habit of making the obligatory reference to Aristotle's *Nicomachean Ethics* before trying to explain why the subject had not attracted sustained attention in their own discipline. In anthropology as well, the landmarks were few and far between, including perhaps Raymond Firth's 1936 tribute to Marett, 'Bond-Friendship in Tikopia', Eric Wolf's paper in an early Association of Social Anthropologists volume (Banton 1966) dealing with 'Kinship, Friendship, and Patron-Client Relations in Complex Societies', and of course Robert Paine's work on middle-class friendship in the late 1960s and early 1970s, where among other things Paine complained that anthropologists lived lives dominated by friendship but instead wrote about kinship (1969: 505).

Sandra and I had tried to open up the topic again in the late 1990s by providing a comparative approach, incorporating but also taking the topic away from its frequent association with the West, or at least asking whether that was a possibility. But when I was asked to reflect on the contributions to this volume I realized that I had fallen into my own trap: after that volume I had not really written anything on friendship at all, with the exception of a passage in a paper on dealing with the methodological implications of having Pentecostal informants as both friends and informants (Coleman 2006).

So I start by pleading guilty to a charge of neglect. But in my defence let me say that putting together the introduction to *The Anthropology of Friendship* was one of the hardest pieces of writing I have done so far, and it was one I was never particularly satisfied with. Part of the problem was hunting around for a decent amount of comparative ethnographic material, other than what could be gleaned, often implicitly, from works ostensibly on other topics. Or, to put it another way, a topic that was itself so often about the apparently non-institutional was itself non-institutionalized within the discipline, and so finding a vocabulary and a set of at least potentially coherent theoretical concerns was not easy. Graham Allan has indeed satirized the difficulties and advantages of using friendship as an analytical term by suggesting and then emphatically rejecting what he presents as its alternative (2001: 583), expressed as 'informal, non-institutionalized personal solidarities'.

All of that is by way of a preface to the fact that I welcome Desai and Killick's initiative in focusing us again on friendship. I still think that the topic is important and neglected – possibly more important now than ever within a discipline concerned with examining constantly shifting grounds of sociality. In the following I want to begin by reflecting on the status of the anthropology of friendship before moving on to making some specific comments on the chapters themselves. So what of the status – and, one might say, fate – of the anthropology of friendship so far? For argument's sake I am going to suggest that we can discern at least three, interrelated fates during the halting history of the topic.

Fate Number One: Looking *Through* Friendship

This outcome can be explained very briefly. In an essay on the Kuria, Malcolm Ruel draws on his teacher F.R. Leavis to make a distinction between looking at categories and looking through them. The former, objectivist position – 'looking at' – contrasts with the more phenomenological approach of the latter – 'looking through'. But as Ruel says, in reflecting on our own perceptions as anthropologists (1997: 239), 'the problem … is making visible what one so easily looks through'. Applying this warning to the topic at hand, one danger is an over-confident assumption that we can form mutually comprehensible bonds of friendship in the field as a means of gathering data, of unravelling the mysteries of such well-established topics as, say, kinship or ritual. Friendship in its apparent ubiquity can be taken for granted as a methodological lens, a tool *through* which we gain 'in depth' information about the worlds we study. It might only really make its presence felt in the cultural disjunctions that sometimes cause us to re-examine the character of the relationships on which our fieldwork depends. Thus in her work on Pentecostal women preachers in Missouri, Elaine Lawless (1992) has talked of the political and epistemological problems of becoming a close friend of a woman who is also a source of deep frustration to her, as social proximity combines with unsettling ideological distance. Whenever Lawless's long-suffering but devout friend Anna refers to 'God giving her strength' to withstand illness, Lawless finds herself guiltily wanting simply to ignore this conclusion, wanting openly to insist that the strength should be seen as coming from Anna herself. Or, more dramatically, in an essay called 'The Intimacy of Violence' (2006), Begona Aretxaga explores her shock at realizing that a friend/informant in the field is committing acts of terrorism. On such occasions our feelings of epistemological and social access, our confidence in our ability knowingly to look at and through indigenous categories by gaining proximity to informants as friends, may and indeed should be challenged.

Fate Number Two: *Relegating* Friendship to a Residual Status

What I mean by 'relegation' is the tendency to see friendship purely as an institutionalized non-institution, for instance the informal negative to kinship's formal positive. More broadly, this point raises the question of whether friendship is to be seen as a set of activities, sentiments and attitudes that take their particular character in any given cultural context from whichever structural conditions they are opposing. In the introduction to our book (1999: 16) Sandra Bell and I actually referred to our desire 'to locate and analyse the social space that exists once such factors as kinship, territory and fixed hierarchies have been accounted for', as part of a wider exploration of constraint and voluntarism in the formation of social relations. I still think there is something in this observation (or aspiration), but of course if taken to an extreme it can present friendship as a blank or at least infinitely malleable social space, and one that cannot be compared cross-culturally in any particularly meaningful way.

I think it also runs the danger of leaving the still functionalist assumptions behind much of ethnography untouched, allowing friendship to remain a very faint ghost in a much more powerful machine constituted by the social structures we have been accustomed to examine. In fact, one of the antidotes to such an approach came from Mario Aguilar's chapter in the Bell and Coleman volume, where he showed (1999: 170ff) how kinship, friendship and cultural diversification could be seen as complementary notions within the ideological construction of contemporary pastoralism amongst the Boorana. Aguilar's piece about friendship was also therefore concerned with tracing the expansion of the post-colonialist pastoralist world into new social landscapes, such as urban and educational centres, and indeed with the attempt to create transnational friendships that played on transcending spatial delimitations of culture and the language of kinship. Friendship in these terms could be seen as adopting a far from residual role in reconstituting social relations, in a way that I think is paralleled by some of the contributions to this book, such as those of Froerer and Course.

Fate Number Three: 'Purifying' Friendship Out of Existence

Parallel to the idea of friendship as non-institution is a depiction of friendship that has proved highly influential in Western discourse and analysis, and it is one that has at least presented friendship as containing positive characteristics rather than merely existing as a kind of reverse parasite in relation to other social roles. In Sandra's and my book it is represented initially by James Carrier's piece on 'People Who Can be Friends', which adopts a deliberately polemical and uncompromising – one might say 'purist' – stance in arguing that friendship involves a mode of thought about affective relationships that requires a notion of the self as autonomous person (see also Allan 2001: 582). Spontaneous and unconstrained sentiment are said to emerge from the notionally free and independent actors of modern, Western, liberal thought. This approach has various roots and resonances. The attempt to remove utility from the picture does indeed recall Aristotle's notion of perfect friendship as justified in and for its own sake. And, as Carrier points out, it also invites rich comparison with the notion of the gift and Parry's (1986) claim that altruistic giver and morally autonomous friend are products of the same ideological perspective, according to which purity of purpose and spontaneity can be contrasted with assumptions of the marketplace (see also Killick and Desai's comments in their introduction). We might also point to parallel developments in ideas of sincerity that depended on the conviction that transparency of thought and motive could be articulated in public and private spheres in eighteenth- and nineteenth-century Europe (e.g. Keane 2002). The general point is that freely chosen relationships could be seen as reflecting the new universalism emerging in civil society – a society that required the presence of 'authentically indifferent' and free co-citizens (Pahl 2000: 57). Paine's work takes the idea of freedom further by arguing that, in idealized Western friendship (1999: 41), the very rules of relevancy as to what is permissible and/or desirable are remarkably implicit, appearing not to be imposed from the outside, and largely hidden from view to all outside the relationship.

Reciprocity itself should appear uncalculating and without compulsion in unique processes of mutual verification.

If Carrier's and Paine's pieces are about friendship as a relationship rooted in a certain, purified vision of modernity (Allan 2001: 582), we can also see how such ideals parallel Pitt-Rivers's point, criticized by some contributors to the present volume, that sentiment among friends is socially unconfined and therefore socially unimportant. They also perhaps explain why there has been such a vast literature on friendship phrased in terms of emotional or psychological processes, rather than in more social terms, thus reflecting Western middle-class notions of friendship as private and personal (Reed-Danahay 1999: 137). If friendship is to be so pure it is not surprising it is so residual in the ethnographic record. But we should also remember that Carrier (1999: 31) in effect goes on to accuse himself of a kind of Occidentalism, an over-simplification and stylization of Western society and selves that, for instance, fails to examine issues of gender and class in constructing the ideal of the autonomous, post-Romantic actor and friend.

So what I think Carrier is doing is luring us initially into looking *through*, before looking *at*, the classic Western, purified category of friendship, showing its utility but then going on to expose its deep limitations. His position surely prepares the ground for appreciating the challenge of this volume, which is to provide ethnographically deeply rooted presentations of friendship and amity, and to do so in a way that challenges the Occidentalism that Carrier describes. Thus the chapters look at how 'friendship' relates to issues of space, age, gender, selfhood, mutual understanding, aggression, wider networks and institutions and so on in ways that have the potential to bring to friendship the attention that I am still convinced it deserves.

Friendship: An Alternative Destiny?

In reflecting on what the contributors to this volume have achieved, I want to begin by going back to Pitt-Rivers' image of friendship as private and of no social significance, or the idea of it as an opt-out from society – both forms of what I would see as purificationist rhetoric. One of the messages that emerges very strongly from contributors is an emphasis on friendship often on the borders, crossing boundaries, perhaps indeed associated with an ideology of free social space – but of great social significance precisely because of, not despite, its cross-cutting or interstitial location. Thus Peggy Froerer explores voluntary ties in India that have their own cultural character and impact beyond and across ties of blood and heredity, including of course caste, while, in the same sub-continent, Amit Desai explores the ways in which ritual friendship can be opposed or alternative to ideologies of caste and brotherhood, transcending class positions; and in both contexts we see how such ties can also bring families together.

Other work explores the cross-cutting role of friendship in disrupted, fragmenting social contexts, or contexts that informants present as disrupted. Graeme Rodgers focuses explicitly on the ambiguities of friendship in relation to Mozambican settlement in South Africa, as profound social and spatial changes not only place strains on older ties but also prompt new possibilities for friendships, and moreover ones that develop beyond the logic of kinship. Thus he reveals one of the ambiguous characteristics of friendship, as both social glue and social solvent. In Evan Killick's piece the social and economic spaces traversed are perhaps more benign in the short term but again here we see friendship crossing social domains, even incorporating different understandings of the nature of the relationship, as the category of *ayompari*, for instance, forms a category allowing the person to create relationships with unknown others.

Such interstitiality, flexibility, adaptiveness, all indicate the contemporary salience of friendship for anthropologists, but also indicate its potential role in what one might call the domestication of strangerhood or potential enmity, its ability to form ties where either no or radically different relations might be expected. Given such interstitiality it is no surprise that informants often try themselves to domesticate it with metaphors of kinship, ritualization, and so on. But of course anthropologists have also carried out their own forms of domestication, for instance through finding that friendship is somehow derivative of kinship, or alternatively through processes of purification that render 'true' friendship difficult to discover in the ethnographic world beyond middle-class Western contexts. As Gonçalo Santos implies, much may depend on how literally we or our informants take kinship metaphors, and equally much may depend on how pure we want our image of friendship to be. It is notable here that many contributors refer to Janet Carsten's (2000, 2004) attempts to ground kinship itself within broader notions of 'relatedness'. Michelle Obeid, meanwhile, does not collapse one into the other but sees both kinship and friendship in the Lebanese village that she studies as emerging from and expressing 'a single principle of sociality'.

In fact, all of the chapters do a fine job of locating friendship within other forms of social tie, but I was also fascinated to observe how they root friendship in physical and material terms as well. The most obvious manifestation of this tendency is in the various references to the spatial grounding of much friendship behaviour. The point is explored in Peggy Froerer's piece, for example, where space provides an alternative catalyst for association to that of blood ties but also entails its own constraints, since contact and proximity are important to the setting up of relationships. Proximity and space form the backgrounds to mimetic social practices – play, doing the chores, and so on – that under certain circumstances can override official caste distinctions.

The spatial dimension is taken in other directions as well. Amit Desai traces how physical proximity can be translated into social proximity but also how physical distance as mitigated by ritual friendship cements a bond originally formed by the anthropologist in the field. And, as I noted, Graeme Rodgers's piece is in many ways a study of displacement and the role of friendship as symptom and response to such a situation, both rooted in idioms of tradition and pointing towards a mistrusted 'modernity'. Magnus Course's work, meanwhile, takes the intersection of friendship and spatiality into a discussion of personhood, with the Mapuche depicted in 'centrifugal' motion, away from given kin relations towards chosen friendship relations. Indeed, to be a true person one must act centrifugally, must realize a form of autonomous volition that is part of the sociality of exchange and helps to constitute a constant movement outwards that is largely metaphorical in terms of social proximity but also has literal referents in geographical space.

Space is not the only way in which these authors 'ground' friendship, of course. For instance Magnus Course's discussion of wine-drinking roots friendship in the social and material practice of a form of exchange – in this case between adult males – where direct reciprocation is avoided in a moral economy where wine acts as currency. The significance of delayed reciprocity is also evident in Evan Killick's work, where it forms part of inter-ethnic relations in Peru. Amit Desai talks of the various substances (*prasād*, holy water, and so on) potentially exchanged between friends during the ritual forming the relationship. Gillian Evans notes that 'without exchange relations there can be no social participation and, without exchange relations humans cannot learn whom it is possible for them to become'. In addition, she provides a striking example of how the very objects children attend to become bridges over and through which they encounter and make sense of each other – and also of the ethnographer, as it turns out. As she points out, there are parallels here with Nigel Rapport's (1999) discussion in my and Sandra's book of playing dominoes as a foundation for sociality, opening on to an intimacy framed by a particular form of physical expression where, as in Evans's case, the value of objects and subjects become mutually specified.

A significant grounding of friendship is also evident in the chapters that link the formation of friendships with physical socialization, especially of the young. Thus the children described by Froerer do things together from a young age, as do the future ritual friends who feature in Desai's account. Both Evans and Santos talk of schools as important contexts of shared activity, involving what Evans sees as an alternative economy of becoming.

But this discussion of space, physicality and materiality leads me on to another significant contribution of this volume: the sense that is given of friendship acted out or located in the public realm, and not merely an occasion for the private or secret. Santos notes that rituals associated with same-year siblingship in China are explicitly visible and noisy, announced to the world of the living and the dead, even as a dyadic relationship also brings into it the respective families of the friends. I wonder whether there is also something of the quality of this public performance in Course's discussion of Mapuche wine drinking: he talks of the ideological suppression of communal sharing in a social process emphasizing the exchanges between two persons, but this is after all a performance with an audience, so that perhaps the exchange demonstrably excludes the wider circle in one sense but requires its presence in another. On the other hand, while Course describes a public celebration of a dyadic relationship, Desai illustrates something of the reverse process, as an original bond made with Radhelal, the village shopkeeper, attracts social pressure to become ritualized – as Desai states: 'Becoming a ritual friend is not necessarily an individual act.'

The making public of friendship ties may, in the imagery I have used before, help to domesticate them, render them socially sanctioned, and take us further from the purist ideology of friendship as private, free and unconstrained. The process also takes us away from the Western, middle-class valorization of friendship as a cultivation of the unpredictable. In most of the cases we read about in this volume the last thing people want is a relationship that will take them into realms they cannot control. Killick describes a form of relationship that is about mutual assistance even if it cannot be reduced to just that, and Peggy Froerer talks of the trust that can be gained from people of your own *para*. Predictability can also link with time and duration, of course, and it is notable that amongst the villagers discussed by Obeid friendship can seem inferior to kinship on the grounds of its lesser capacity for long-term endurance.

This sense of friendship as sometimes precariously expressive of trust, poised between or cross-cutting kinship and strangerhood, points us to its ambiguous character as a form of sociality, as we see how it is balanced and defined not only in relationship, say, to kinship, but also to idioms of aggression and potential distance. Froerer writes of mistrust for people in another *para*, while Gillian Evans refers to friendships not only formed out of aggression – boys in effect fight their friendship into existence – but also to the perception of violence as a kind of social good in opposition to the mainstream values of education. Perhaps such views and actions provide a rather less elegant, if more contemporary, manifestation of the remark often attributed to Oscar Wilde, to the effect that 'A true friend stabs you in the front.'

More could be said but I shall finish by simply stating that if some of the issues surrounding the anthropology of friendship have raised questions relating to its 'residuality' and supposed 'purity', this book does an excellent job in presenting the cultural contexts in which we are to understand voluntarism as well as constraint in the formation of relationships. We see how being (apparently) residual has its own power, but also how the dual-edged task of bringing friendship firmly into social realms has the effect of rendering it deeply and satisfyingly impure.

References

Aguilar, M. 1999. 'Localized Kin and Globalized Friends: Religious Modernity and the "Educated Self" in East Africa', in Sandra Bell and Simon Coleman (eds), *The Anthropology of Friendship*. Oxford: Berg.

Allan, G. 2001. 'Review of The Anthropology of Friendship (Bell and Coleman)', *The Journal of the Royal Anthropological Institute* 7(3): 582–3.

Aretxaga, B. 2006. *States of Terror*. Reno: University of Nevada Press.

Bell, S. and S. Coleman. 1999. 'The Anthropology of Friendship: Enduring Themes and Future Possibilities', in Sandra Bell and Simon Coleman (eds), *The Anthropology of Friendship*. Oxford: Berg.

Carrier, J. 1999. 'People Who Can Be Friends: Selves and Social Relationships', in Sandra Bell and Simon Coleman (eds), *The Anthropology of Friendship*. Oxford: Berg.

Carsten, J. (ed.). 2000. *Cultures of Relatedness: New Approaches to the Study of Kinship*. Cambridge: Cambridge University Press.

———. 2004. *After Kinship*. Cambridge: Cambridge University Press.

Coleman, S. 2006. 'Studying "Global" Pentecostalism: Tensions, Representations and Opportunities', *PentecoStudies* 5(1): 1–17.

Firth, R. 1936. 'Bond Friendship in Tikopia', in L.H. Dudley-Buxton (ed.), *Custom is King: Essays Presented to R. R. Marett on his 70th Birthday*. London: Hutchinson.

Keane, W. 2002. 'Sincerity, "Modernity", and the Protestants', *Cultural Anthropology* 17: 65–92.

Lawless, E. 1992. '"I Was Afraid Someone Like You... An Outsider, Would Misunderstand": Negotiating Interpretive Differences Between Ethnographers and Subjects', *The Journal of American Folklore* 105(417): 302–14.

Pahl, R. 2000. *On Friendship*. Cambridge: Polity.

Paine, R. 1969. 'In Search of Friendship: An Exploratory Analysis in "Middle-Class" Culture', *Man* 4(4): 505–24.

Paine, R. 1999. 'Friendship: The Hazards of an Ideal Relationship', in Sandra Bell and Simon Coleman (eds), *The Anthropology of Friendship*. Oxford: Berg.

Parry, J. 1986. 'The Gift, the "Indian" Gift, and the "Indian Gift"', *Man* 21(3): 453–73.

Pitt-Rivers, J. 1973. 'The Kith and the Kin', in Jack Goody (ed.), *The Character of Kinship*. Cambridge: Cambridge University Press.

Rapport, N. 1999. 'The "Bones" of Friendship: Playing Dominoes with Arthur of an Evening in the Eagle Pub', in Sandra Bell and Simon Coleman (eds), *The Anthropology of Friendship*. Oxford: Berg.

Reed-Danahay, D. 1999. 'Friendship, Kinship and the Life Course in Rural Auvergne', in Sandra Bell and Simon Coleman (eds), *The Anthropology of Friendship*. Oxford: Berg.

Ruel, M. 1997. *Ritual and the Securing of Life: Reflexive Essays on a Bantu Religion*. Leiden: E.J. Brill.

Wolf, E. 1966. 'Kinship, Friendship, and Patron-Client Relations in Complex Societies', in Michael Banton (ed.), *The Social Anthropology of Complex Societies*. Association of Social Anthropologist of the Commonwealth Monographs. No. 4. London: Tavistock Publications.

Notes on Contributors

SIMON COLEMAN is Professor of Anthropology at the University of Sussex. He has conducted research in a number of locations including Sweden, the UK and Nigeria on a range of topics from pilgrimage to biomedical discourses and tourism to art. His numerous publications include *The Globalisation of Charismatic Christianity: Spreading the Gospel of Prosperity* (CUP, 2000), as well as the edited volumes *Space, Movement and Health* (edited with K. Hampshire, Berghahn, 2008) and *The Anthropology of Friendship* (edited with S. Bell, Berg, 1999). He is currently Editor of the *Journal of the Royal Anthropological Institute*.

MAGNUS COURSE is Lecturer in Social Anthropology at the University of Edinburgh. His research is concerned with the relations between kinship, personhood, power and language in the context of Native South American socialities. He is the author of a number of articles on kinship, ritual, death and song.

AMIT DESAI is a Lecturer in the Anthropology Department at the London School of Economics. His research explores the connections between religious experience and nationalist identification among people in central India, and has led him to consider questions of religious subjectivity, moral practice, power and transformations in personhood and sociality.

GILLIAN EVANS is a Research Council Fellow and Lecturer in Social Anthropology at the University of Manchester. She is author of *Educational Failure and Working Class White Children in Britain* (Palgrave Macmillan, 2006) as well as a number of articles on social class, education and learning and children, childhood and youth. Her new research will explore the effects of the 2012 Olympics on the East End of London.

PEGGY FROERER is Lecturer in Anthropology at Brunel University. Her book, *Religious Division and Social Conflict* (Berghahn Books, 2007), and various articles consider the emergence of Hindu nationalism in rural India. Her current research interests include education and schooling; childhood, learning and cognition; and illness and healing.

EVAN KILLICK is a Nuffield Foundation New Careers Development Fellow and Lecturer in Development Studies in the Department of Anthropology at the University of Sussex. He specializes in the study of Lowland South American societies. Working with both indigenous and mixed-heritage peoples in Amazonia, he considers social and economic relations as well as issues of race, indigenity and land rights.

MICHELLE OBEID is a Research Fellow at the Centre for the Advanced Study of the Arab World and Department of Anthropology, University of Manchester. She specializes in research on the Middle East and Middle Eastern diaspora populations and considers issues of kinship, social, economic and political change, migration and diaspora.

GRAEME RODGERS is an independent researcher and Research Fellow at the Refugee Studies Centre, University of Oxford and the Forced Migration Studies Programme, University of the Witwatersrand, Johannesburg. His work amongst Mozambican refugees in South Africa focuses on humanitarian aid and repatriation, transnationalism and reconstructions of everyday life.

GONÇALO D. SANTOS is an LSE Fellow in the Department of Anthropology at the London School of Economics. His work on South China centres on questions of kinship, family, sociality, technology and environment. He is the editor of *Chinese Kinship. Contemporary Anthropological Perspectives* (with S. Brandtstadter, Routledge, 2009). He has also recently undertaken comparative field research in the Toraja highlands of Sulawesi.

Index

Lightning Source UK Ltd.
Milton Keynes UK
UKOW031245091212

203353UK00003B/58/P